Goethe's Allegories of Identity

Goethe's Allegories of Identity

Jane K. Brown

PENN

UNIVERSITY OF PENNSYLVANIA PRESS

PHILADELPHIA

A volume in the Haney Foundation Series, established in 1961
with the generous support of Dr. John Louis Haney

Published by
University of Pennsylvania Press
Philadelphia, Pennsylvania 19104-4112
www.upenn.edu/pennpress

Printed in the United States of America on acid-free paper
10 9 8 7 6 5 4 3 2 1

Library of Congress Cataloging-in-Publication Data
Brown, Jane K., 1943–
   Goethe's allegories of identity / Jane K. Brown.—1st ed.
     p. cm.—(Haney Foundation series)
   Includes bibliographical references and index.
   ISBN 978-0-8122-4582-0 (hardcover : alk. paper)
   1. Goethe, Johann Wolfgang von, 1749–1832—Criticism
and interpretation. 2. Goethe, Johann Wolfgang von, 1749–
1832—Language. 3. Identity in literature. 4. Self in literature.
5. Subconsciousness in literature. 6. Subjectivity in literature.
I. Title. II. Series: Haney Foundation series.
PT2193.B76 2014
831'.6—dc23

                                          2013031265

Frontispiece: Bust of Goethe
by Pierre-Jean David d'Angers (1829).
© RMN-Grand Palais/Art Resource, NY.

CONTENTS

For Marshall, Dorrit, and Benedict

PART I

The Problem

CHAPTER I

Representing Subjectivity

Il fallait Freud pour penser les sentiments de Rousseau.
—Jean Starobinski, *Jean-Jacques Rousseau:*
La transparence et l'obstacle

European culture underwent a paradigm shift in the last third of the eighteenth century that, depending on point of view and disciplinary focus, goes by various names—the displacement of classicism (or Enlightenment) by Romanticism, a fundamental change in literary style, the emergence of historicism, an epistemological shift from surface to depth, and above all the emergence of a subjectivity that locates meaning within the individual. It has become clear in the last fifty years that the issue is not just the period's focus on emotion, its "cult of feeling," but a profound change in the way in which emotion was understood and represented. Jean-Jacques Rousseau, identified by Hannah Arendt as the first "theorist of intimacy," and Johann Wolfgang Goethe, often seen as the father of modernity and creator of the iconic heroes for the nineteenth century (Werther, Wilhelm Meister, and Faust) have long been acknowledged as the major players in this shift, which was then fully conceptualized by Sigmund Freud, such an effective theorist and popularizer of the unconscious that it is practically synonymous with his name.[1] This book focuses on Goethe's contribution to this history between the beginning and end points so cogently identified in my epigraph. Not a study of Freud or Rousseau per se, the argument here addresses Goethe's trajectory between the asymptotes defined by his great predecessor and successor.

Why come back, yet again, to a narrative that has been told often and well? There are two reasons. First, Goethe's role is widely acknowledged but has not been the subject of detailed analysis. And second, the topic has been treated largely as one of the history of psychology or of general intellectual history. But it is also an issue of literary history and will be treated here as such, by focusing on Goethe's rewritings of important works of Rousseau (the topics of Part I, especially Chapters 2 and 3), his struggle to develop a specific allegorical technique to represent the unconscious (Part II), and the transmission of his new style through his Romantic contemporaries to the most influential formulators of the modern notion of the unconscious (Part III). Let me comment on each of these points in turn.

Goethe's Role in the Emergence of Psychoanalysis

It is widely accepted that Goethe contributed immensely to the depth psychology that corresponds to the shift to interiorized subjectivity.[2] According to Henri Ellenberger, historian of psychoanalysis, Freud intended "to incorporate into scientific psychology those hidden realms of the human psyche that had been grasped intuitively by the Greek tragedians, Shakespeare, Goethe, and other great writers."[3] But none of the early psychoanalysts identified with the Greeks or Shakespeare in the same way as they did with Goethe, who served many as their ego ideal.[4] Freud said he was inspired to study medicine by an essay on nature attributed at the time to Goethe, and he cited Goethe (particularly *Faust* but also other works) so frequently that only two of the eleven volumes in the Fischer *Studienausgabe* do not include him in the index.[5] Theodor Reik echoed Goethe's famous phrase about his own works in the title of his autobiography *Fragment of a Great Confession*, which begins with his adolescent obsession to read every word Goethe wrote in the authoritative 144–volume Weimarer Ausgabe of Goethe's works.[6] And Carl Gustav Jung, who "quoted from Faust on almost any occasion,"[7] begins his autobiography, *Memories, Dreams, Reflections*, by denying the rumor that he was an illegitimate grandson of Goethe—a rumor that the denial, of course, did much to propagate.[8]

This impact was part of Goethe's overwhelming status as adopted cultural father of the German Empire beginning in the 1870s (though the fathers of psychoanalysis came, strikingly, from outside the empire—from Vienna and Zurich and Budapest). The first half of the nineteenth century had turned its back on him as too cosmopolitan, too radical, too hostile to the ideals of Biedermeier calm, the tight family, religion, and daily morality;

in a phrase, he was too modern. But for the newly unified German state aiming to become a modern power the figure once considered pagan, immoral, and un-German was made its cultural model.[9] The ensuing Goethe cult crystallized primarily around "the young Goethe," the youthful rebel, and secondarily around the dignified humane classicist. Focusing on the lover of young women, the genius, the *Lebenskünstler* (artist of life) it dealt as much with Goethe the person as with his works. Plaster and marble busts still visible in antique stores, on Longfellow's desk in Cambridge, Massachusetts, or towering over the nineteenth-century hall of the Quai d'Orsay Museum in Paris, reproduced in the frontispiece to this book, testify to the magnitude of this influence.

Indeed, the difficulty with the topic is that Goethe's influence at the turn of the twentieth century, the foundational period for depth psychology, has seemed so diffuse. Despite their obvious devotion to Goethe and his poetic writings, Freud and the other depth psychologists wrote remarkably little about Goethe's works per se—especially compared with their output on Shakespeare and on the Romantic writer E. T. A. Hoffmann.[10] Goethe wrote scholarly essays in many fields of science, but psychology was not among them. Even so, direct scientific transmission of this generalized Goethe for psychology has been traced through Carl Gustav Carus (1789–1869)—gynecologist, psychologist, *Naturphilosoph*, painter, and important contributor to the emerging scientific formulation of the unconscious still being read by the first generation of psychoanalysts.[11] Carus proselytized enthusiastically for Goethe's scientific method (morphology) and for his work in general in the first decades after the poet's death. He wrote three books about Goethe and also referred to him repeatedly in *Psyche*, his treatise on psychology. This explanation of Goethe's *Lebenskunst* from *Goethe: Zu dessen näherem Verständnis* (Toward Better Understanding of Goethe, 1843) illustrates the typical generality of such transmissions:

> It is on the one hand the first and purest task of man to renounce
> all disruptive influences and to keep building the pyramid of his
> own existence without discouragement and without hesitation from
> base to peak ever larger and more complete, and yet, under certain
> circumstances, there is something so mighty and so beautiful in
> risking this whole existence, in being so captivated by love, that the
> entire building might collapse into ruins, all renunciation be given
> up, and the self be entirely delivered over to what is loved.

(Dem Menschen ist es einerseits allerdings die reinste und erste Auf-
gabe, durch Entsagung gegen alle störenden Einflüsse die Pyramide
seines eigenen Daseins unverdrossen und unverzagt von der Basis
bis gegen die Spitze hin vollständiger und größer auszubauen, und
andererseits liegt wieder etwas so Mächtiges und Schönes darin, dies
ganze Dasein unter gewissen Umständen dran zu wagen, von Liebe
so ergriffen zu sein, daß auf die Gefahr hin, daß dieser ganze Bau
zu Trümmern gehe, alle Entsagung aufgegeben werde und die volle
Hingebung des eignen Selbst an das Geliebte erfolge.)[12]

Goethe represents here the ideal example of developing one's full potential,
for Carus the task of every individual; so important and concrete is it that
Carus reifies it with his pyramid metaphor. For all his devotion to Goethe's
morphology, probably the more important object of Carus's transmission was
this focus on self-development, which remained the central preoccupation of
much of modern psychology.

Two points follow from the diffuseness of Goethe's influence. First, it
translates into general more than specific impacts. When the name "Freud" or
the term "psychoanalysis" appears below, both are to be understood as place-
holders for a widespread notion of depth psychology that varied consider-
ably in its details in different places at different times. I do not seek to trace
Goethe's influence on the specifics of Freud's or anyone else's terminology; my
goal is rather to identify what in Goethe's writing led to this enormous yet
vague attribution of influence and thus to specify Goethe's contribution to
the modern subject. Second, the diffuseness has left a blank spot in discussions
on the history and origins of psychoanalysis, in the significant psychoanalytic
interpretation of Goethe by biographers and scholars, and, in the last twenty
years, important discussions of the development of the modern interior self
in the eighteenth century—namely the specific language of his literary works
that made them seem so pregnant with psychological meaning to his contemporaries and later admirers. The issue here is not what psychoanalysis can tell
about European cultural history or about Goethe, nor how Goethe anticipates
psychoanalysis. Rather, this book will show his contribution to the language
that made it possible to formulate the tenets of psychoanalysis in scientific
terms; in effect, the discourse of modern psychology owes much to a literary language of depth psychology that Goethe developed in his response to
Rousseau.

Despite the importance of Carus and the Goethe cult, the transmission from Goethe to the early psychoanalysts was also direct, through his great literary works—especially *Die Leiden des jungen Werther* (*The Sorrows of Young Werther*), *Iphigenie auf Tauris* (*Iphigenia in Tauris*), *Wilhelm Meisters Lehrjahre* (*Wilhelm Meisters Apprenticeship*), and *Faust*, all of which were widely read at the beginning of the twentieth century. *Werther* has been generally recognized as a landmark portrayal of the modern psychological subject. Together with the *Lehrjahre* it pervasively shaped the conception of selfhood in the nineteenth and twentieth centuries. *Werther* offers the most lucid and complete picture of eighteenth-century melancholy, but also of its rationalist psychology. *Iphigenie* presents an early version of a talking cure, *Wilhelm Meister* and *Faust* forms for describing and analyzing the development of the individual psyche that were at the heart of the psychoanalytic project. Not only do all these texts involve a notion of personhood with depth psychology, with a subconscious or unconscious part of the psyche whose workings are largely inaccessible to the conscious or rational part of the mind—the notion of subjectivity described scientifically a century later by Freud—but more important, they invent a language for discussing and eventually conceptualizing it. If Rousseau was the first to think the thoughts later conceptualized by Freud, as the epigraph suggests, it was Goethe's achievement to find a new language independent of the conscious and (as Freud taught) censoring self for representing and exploring the first traces of the unconscious identified by Rousseau in his *Confessions* and *Reveries*. As a result this book will point both forward and back; in order to lay out Goethe's achievement in making the unconscious accessible to language, it will need to examine first how he came to terms with the legacy of Rousseau.

Literary History

Depending on scholars' disciplinary background and particular national foci, the emergence of modern subjectivity has been narrated in a variety of mutually complementary forms, ranging from broad social focus (character and morality) through largely philosophical (more epistemological, with more emphasis on consciousness and unconsciousness as such) to psychological and psychiatric.[13] The various discourses engaged by these studies as a group were not so clearly distinguished from one another in the eighteenth century as they are today, and they all came together in literary texts: the argument of this book is predicated on the idea that many issues are, if not thought through, at least talked through in literature before they are clearly conceptu-

alized in scientific discourses—of whatever stripe. From that point of view it
makes sense to discuss the emergence of modern depth psychology by analyzing Goethe's response to Rousseau, and the specifically literary methodology
distinguishes my work from the broad and distinguished assemblage of discussion on which it rests. But it is important to show not just how concepts
were thought through or talked through or anticipated in nonscientific texts.
This book demonstrates furthermore how Goethe actually developed important parts of the language in which the concepts of modern identity could be
conceptualized. That the first generation of psychoanalysts mined literature
and mythology for their psychological insights is well known, as is also the
powerful influence of their hermeneutic techniques on much contemporary
critical practice.

As a literary historian I have formulated the problem in the terms of my
discipline, and approach it in terms of what I understand to be literary methodology. First, it involves taking individual examples as typical for larger trends:
Rousseau, Goethe, Freud stand in here for intellectual developments going on
all around them. One can claim that they were geniuses, or less dogmatically
that they happened to be particularly sensitive figures who formulated what
those around them were thinking and feeling less articulately—it doesn't matter. We are at sufficient historical distance from all three to see them as paradigmatic for their times, and on that basis we understand trends. Second, as a
literary study this book is interested in parallels, underlying patterns, and conversations between texts. It is interested in intertextuality (in literary terms) and
morphology (in analytical terms). It seeks to understand relations among phenomena and implicit patterns rather than causality. It follows then, that Rousseau is represented here only by the aspects of his work that absorbed Goethe's
attention—his novels and biographical texts, and these only piecemeal. The
last century has learned from Freud ways to read both Goethe and Rousseau
not open to earlier scholars; the reading here explains why Freud works so well
on both. Third, I operate on the premise that telling stories is a way to focus
on issues not yet identified in conceptual terms by a culture—that, in effect,
literature can do intellectual work as much as philosophy does. Because it deals
with intuitions, perhaps notions, it narrates rather than conceptualizes. As a
literary critic rather than as a historian, I see my task as teasing the notions out
of intuitions, and perhaps occasionally teasing concepts out of notions. I seek
not to define terms, but in a sense to undefine them, to elicit the polysemy of
a discourse not quite sure of its object or, consistently in Goethe, of an object
that loses its significance when pinned to a single spot.

The notion of text used in the argument that follows is deliberately expansive. Ultimately, I describe a stylistic development in Goethe's work between roughly 1790 and 1810, the period of his "classicism." By the time he began publishing his autobiography, *Dichtung und Wahrheit* (*Poetry and Truth*) in 1811 it was already an obvious point to be made only in passing that the central function of poetry was "the representation of manners, characters, passions, in short, the interior self" (die Darstellung der Sitten, Charaktere, Leidenschaften, kurz des innern Menschen).[14] Because, however, Goethe constantly returned to certain themes and elaborated his meanings in major sequels to the two most important works of this period, *Wilhelm Meister* and *Faust*, I have found it necessary to document the presence of the images and techniques of this classical period in other works in order to justify my assertion that the shift is pervasive and central to Goethe's impact on his later readers. Furthermore, the analysis is intended not only as a summary reading of Goethe's major work, but deliberately includes his life as an interpretable part of his oeuvre. As Chapter 4 will demonstrate, Goethe operated at times with a theatrical notion of personal identity—that one's life was a role that one played, shaped, and even changed from time to time. Imitation of Rousseau became a role that Goethe took on, explored and tested, and, like an imitated text, eventually reshaped and rewrote. Similarly, something our century has certainly learned from psychoanalysis is how the different parts of the psyche compete with one another to shape and control our identity. Our lives are our life's work, especially for a thinker like Jung, the achievement of our own applied creative powers. Rousseau advocated a new standard for sincerity in autobiography, but one of the things Goethe learned from him was the need to shape the life that would be read by his future audience. Hence the argument here will offer not an explanation of Goethe's works in terms of his life, but a parallel reading of works and life that treats both as texts *in statu nascendi*.

Finally, a word about allegory is in order here. This book argues that Goethe's solution to the stylistic problem of representing the part of the psyche that lacked its own voice was a modernized version of allegory. Goethe still worked comfortably in the tradition of allegorical world theater that I have analyzed in an earlier book. It descended ultimately from morality drama and reached its peak in the seventeenth century. In this form of dramatic allegory the focus was not on the discrepancy between the allegorical tenor or meaning and its vehicle (as in the medieval theological and poetic allegory most familiar from Dante), but rather on truth made concretely visible via allegorical representation: what you see is what it means. It traded in characters with

names like "Hypocrisy," "Faith," "Understanding," even "Vision" or "Smell."
It worked so long as the cosmic (religious) referent of its semiotic system was
universally understood by its audience. Under the pressure of secularization,
the system started to break down. In *The Persistence of Allegory* I analyzed the
interplay between this mode of drama and the rising tide of Aristotelian mimetic drama. Apart from a few outliers in Vienna in the first half of the nineteenth century, Goethe was the last European writer who still understood and
used the older allegorical mode. But he understood that it meant something
different in a Kantian world in which the transcendent order of the cosmos,
what the late eighteenth century in Germany liked to call "the Absolute," was
by definition unknowable. The older form of allegory, largely trivialized in
the eighteenth century, takes on a new life in Goethe's use under the name
"symbol," in which a sign combines within itself its concrete reality and its
ineffable referent. Goethe used this new technique to suggest what cannot
be known (the first scene of *Faust*, part 2, as I have argued elsewhere, offers
an excellent example).[15] In this book I argue that he learned from this older
tradition of moral allegory to substitute the inner self, or what we now call the
unconscious, for the former cosmic referent. In effect, it relocates God into
the human breast. Readers of Goethe are surely all familiar with the famous
assertion in *Iphigenie auf Tauris* that the gods speak only through the human
heart (HA 5:494); in effect Goethe turns this assertion into a principle of style.

The need for this allegorical technique has little to do with our contemporary knowledge of Rousseau; it rises rather from the general enthusiasm for
him as the consummate writer of feeling in Goethe's circles, manifested not
in analysis but in the urge to imitate and, increasingly, to rewrite. The Rousseau that interested Goethe and his friends first was not the political theorist
but the author of *Julie* and of *Emile*, and then, second, the autobiographical
work—the *Confessions* and the *Reveries*. These works posed in particularly cogent form what was coming to bother most eighteenth-century writers, the
problem that the new self of the eighteenth century was unconscious, not
known to itself. Although the insight has become so obvious today that we
gloss over the problems, there is the real question of how to represent in language what by definition cannot be known rationally. Goethe justifies his allegorical approach to representing the new subjectivity in capsule form in one
of his late aphorisms:

> Nothing can be easily represented with complete impartiality. One
> might say the mirror offers an exception to this, and yet we never

see our face quite accurately in it; indeed, the mirror reverses our form and makes our left hand the right. Let this be an image for all observations about ourselves.

(Nichts wird leicht ganz unparteiisch wieder dargestellt. Man könnte sagen: hievon mache der Spiegel eine Ausnahme, und doch sehen wir unser Angesicht niemals ganz richtig darin; ja der Spiegel kehrt unsre Gestalt um und macht unsre linke Hand zur rechten. Dieß mag ein Bild sein für alle Betrachtungen über uns selbst.)[16]

On the surface the representation of the visible self seems to be at issue: normally a mirror is understood to reflect reality exactly. But Goethe shifts away from the common mimetic understanding of the mirror to its unavoidable reversal of the image. In effect the mirror alienates the self from itself; it is the same but different. The effect of representation and yet alienation is what I attribute to Goethe's transmutation of older forms of allegory.

The ramifications of my argument are more complex than would first appear. For a general audience interested in the roots of modern psychology, it demonstrates the importance of Goethe's works in specific terms. Because it demonstrates how Goethe's psychological writing developed explicitly as a reaction to Rousseau, the book also fills in a long incomplete analysis of the interaction between these dominant writers of European Romanticism. Because, finally, the primary development of this language turns out to take place in the 1790s, the discussion also forces a reconsideration of Goethe's classicism in more psychological terms.[17]

Eighteenth-Century Interiority

As background to the analysis the remainder of this chapter describes how the problem of subjectivity developed in belles lettres to reach Goethe in the late eighteenth century. Because the topic has elicited much discussion for the last several decades, I will focus here only on the issues relevant to the unconscious as a specifically literary problem for Goethe.[18] It can in fact be summarized in the following three characteristic statements:

- "Ego cogito ergo sum" (Descartes, *Principia philosophiae*, 1644)
- "Le premier sentiment de l'homme fut celui de son existence"

(Rousseau, *Discourse on the Origin of Inequality*, 1754; The first sentiment of man was that of his existence)[19]

- "Der Handelnde ist immer gewissenlos, es hat niemand Gewissen als der Betrachtende (Goethe, *Maxims and Reflections*, 1820; One always acts without conscience; only the observer has a conscience)

Descartes offers the obvious starting point for seventeenth-century anthropocentrism by grounding identity in the self rather than in a cosmic frame of reference. Rousseau grounds selfhood not in thought, as in Descartes, but in feeling. Indeed, in his *Discourse*, Rousseau has already attacked Descartes's *Meditations* when he writes, "the state of reflection is a state against nature and the man who meditates is a depraved animal" (*ŒC* 3:138; l'état de réflexion est un état contre Nature, et l'homme qui médite est un animal dépravé, 22). If Descartes and Rousseau reveal the shift from thought to feeling, Goethe pinpoints the moral question that was to dominate his struggles with Rousseau: what is the relation of conscience to consciousness? The sequence raises in capsule form the twin issues of the new nature of selfhood and the problematic relation of the self to the world caused by the change.

Two main categories characterize subjectivity in this context, interiority and consciousness. Interiority is the sense clearly visible in Descartes and increasing throughout the eighteenth century that the real self is inside, underneath the public self.[20] Increasingly this selfhood was grounded less in thought than in the new, less rational categories of feeling and then consciousness. This is the development outlined in the three quotations. But as selfhood became divorced from thought and receded beneath the threshold of sensory perception, it also became less of an ontological issue and more of an epistemological one, less something that knowably exists and more a psychic construct.

Goethe found the genealogy of identity as interiorized consciousness of one's being in the English novel and in Rousseau, but not in a simple direct line. Daniel Defoe's *Robinson Crusoe* stands in the seventeenth-century tradition of self-examination: it focuses in Cartesian fashion on the inner self defined by what itself thinks. Crusoe lives isolated on his island from all normal social contacts and from most outer constraints. Shipwreck has reduced him to pure selfhood thinking in the middle of nowhere; only gradually does he recover contact with the world, first in the basic conditions of life, then in rudimentary human contact, finally in returning to his accustomed outer world. His closing resumption of effective functioning in society becomes paradigmatic for novels of this tradition, most obviously, of course, as the model of the bildungsroman. With their shared conversion structure Samuel Richardson's *Pamela* and *Clarissa* continue the tradition of self-examination. Clarissa ends as a kind of saint as she withdraws from the world, obsessively prepares for her death, and seems to have become a being of a different order. Pamela's conversion is more secular, but after fleeing B. for most of the novel she finally converts to being Mrs. B.; at the same time she becomes the humble wife who no longer tries to withstand temptation on her own without the help of father or husband. Beyond this religious structure the novels develop an increased sense of interiority. Letter writing implies the isolation of letter writer from receiver, a situation dramatically heightened by the abduction element in both plots, which separates Richardson's heroines from everyone who can help them.[21] Because their being is contained entirely in writing, they seem to possess a new form of psychological depth.

The identity of Richardson's protagonists is tied to their writing. Pamela is stripped at one point in a search for her letters: the motif suggests, first, that the real Pamela is her letters, and, second, that her exterior must be removed to locate that real self. In *Clarissa* the motif is more abstract: there the heroine has to deal with letters forged in her name and with letters forged in others' names sent to her. Both types test her integrity. Yet the letters often contain unreasoned outpourings of feelings. The heroines do not always seem to know exactly what they mean, especially whether they love or hate their abductors. Nor do they always seem to mean what they say. We might even speak of a primitive unconscious here. But there is also a strong ethical element, as when Robinson Crusoe returns to the world. Despite their social isolation and their strong interiority, acting properly is crucial for both Clarissa and Pamela. They worry constantly about the correctness of their decisions and of their actions; they worry about whether their actions will be properly understood. While the novels build up a cult of interiority and subjectivity, at the same time they are preoccupied with action and with externalizing the self. The balance between conscience and consciousness is an unsolved, indeed, barely recognized, problem.

Interiority is yet more obvious in Laurence Sterne's *The Life and Opinions of Tristram Shandy*, which began to appear around 1760. Despite the apparent balance of the title, the focus in the novel is entirely on sentiments and mental activity. Its Greek epigraph means "It is not actions, but opinions concerning actions, which disturb men." Much of the book records meandering conversations between Tristram's father, Walter, who pins his faith on words, and

Tristram's uncle Toby, who depends more on things. As it turns out, neither is really adequate to the vagaries of human thought, which find their most telling expression in the actions—strategic silences and gestures—of its sentimental heroes Trim and Yorick. Words and things, thought and action are problematically separate in the novel; the whole first half is devoted to setting up the oppositions and exploring the comic ways they impinge on one another. The novel originally defines thought and thing as the poles between which all issues can be defined, but this opposition gradually modulates into one between mind and body, cerebral and sexual, and becomes ever fuzzier. Thus the gap between oppositions is increasingly bridged (bridges are an important motif), nowhere more cogently than in the delicate expressions of sentiment that grow in importance as the novel progresses. While the hyperintellectual Walter loses status as spokesman to Uncle Toby, Trim, and Yorick, the vaguer in-between realm of heart and feeling comes increasingly to the fore: the bridge becomes the significant locus of human activity, and sentiment becomes the real motivator of human action, not logic or physical drive. Identity is notoriously diffuse in *Tristram Shandy*, not just because the hero doesn't even manage to get born until book 3, chapter 23, but because of the difficulty of connecting thought to action and word; identity is so interiorized as to be almost inaccessible.

Contemporary with *Tristram Shandy*, Rousseau's *Julie, ou La nouvelle Héloïse* (1761) established the rhetoric of sensibility, that is, of selfhood grounded in feeling, and simultaneously explored the kind of society (as always a necessary evil) that can preserve most of what is natural to mankind. In the *Discourse on the Origin of Inequality* (1754) there was already a strong sense of the natural self being superior, as the following typical examples suggest: "ce que nous serions devenus, abandonnés à nous mêmes" (*ŒC* 3:127; what we would have become, left to ourselves), "dépouillant cet Etre . . . de tous les dons surnaturels qu'il a pu recevoir, et de toutes les facultés artificielles, qu'il n'a pu acquerir que par de longs progrès (*ŒC* 3:134; stripping this being . . . of all the supernatural gifts that he might have received, and of all the artificial faculties he could have acquired only through slow progress). As Ernst Cassirer argued, the sole source of knowledge of natural man in the *Discourse* is self-knowledge and self-examination.[22] So deeply buried is the self even in early Rousseau that natural cataclysms (enumerated *ŒC* 3:168) are required to bring about the origin of speech in the *Discourse*. Furthermore, Rousseau repeatedly redefined the Cartesian *cogito* by setting feeling above reason: for Rousseau feeling is both anterior to and superior to reason, which is associated with the origin of society and therefore of evil. To be sure, feeling does not belong to natural man either, but it at least only accompanies an earlier, less pernicious form of existence between natural man and society. Indeed, to the end of his life Rousseau considered any kind of rememberable mental activity, anything beyond the pure consciousness of existence described in the fifth of the *Reveries of the Solitary Walker*, to be imperfect, if not downright evil.

Rousseau was deeply concerned with ethics: what kind of society is appropriate to man and what is proper action were always burning questions for him. It is not surprising that he so admired the moralist Richardson. The tension between pure selfhood and right action developed into a central paradox in Rousseau that Goethe later struggled with at length. For Rousseau's new subjectivity contains a fundamental contradiction. On the one hand it involves the drive toward what Jean Starobinski called "transparency," the pure visibility of truth, manifested in the *Nouvelle Héloïse* as an ideal to be realized in the world, but also as pure, completely open, communication between souls; in the *Confessions* it appears as the insistence on revealing the entire truth about the autobiographical subject. But, as Rousseau himself repeatedly recognizes, transparency cannot ever be achieved—it is always interrupted by the inherent opacity of the world, what Starobinski calls "l'obstacle." In the *Confessions* this opacity takes the form of an inevitable discrepancy between intention (one's inner true self) and action (the self visible to others). Over and over again Rousseau justifies himself by the purity of his intentions, which may, however, be incommensurate with his incomprehensible, irrational actions. The episode in book 2 of the *Confessions*, in which the young Rousseau spontaneously steals a ribbon and, when caught, blames the theft on the innocent fellow servant to whom he intended to give it, is only the most famous example. In the fourth promenade of the *Reveries of the Solitary Walker* Rousseau goes so far as to ground his "professed truthfulness" in the *Confessions* "more on feelings of integrity and justice than on factual truth."[23] Thus he can say in an essay devoted to establishing principles of truthfulness, "I have hardly ever acted according to rules—or have hardly ever followed any other rules than the promptings of my nature" (*Reveries*, 73). Abstract moral truth has been so fully internalized that it risks becoming totally invisible. Some version of this paradox underlies many versions of what scholars have found interesting about Rousseau, whether they have formulated it as a problem of language, of psychosocial positioning, or of the nature of existence.[24]

In *Die Leiden des jungen Werther* (1774) Goethe critiqued the extreme cult of subjectivity around him in the 1770s.[25] The name of the main character,

Werther, which means "valuable one," and the central love triangle obviously derive from the *Nouvelle Héloïse*, whose hero is named Saint-Preux. The novel alludes repeatedly to other important texts of sensibility by figures such as Oliver Goldsmith, Ossian, and Friedrich Gottlieb Klopstock. *Werther* portrays the cult of sensibility with great sympathy: the famous moment is Charlotte putting her hand on Werther's arm and saying "Klopstock" during a thunderstorm on their first evening together. Indeed, the novel communicated so much sympathy that Goethe was distressed that it was first misunderstood only to be glorifying sentiment, and indeed that suicides were committed in its name. Goethe thought he had intended—and he clarified it when he revised *Werther* for the 1787 version—to reveal the dangerous solipsism of extreme interiority and the tragic outcome when sentiment loses contact with reality. For Werther's view of Charlotte has little to do with the real Charlotte, or with her own view of herself; Werther has created his own goddess. His selfhood has become so interiorized, so out of touch with the realities around him, that, as less urgently in Sterne, it has become inaccessible, and the world has become inaccessible to it. He is unable to act or even to live in the world, and the novel can only end with suicide.

Whereas Defoe, Richardson, and Sterne develop the novelistic subject from a tradition of religious introspection, Rousseau drives the discussion to its extremes both in the genre of the novel and also in genres closer to religious self-examination, the passionate essay and above all autobiography. In his autobiography he is particularly concerned about his own truthfulness, both as protagonist and as narrator. Rousseau's uneasy extremity links the general concerns about the truthfulness of the novel in this period of its emergence to new concerns about the validity (transparency) of all narrative prose, confessional or novelistic, spoken or written. After *Werther* Goethe did not publish another novel for twenty years; but the thematics of subjectivity suddenly emerged as a crucial theme in his plays. Furthermore, his next novel, *Wilhelm Meisters Lehrjahre* (1795–96), the paradigmatic bildungsroman, concerns itself largely with the theater. And in his plays Goethe transformed drama into just as important a vehicle for exploring subjectivity as the novel was, so that *Faust*, first published as a fragment in 1790, then in full as part 1 in 1808 and part 2 in 1832, is really the ultimate analysis of subjectivity in Goethe's lifetime.[26]

There was considerable cross-influence between novel and drama in the eighteenth century that does not need to be discussed here. Suffice it to say that the discursiveness and sentimentality of the epistolary novel emerge as talkiness, much weeping, effusive and often incoherent emotionalism on stage, incoherent or virtually absent plotting in the genres known as bourgeois tragedy, *comédie larmoyante*, and Sturm und Drang (associated with names such as Gotthold Ephraim Lessing, Denis Diderot, Pierre Augustin Caron de Beaumarchais, George Lillo). After some trendsetting experiments in this style, Goethe took a different, and, as it turns out, extremely important alternative approach to the relationship of drama to feeling. His new form is usually called "classical" and associated with his journey to Italy in 1786. It actually has more to do with his unique insight that the decisive development of European dramaturgy in the previous century had been the emergence of opera and that neoclassical plays resembled opera libretti more than Aristotelian tragedies. As a result, they were not mimetic or verisimilar; they did not represent humans as they appeared in the world, but rather created illusions of a truth not normally visible in reality.[27] How Goethe understood it is best illustrated by the praise of Shakespeare's representation of character in *Wilhelm Meisters Lehrjahre*:

The most secret and most complex creations of nature behave before us in his plays as if they were clocks, whose faces and housing were made of crystal; they would show the passing hours as they were meant to, and at the same time the wheels and springs that drive it are visible. (HA 6:192)

(Diese geheimnißvollsten und zusammengesetztesten Geschöpfe der Natur handeln vor uns in seinen Stücken, als wenn sie Uhren wären, deren Zifferblatt und Gehäuse man von Kristall gebildet hätte, sie zeigten nach ihrer Bestimmung den Lauf der Stunden an, und man kann zugleich das Räder- und Federwerk erkennen, das sie treibt.)

This passage seems already to have been drafted in 1784, just a few years before Goethe rewrote his classical dramas in the late 1780s. The capacity to let the interior show visibly through the exterior skin is precisely the skill Goethe honed in the 1780s. With this move Goethe shifted the psychology of the literary text from the language of passion and emotion accessible to rational discussion to an apparently de-psychologized, externalized representation. In effect, as the analyses below intend to demonstrate, Goethe transformed allegory from a tool of moral analysis to one of psychological analysis and thus enabled himself to lay out otherwise hidden, too interiorized, parts of the psyche to achieve a fuller representation of interiority not mediated by the thoughts of the characters.

CHAPTER 2

Goethe Contra Rousseau on Passion

Interiority hardly begins with Rousseau, but the notion of a self inaccessible to the light of reason, knowable at best through dreams and inchoate feelings, does find its earliest widely influential formulation in his work, especially in *Julie, ou La nouvelle Héloïse* of 1761, in which the heroine renounces her lover, marries the older, rational husband selected by her father, and settles down to an apparently happy and virtuous ménage à trois with both lover and husband—a ménage in which, however, the renounced passion continues (at least to modern eyes) to burn beneath the surface. Passion has always had to be controlled in European culture—think of Euripides' *Phaedra*. Special in Rousseau is what is now called "repression," the characters' insistent belief that they have conquered their passion when they really haven't. Goethe was not alone in his interest in the novel, but probably unique in that he rewrote *Julie* twice in his own novels of passion—first in *Die Leiden des jungen Werther* (1774), the novel that made his own reputation, and again in *Die Wahlverwandtschaften* (*Elective Affinities*, 1809). As a result, the two novels form a clear point of entry into Goethe's struggles to come to terms with Rousseau and with his elusive, inarticulate unconscious, and they thus determine the beginning and ending points of the larger argument made in this book.

Although Goethe's role in the reception of Rousseau has been an obvious topic from the earliest days of comparative literary study,[1] and although Rousseau's influence on Goethe has been surveyed and a few connections explored in detail,[2] it has been less common to take careful account of Goethe's ambivalence toward his predecessor.[3] *Werther* has long been recognized as a response to *Julie*, but the argument made below demonstrates that he was still driven to confront the novel again thirty-five years later (and thirty years after Rousseau's death) in *Die Wahlverwandtschaften*. Furthermore, the ambivalence resides not only in the interplay among the novels, but also in the writers' lives, both as lived and as described in their autobiographies. The complexity of the surreptitious conversations among these three novels and their implications for Goethe's efforts to understand and represent the unconscious requires an initial discussion of Goethe's more overt expressions of ambivalence toward Rousseau in his autobiographical writing, an examination of the relations among the novels, then a return to Goethe's lived "rewriting" of aspects of Rousseau's love life. On that basis the stylistic implications of the conversation among life text and written text become visible.

Innumerable elements connect Goethe and Rousseau. Born into the free citizenry of the independent city-states Frankfurt and Geneva, each maintained this social identity and even local speech habits for his entire life. Although Goethe's circumstances were more privileged, his paternal grandfather belonged to the artisan class that spawned Rousseau, and his father remained marginal to the Frankfurt patriciate despite his marriage into it. Both were educated at home by devoted fathers, Goethe, to be sure, more systematically. Both left their home and (to different degrees) ideal state to return only ambivalently for visits. Both prepared to become officials, though only Goethe actually did so; both moved in aristocratic circles toward which they had strong reservations and from which they maintained a certain independence. For both there was a significant tension between writing as an art and as a tool to earn a more dependable, if more mundane, income. There is too much and too little known about the love lives of each, which in both cases crossed class boundaries upward and downward. Both were noted hypochondriacs.[4] While Goethe's life was more comfortable, secure, and stable—economically, socially, and emotionally—the multifarious connections suggest an intriguing mix of general cultural patterns, unconscious affinities, and deliberate response that make these two both representative of their time and significant partners in conversation.

Like many of his contemporaries, Goethe unquestionably sometimes modeled himself on, and even cast himself explicitly as, Rousseau, as Carl Hammer has detailed in *Goethe and Rousseau*. While a student in Leipzig, for example, Goethe tried to simplify his life and harden himself along the lines prescribed by *Emile* (Hammer 45). Later he undertook to educate Fritz von Stein, son of his beloved Charlotte von Stein, according to the same book (Hammer 123). Until 1782 Goethe's primary residence in Weimar was a small garden house given him by Duke Karl August of Weimar, Goethe's lifelong friend and patron, in 1776, and there Goethe led a Spartan life modeled on

Rousseau's glorification of simple country retirement in *Julie*, the *Reveries* (Hammer 102), and perhaps even the *Confessions*. In *Briefe aus der Schweiz* (*Letters from Switzerland*, 1808) Goethe describes a visit to the Île St. Pierre in Switzerland, where Rousseau had spent the autumn of 1765 as French-speaking Europe was becoming closed to him. Hammer suggests that Goethe's special pleasure in traveling in Switzerland may even be understood as direct imitation (94–95).

Passing allusions to the *Confessions* in *Dichtung und Wahrheit* imply that Goethe not only stylized his biography in response to Rousseau, but also wanted the reader to evaluate his conduct in contrast to Rousseau's.[5] Eugene Stelzig has examined this issue at some length, so I will discuss only one example here. In book 6 of the *Confessions* Rousseau allays his anxiety about salvation by trying to hit a tree with a stone: if he succeeds, he will be saved, if not, he will be damned. Having chosen a very large tree close by, he hits it—and is never troubled by doubts of his salvation again, though he cannot decide whether to laugh or weep at the episode. Book 13 of *Dichtung und Wahrheit* opens with Goethe impulsively casting a knife into the Lahn River to test whether he will become a painter: if he sees it enter the water he will, otherwise he won't. He misses the entry into the water but can see the splash and comments ironically on the ambiguity of omens. The connection is obvious from the motifs of casting, important life decision, idyllic context, and ambiguity; yet the differences reveal the essence of Goethe's ambivalence. Rousseau broods on his moral condition, for which he takes little or no responsibility, while Goethe's more secular question concerns his achievement rather than his fate. Rousseau's ambivalence at the end of the passage involves judgment and emotions; Goethe's is epistemological—not whether what he did was silly, but why it was silly. Sudden impulses in Rousseau, the location of acts that we would now see as rising from the unconscious, are uniformly problematic and usually serve for self-justification. Although this one seems relatively harmless, it belongs to a more sinister pattern in the *Confessions* that the intention within always justifies the impulsive action, even if the latter is immoral—as in the famous ribbon episode (referred to in the previous chapter) or when he excuses the consummation of his affair with his "Maman," Mme de Warens, by asserting the purity of her intentions even though her ideas were faulty.[6] When Goethe describes his impulse welling up "imperiously from the depths of his soul" (HA 9:536; aus dem tiefen Grunde der Seele befehlshaberisch hervor), he parodies Rousseau's problematic immorality. By the period of *Dichtung und Wahrheit* (which began to appear in 1811), Goethe had explored Rousseau's location of moral identity in intention rather than in action, and indeed at greater depth than implied by these examples, which recapture the narrated rather than the narrating Goethe.

Goethe's Novels of Passion and *Julie*

The real analysis took place most explicitly in his novels of passion and in his own love life. Goethe's novels of passion, *Werther* and *Die Wahlverwandtschaften*, are rarely read together, because, written decades apart in different styles, they seem to tell different stories. In the emotional tone of the age of sensibility Werther narrates his own tale in a series of letters until his emotion reaches such a pitch that a third-person narrator intervenes in the last quarter of the novel. Unlike most eighteenth-century love plots, the issue is not conflict between father and daughter, but the adulterous love triangle that was to become typical of the nineteenth century. Passionate Werther arrives after an emotional mix-up of his own creation to arrange some family business in a distant town. In the lovely countryside around it he falls in love with Charlotte, daughter of a bailiff, who is already engaged to Albert; the couple enthusiastically accepts Werther into their friendship. The situation becomes tense, and Werther leaves to become private secretary to a nobleman in a different city, where he is miserable. He returns to Charlotte, is less and less able to remain within the bounds of friendship, and finally takes his own life.

Die Wahlverwandtschaften is a more obviously nineteenth-century novel. Its dry, elusive third-person narrator wanders in and out of the consciousness of four central characters in a vaguely gothic novel of manners. Eduard and Charlotte, the handsomest pair at court in their adolescence, have now married after each has survived a marriage of convenience to an older, wealthy partner. They invite Eduard's closest friend, a Captain, to help them improve their estate, and Charlotte's ward, Ottilie, to live with them, and speculate jokingly about a possible marriage. Instead, Eduard and Ottilie fall passionately in love, while Charlotte and the Captain become warmly attached. In a paradoxically adulterous moment Charlotte and Eduard conceive a child, each thinking of the absent beloved, and at birth the child resembles the two absent partners. Charlotte is prepared to renounce the Captain in the interests of the child's future, while Eduard is desperate to marry Ottilie. Ottilie inadvertently drowns the child, then gives up Eduard; in order to enforce her renunciation she stops speaking and eating. Eduard dies shortly after Ottilie and the two are buried together. Both novels have tended to be situated in their unique biographical circumstances,[7] the more so as Goethe asserted such a uniqueness for *Werther,* when he told Johann Peter Eckermann, not quite accurately, that he had read it only once since its publication.[8] Yet, in both novels, outsiders (Werther, Ottilie) threaten an established marriage that constitutes an insurmountable barrier to their passion. Suicide becomes the only solution for the person who oversteps the limits of humanity.[9] At the same time passion is figured as an unavoidable force, as a manifestation of what Goethe much later called "the demonic." Although virtue thus becomes secondary, neither protagonist ends with the narrator's full approbation, for passion culminates in an ironically heightened perception of the absolute—Werther casts himself as the prodigal son of God, while Ottilie appears to be sainted. Ignoring the gender of the protagonist for the moment, the plots of the two novels are identical.

Shared motifs and organization enhance the connection. Isolation from normal society is the basic premise of both. Werther flees family, friends, and the town for Charlotte's little country world, while in *Die Wahlverwandtschaften* Eduard and Charlotte cultivate their marriage in isolation on their estate. The Charlottes in both novels are similarly efficient, kind, attractive managers of their isolated realms, even though the Charlotte of the second is no longer the love interest. In both novels the heroine (Charlotte in the first, Ottilie in the second) has remarkable dark eyes; there are emotional relationships to trees planted on the birthday of a loved one; music is a mode of immediate communication between passionate lovers even when the passion is unrecognized; a man wastes his talents keeping an aristocrat company and finds it dull. Although Goethe often repeated motifs, none in this list except isolation is prominent in his other works, so that the repetition of several together is significant. Furthermore, both novels fall into symmetrical parts of equal length, one treating the growth of passion and the second its tragic conclusion. Each part closes with death, the first symbolically (a conversation on the afterlife in *Werther,* fall flowers in *Die Wahlverwandtschaften*) and the second with the death of the protagonist. The novels begin, climax, and end at the same times of year, and equivalent actions occur at the same season—new relationships in spring, passions in summer, a pause in fall and winter for a social interlude at the beginning of part 2, revival in the following spring and summer, a different narrator entering at the middle of part 2, and death at the end of the fall.

Die Wahlverwandtschaften is known for its objective detail, *Werther* for its subjectivity. Yet Werther's letters abound in concrete descriptions and what he calls "historical" narrative, and like the narrator of *Die Wahlverwandtschaften,* Werther has a sharp eye for characterizing gestures like Charlotte cutting bread for her siblings. Though less elusive than the narrator of *Die Wahlverwandtschaften,* the narrator who intervenes at the end of *Werther* shares both the apparent objectivity and the tendency to subtle bias and ironic distance characteristic of the later novel. As Ottilie is "das liebe Kind" (the dear child), so too Charlotte is "die liebe Frau" (118; the dear woman), and despite his avowed sympathy for his hero, the third-person narrator quietly distances the reader from Werther's overwrought views.[10] Finally, both novels use parallel situations and inset narratives to achieve distance.[11]

The link between the two novels is to be found in Rousseau's *Julie.* Erich Schmidt demonstrated long since the essential similarities between *Julie* and *Werther* and compared them with respect to style and treatment of passion, nature, art, and suicide. Clearly the motifs and structures of the two are similar—passion treated in a love triangle in a two-part novel in which the lover returns after the marriage of the beloved has made the desired relationship impossible. This special community of love is isolated from the world at large, and each contains an ideal adored woman, a reasonable husband, and a talented lover. The heroes' speaking names, Werther and Saint-Preux, have the same implications. Although Goethe tightened Rousseau's epistolary form by presenting only one side of the correspondence, the narrative intervention so crucial to *Werther* already occurs in *Julie.* There, too, Goethe found the tendency to project emotional states onto the landscape, a technique that enables both writers to make human passion but a specific example of the drive to connect oneself to nature, God, and the absolute.

Nevertheless, *Werther* is not just a more efficient *Julie,* for Goethe shifts the focus from two passionate lovers to one and also moves into an essentially negative mode: Saint-Preux and Julie struggle actively to control their passion, but Werther flees, beginning with his first words, "How glad I am to be away!" (7; Wie froh bin ich, daß ich weg bin). While Julie is torn from her family by an unfortunate accident (she drowns), Werther dies by conscious choice. Unlike Saint-Preux, Werther cannot successfully engage in constructive activity away from his beloved, nor can he return to a comfortable relationship with her and her husband in part 2. Julie becomes a religious mediator, especially for her husband Wolmar and her friend Claire. The self-centered Werther, by contrast, must forgo the final religious tie—"No clergyman was present" (124; Kein Geistlicher hat ihn begleitet) are the closing words. As Werther rejects everything around him, so too the editor implicitly rejects Werther's negative attitude and his suicide. "Be a man and follow me not" (Sei ein Mann und folge mir nicht nach) admonished the motto to part 2 in the 1775 edition.[12] *Werther* is without doubt an emphatic "no," not only to the fashionable English sentimentalism of the day, but especially to that of *Julie*.[13]

While the achievement of virtue in *Julie* ultimately depends on a belief in transcendence,[14] Werther's solipsism denies him a transcendent solution, since he sees God in the same self-centered terms as everything else. At the same time the collapse or endangering of all the social relationships in the novel at the end—those in the subplots as well as those of the main characters—implicitly rejects the fragile virtuous community Rousseau portrays in the second half of *Julie*.[15] However admirable she is, Charlotte lacks the moral and religious strength to hold together such a community as Julie leads. Moreover, she has no feelings that she cannot restrain. Goethe rejects Rousseau's presentation of a relationship transcending time and natural change in favor of the realism articulated about the same time in the poem "Auf dem See" (On the Lake): "Out, you dream, gold as you are, / Here too are love and life" (HA 1:102; Weg du Traum, so gold du bist, / Hier auch Lieb und Leben ist). The virtue of *Julie* is revealed in *Werther* to be a sentimental fantasy, intention rather than action.

Goethe in the Role of Rousseau

Goethe's revision of his critique thirty-five years later rests on his subsequent interaction with Rousseau's morality in his own life. Goethe's bourgeois existence seems a far cry from the love life described in Rousseau's *Confessions*, which includes masochism, masturbation, explicit homosexual encounters, incestuous love for Mme de Warens (whom he consistently refers to as "Maman" and for whose other live-in lover, Claude Anet, he felt the devotion of a son), and a long-term affectionate but passionless relationship of sexual convenience with Thérèse Levasseur, the offspring of which were deposited at the foundling hospital. His most stable and significant relationships were those with his "Maman" and with Thérèse. They were also the most scandalous—to Rousseau's contemporaries, to himself, to us—since they comprised incestuous emotion and the rejection of his own children by the most visible European proponent of the sanctity of childhood. Nevertheless Goethe's long and significant relationships with Charlotte von Stein, a (married) court lady with whom Goethe began a rarefied love affair shortly after he settled in Weimar in late 1775, and his mistress Christiane Vulpius stand out as analogues to

Rousseau's—the first with an older aristocratic and idolized woman who educated him, and the second with a woman beneath him in social status who
kept him happy.

It may seem odd to compare the rigidly virtuous Frau von Stein to Mme
de Warens, with whom Rousseau lived in a ménage à trois as his initiation
into the love of women. There is no evidence of any physical consummation,
and Goethe educated her son (of which more in Chapter 3). Yet Rousseau is
eerily present in Goethe's correspondence with Charlotte von Stein, according
to Hanna Fischer-Lamberg, who demonstrates how Stein cast herself as Julie
in a gesture typical of the period.[16] Goethe, Fischer-Lamberg argues further,
could not have overlooked how he played the role of Saint-Preux. Nor, as
she only obliquely hints, could he have overlooked the parallels to his own
Werther, the more so since his beloved just happened to be named Charlotte.
This subtle element of role-playing enhanced perhaps the parallel role-playing
from Rousseau's Confessions. Yet the Steins' marriage did not much resemble
that of Charlotte and Albert in Werther, and Goethe did not resort to suicide.
In view of Goethe's critique of Julie in Werther, the relationship with Charlotte
von Stein appears as a living correction of both Rousseau's novel and of the
sentimental excesses of his own.

Yet Goethe fled Charlotte von Stein just as he finished revising Werther
in 1786 (published 1787); in late summer he abruptly left the court and Frau
von Stein for Italy. Fischer-Lamberg argues that Bildung, the heart of the affair
with Charlotte von Stein, ultimately ran aground on Goethe's sensuality, but
Rousseau surely also played a role. In the late 1770s it may reasonably have
appeared to Stein that she played Julie to Goethe's Saint-Preux, or a sister to a
beloved brother. But already in 1776 Goethe wrote a little play, Die Geschwister
(Siblings), in which a sister is too devoted to the older brother who has reared
her to accept a lover—only to learn that he is not her brother at all but the unsuccessful lover of her mother and now her (successful) lover. "Warum gabst
du uns die tiefen Blicke" (1776; Why did you give us deep insight) , a poem
to Frau von Stein, hints at the incest prohibition at the end of the fourth
stanza with "Ah, in the past you were, / My sister or my wife" (HA 1:123;
Ach, du warst in abgelebten Zeiten / Meine Schwester oder meine Frau). In
both these texts the reader is expected to understand the use of "sister" only
as a metaphor, "sister of my soul." Nevertheless, having already written these
texts, Goethe would have found it impossible after reading the Confessions as
soon as it appeared in 1781 to ignore the parallel between his affair and Rousseau's great Bildungserlebnis, his passage from adolescence to sexual maturity

under the tutelage of Mme de Warens. If Goethe suppressed his sensuality with Charlotte von Stein, Rousseau certainly did not with Mme de Warens. Goethe left behind too little commentary on Rousseau, and most of it characteristically too tactful, to assess the impact of the *Confessions* directly, yet his relationship with Stein became increasingly strained in the eighties. To what extent did Rousseau mirror for Goethe his own suppressed wishes? To what extent did the *Confessions* reveal to him an underlying immorality in his supposedly pure relationship with Stein, whom he called "muse"? And to what extent did the discrepancy between Rousseau's idealized *Julie* and his own reality reinforce Goethe's questioning of the apparently easy idealism of the novel he admired so much? The analogies between Mme de Warens and Frau von Stein may have been fortuitous, but they must have shocked so sensitive a reader as Goethe.

When he returned from Italy in 1788 he soon made his petite bourgeoise mistress, Christiane Vulpius, head of his household. The second half of the *Confessions* appeared in 1789; whether or not Goethe read it, the subject of Rousseau's relations with Thérèse Levasseur was widely known.[17] In the common view, Italy enabled Goethe to break the chains of Charlotte von Stein and enter into a free, nonbinding relationship with Christiane. But consider first the alternative models for conducting love relationships available to Goethe around 1790. For whatever reasons, as *Dichtung und Wahrheit* makes amply clear, entering into marriage seems to have terrified him. A second possibility was a platonic relationship like that with Charlotte von Stein, in which the metaphor of incest preserves the virtue of the connection; the "brother-sister" relationship he describes with a girl named Gretchen in *Dichtung und Wahrheit* and even more so that in *Die Geschwister* (where the incest impediment evaporates when the "sister" is revealed not to be a sister after all) offer literary versions. Both Goethe's flight to Italy and Rousseau's *Confessions* reveal the threat of uncontrollable sexuality that rendered this alternative untenable for Goethe. Third, now that Goethe had become in effect an aristocratic gentleman of leisure he could simply take a mistress—either discreetly, along the lines described in his *Römische Elegien* (*Roman Elegies*), or openly, as his employer, Duke Karl August, himself did, with a separate public household for mistress and children.[18] Goethe opted rather for a daring fourth alternative: he adopted the model of Rousseau, who took up with Thérèse in 1743 and lived with her until his death in a relationship that was only questionably regularized around 1770. Shortly after their first meeting Goethe installed Christiane in his garden house and all succeeding homes until her death in 1816 and, as Rousseau did with Thérèse, thereby adopted her relatives as well. Even more than Rousseau, Goethe treated Christiane as his wife in all but name, and the strains were greater because Goethe had much stronger ties to the court at which Christiane was unwelcome. However difficult Goethe may have been to live with (as Sigrid Damm argues), Nicholas Boyle has demonstrated that Goethe not only loved Christiane devotedly, but that he also made major sacrifices for her in his turn.[19] Goethe consistently stylizes relationships and marriages in his works of this period—*Hermann und Dorothea*, the elderly couple in "Das Märchen" (Fairy Tale), Baucis and Philemon in *Was wir bringen* (Our Offering)—in terms of the rural idyll that is the ground bass of Rousseau's *Confessions*. It is generally agreed that the mother in *Hermann und Dorothea,* heart of an idyllic family life and caretaker of the garden, is Goethe's literary monument to Christiane (they did later briefly own a country estate). Christiane was a gardener and Goethe wrote "Metamorphose der Pflanzen" (Metamorphosis of Plants) for her, a work he later identified specifically with Rousseau.[20]

Yet here above all Goethe's ambivalence toward Rousseau comes to the fore. The great scandal about Thérèse was not her existence, but her children: Rousseau the celebrated pedagogue could not face raising children and delivered five to the orphanage. Goethe by contrast aspired eagerly to fatherhood. However problematic he may have been as a father,[21] his grief at the deaths of the four infants born to them after their surviving son, August, makes evident how desperately he wanted children and how he shared Christiane's pain at their loss. This is, of course, a personality difference from Rousseau, but also a correction. Goethe's refusal to marry participated in Rousseau's rejection of certain cultural institutions, but not in his evasion of responsibility. On the contrary, Goethe's desire for children turned the relationship into a greater personal responsibility—and more trouble to someone who hated the nuisance of daily life—than a sanctioned marriage would have been. Precisely in the 1790s, as Goethe grieved for successive lost infants, his references to Rousseau in his correspondence drop off noticeably, and his praise of the *Confessions* occurs henceforth exclusively in the context of Rousseau's botany. Christiane seems to have exorcised Rousseau.

Die Wahlverwandtschaften and *Julie* Redux

Goethe married Christiane in 1806. One can only speculate on the likelihood that normalizing the relationship to Christiane brought Rousseau back to Goethe's mind, but for whatever reasons, within two years he had begun *Die Wahlverwandtschaften*. If *Werther* is at first level an admiring and competitive critique of *Julie*, in *Die Wahlverwandtschaften* Goethe offers a nuanced reconsideration of Rousseau's novel. The initial impulse seems to be a desire to interpret the conduct of his own life in the years between his two novels of passion, for the question of responsibility in marriage centers on the presence of a child and the actions of yet a third Charlotte, the last half of whose name echoes through the names of the other three protagonists (two Ottos and an Ottilie)—Charlotte yet again and again and again. Consonant with Goethe's increasing reticence about Rousseau, *Die Wahlverwandtschaften* seems to rewrite *Werther*, but for the careful reader, Rousseau is never far from the center of the later novel.

Given its ties to *Werther*, *Die Wahlverwandtschaften* adopts the basic structure and techniques of *Julie*, even though it is not an epistolary novel;[22] furthermore, it exploits several motifs from *Julie* that Goethe ignored in *Werther*. Saint-Preux's profession as educator returns in a pension assistant who loves Ottilie. Rousseau's impulsive English lord Edouard cedes his name to Goethe's impulsive hero, leaving the English lord who visits Charlotte and Ottilie in the second half of the novel nameless. Both novels focus on building a garden house (*Lusthaus*, *pavillon*), and, more important, on taming the landscape, a precarious process associated with the suppression of passion. Water is the site and metaphor for passion in both works (a storm on the lake in Rousseau reevokes the memories of the love between Julie and Saint-Prieux, and later Julie drowns; the Captain kisses Charlotte at the lake, Eduard and Ottlie embrace by the lake, the child drowns there in Goethe). Julie becomes a metaphoric saint at the end of her novel; Ottilie is canonized more explicitly in Goethe. If anything *Die Wahlverwandtschaften* is closer to Rousseau than *Werther* is.

In general *Die Wahlverwandtschaften* uncovers ambiguities in *Julie* of which *Werther* seems unaware. The glorification of true love and transcendence that *Werther* appears to reject in Rousseau does not do justice to the moral complexities of the *Confessions*, and even less to those of Goethe's own relationships. It has been clear since Starobinski's reading that *Julie* is a novel of bipolarities rather than syntheses and has at its heart the unresolvable relationship between nature and culture. The novel itself thus remains an unresolvable problem:

> The will to unity is not well served by perfect conceptual clarity: it is an impulse of the whole person, and not an intellectual method.

Hence there exists in him and in his work more implicit meaning than he himself knows. This fact, which is true of every writer, is eminently true of Rousseau. «It took Kant to think the thoughts of Rousseau,» according to Eric Weil (and we add: it took Freud to think the sentiments of Rousseau).

(La volonté d'unité n'est donc pas servie par une parfaite clarté conceptuelle: c'est un élan de la personne entière, et non pas une méthode intellectuelle. Par conséquent il y a en lui et dans son oeuvre plus de sens implicite qu'il ne le sait lui-même. Ce fait, qui est vrai de tout écrivain, l'est éminemment de Rousseau. "Il fallait Kant pour *penser les pensées de Rousseau,"* écrit Éric Weil [et nous ajouterons: il fallait Freud pour penser les sentiments de Rousseau].)[23]

Die Wahlverwandtschaften makes this complexity nowhere clearer than in foregrounding renunciation. Ottilie's inability to achieve complete renunciation of Eduard after the birth of his and Charlotte's child brings to the surface the ambiguity underlying Julie's successive renunciations of Saint-Preux that begin in part 1, letter 9. The pattern persists throughout the novel, with each successive renunciation more official and each continuation of her love more repressed—first beneath landscape descriptions (the contrast between Julie's artificial "Elysium" and the groves outside the house, part 4, letter 11; the storm on the lake, where it still breaks out, part 4, letter 17) and later beneath Julie's excessive piety.[24] Julie herself recognizes that her renunciation was an illusion (part 4, letter 12). Thus while Rousseau presents on the one hand an ideally virtuous woman and a virtuous community dependent upon her, at the same time the foundation of her virtue—her renunciation—is never achieved and must be constantly renewed. This complex basis for her eventual death and for Eduard's and Ottilie's deaths in *Die Wahlverwandtschaften* makes Werther's suicide look almost callow.

The narrative focus is equally ambivalent. Rousseau exploits the epistolary mode to present different points of view—his correspondents regularly contradict, correct, and interpret one another, the novel's narrator expresses pleasure when some letters are omitted (part 5, letter 6, p. 584), the preface refuses to say whether or not the characters are real and discusses at length who should not read the book. Unlike the discrepancy between Werther and his editor, the accumulated ambivalence does not undermine or correct the point of view of the characters, but instead, as Starobinski demonstrates for the metaphysical issues in the novel, allows opposing possibilities to exist side by side. Despite the shift from the epistolary form, the narrator's extreme reserve, which ultimately robs him of any authority in *Die Wahlverwandtschaften*, is very close to the lack of an authoritative point of view in *Julie*, and elsewhere in Rousseau as well. The heroes of both novels, for example, have arbitrarily assumed names that reflect the hero's hesitation to accommodate to social expectations. With the claim of worthiness implicit in his adopted name, Saint-Preux claims a position from which he can legitimately love Julie; Eduard has rejected not only his given name, Otto, but also, as it turns out, Otto's role, which is to love Charlotte, as the Captain (also named Otto) indeed does. The arbitrary names, further, emphasize the fictionality of both narratives. Goethe makes the connection explicit in the narrator's aside in the first sentence, "thus we shall call a wealthy baron" (242; so nennen wir einen reichen Baron). Ultimately the fictionality signals a truth lurking behind the narrative that is either inaccessible or repressed. Saint-Preux's assumed name asserts his worth, while Julie tries constantly to repress how precious he really is to her. Indeed, one must question whether Saint-Preux or Wolmar is the truly worthy man in the novel: the name marks an essential ambiguous truth in the novel. Similarly Eduard's assumption of his name asserts a false independence of social and natural law. At the same time, his persistent faith that the entwined *E* and *O* on his favorite glass represents his bond to Ottilie, rather than his own name change, conceals his initial wrong act of separating himself from the community of the other protagonists, whose names all include his rejected name "Otto." While *Werther* may question the language of sentiment, *Die Wahlverwandtschaften* uncovers how Rousseau questions what Starobinski calls the "transparency" of language itself.

Die Wahlverwandtschaften reinterprets the motif that most obviously connects these novels, the love triangle. In both *Werther* and *Julie* it consists of a woman between two men, the one a passionate and attractive lover, the other an ideally stable, generous, and beloved fiancé/husband. *Werther* seems almost to lose patience with Julie's lengthy postmarital nonflirtation with Saint-Preux; instead the narrator who intervenes at the end hints that Charlotte cannot willingly pass Werther on to another and allows her realistic guilt to prevent her from interfering with the loan of Albert's pistols to Werther. *Die Wahlverwandtschaften* revisits the triangle in such complex fashion that it has obscured for most readers the fundamental connections among the three books. Charlotte between her husband Eduard and his friend the Captain recalls the basic triangle; but the Captain is no passionate lover, Eduard hardly an ideal husband, and Charlotte's devotion seems more to the institution of marriage than to him. Ottilie shifts the balance entirely, less to the square implied by the chemical analogy that gives the novel its title (elaborated in book 1, chapter 4), than to a second triangle formed by Eduard between the ideal wife Charlotte and the mystifying Ottilie. The situation certainly is more complex than appears in *Werther* and possibly also more than in Rousseau.

The issues identified with the triangle change as well. At the beginning of *Julie* the problem seems typical of eighteenth-century drama and novel: who has the right to dispose of the daughter's hand, and whether she belongs to herself or to her father. In *Werther* Goethe evidently recognizes how Rousseau moves beyond the convention to the moral implications of Julie's position and how the fulfillment of passionate desires inevitably injures the claims of family. Finally, virtue as a self-defined rather than social standard requires adherence to a chosen course of action, like Julie's extreme moral and religious purity. Goethe grants such purity automatically to Charlotte in Werther's first encounter, when he sees her cutting bread for her sibling-children, but otherwise ignores it as Werther's psyche becomes the real center of attention. In *Die Wahlverwandtschaften* the typically eighteenth-century patriarchal issue is relegated to the prehistory of the novel: Charlotte's and Eduard's happiness has been fatally delayed because Eduard's parents insisted on a prudent marriage. Goethe further undermines the convention by restricting the problem to Eduard's choice of mate, while representing Charlotte as a free agent. At the same time, the propriety of divorce is not the central question, a levity that scandalized Goethe's contemporaries. The claims of family seem to play a role when characters, especially Charlotte and Ottilie, worry about one another's feelings, but they soon fall by the wayside as all manners fail in the novel.[25] What remains paramount is the moral problem, particularly for Ottilie. In the climactic scene with Charlotte after the death of the child she criticizes herself for having abandoned the role resolved upon many years before (462–63) and identifies her love for Eduard as a crime that interferes not only with her commitment to her path ("Bahn"), but also with the commitments of the others to their particular destinies. In this respect *Die Wahlverwandtschaften* returns to the passionate moral commitment of Julie's zeal to achieve moral and religious perfection.

Goethe does not, however, simply restore something he perhaps overlooked in writing *Werther*, for the religious elements of *Julie* are taken to much greater extremes in *Die Wahlverwandtschaften*. Where Rousseau operates with the strict Protestantism of his Genevan heritage and with the mimetic imperative of the novel, Goethe moves his novel from moderation to flamboyant Catholicism. Charlotte's position at the beginning, when she straightens up the local graveyard and turns its old tombstones into historical and aesthetic memorials is at best a moderate deism, while the family friend, the former pastor Mittler, has renounced his religious function as a result of winning the lottery. By the middle of the novel Charlotte's reforms have aroused more conservative opposition from the original benefactors of the church and she has to buy them out. Soon after, the visiting architect begins to restore the gothic chapel, and what began as a primarily aesthetic activity transforms the chapel into a space that evokes religious feelings so strong as to arouse discomfort, though of different sorts, in both women. As the angels painted by the architect onto the ceiling come ever more to resemble Ottilie, she is increasingly subsumed into the Catholic ambience of the chapel. She virtually martyrs herself at the end; her protégée, Nanny, is miraculously healed by contact with her corpse as it is carried to the same chapel. Ottilie has become a saint—assuming we trust the dry reserve of the narrative voice. Goethe both elaborates a moral complexity *Werther* apparently overlooked and also calls it into question.

To Rousseau's already considerable ambiguity Goethe adds the further uncertainty of his tone. Given his own efforts to relive and correct the moral failures of Rousseau's marriage, the irony is liable to be substantial. The shift to religious imagery in order to achieve at least an apparently affirmative resolution becomes typical of Goethe in the 1790s in the wake of his engagement with Mozart's *Magic Flute* (*Die Zauberflöte*). The endings of his fairy-tale "Das Märchen" (1795), of the story of Mignon's mother in *Wilhelm Meisters Lehrjahre* (1796), and indeed of *Faust*, part 2 (1832), are obvious examples. Goethe discovered in these texts how to use the existing rhetoric of religion to represent something going on inside his characters. Julie as a kind of secular saint for the family gathered around her appears in Goethe first in much the same way as Charlotte cutting bread for her siblings, but Ottilie now invokes the full panoply of Catholic imagery. Rousseau's novel still operates with the traditional language of passion and virtue; reason is presumed in the very rhetoric of the text to be in control even as Rousseau discovers that the characters do not always know by what forces they are driven. In *Die Wahlverwandtschaften* such language is ostentatiously absent. The characters carefully avoid telling one another how to behave as they avoid explaining themselves. There is awareness of self-control, but when characters go out of control, all of nature seems to do so as well. By the end of the novel all of the characters give up trying to keep Eduard and Ottilie apart, and their affinity for one another has nothing to do with will. It is, instead, "an almost magical attraction" (478; eine fast magische Anziehungskraft). The explicit religious imagery at the end of *Die Wahlverwandtschaften* shows that Goethe's struggles with Rousseau's morality made him adapt and elaborate the imagery in Rousseau that became the food for the thoughts of Freud in Starobinski's reading.

Such development appears especially in the way *Die Wahlverwandtschaften* elaborates the psychological significance of landscape in *Julie* without Goethe's otherwise characteristic distancing or parody, as if Goethe were excavating a metaphor in Rousseau. Julie and her extended ménage enter into the eighteenth-century pleasures of improving their estate. They create a lovely rural idyll in a garden they call "Elysium," and their English friend, Lord Edouard, undertakes to build a pavilion there. The emotional safety of the garden versus the forest, just hinted at in this section of the novel, becomes a dominant motif in Goethe, where the characters' efforts to control the landscape embody their refusal to acknowledge their own illicit passions. In retrospect the actions of Goethe's characters reveal the similar repressive function of the practical improvements at Clarens described at such generous length. Edouard's pavilion, the completion of which is interrupted by Julie's death, scarcely seems to signify more than a dashed hope, while Goethe's pavilion has all the tensions among the characters sealed into it at various ceremonies and comes to represent the characters' failure to form a successful society. Since Julie's death has deprived the ideal society at Clarens of its basis for existence, the pavilion has the same significance; but Goethe has brought what was submerged to the surface. Goethe had briefly evoked these motifs in Werther's patriarchal garden at the beginning of the novel; in *Die Wahlverwandtschaften* he uncovers their real importance. The elaboration of external detail combined with the narrator's general reticence transforms Rousseau's imagery into the more obvious and more legible allegory of *Die Wahlverwandtschaften*: Goethe's allegory makes Rousseau's visible.

The most extreme example is the occasional but crucial water imagery in *Julie*. A storm on Lake Geneva brings the former lovers first to the place from which Saint-Preux had written some of his most passionate letters and thus into renewed danger that they will again succumb to passion. Their insecure boat implies that the lovers have achieved but uncertain control over their feelings, and the waters of the lake suggest the depths of passion, but none of this is articulated explicitly. Julie later falls ill and dies after plunging into the lake to rescue her child. Although basically a pretext to end the novel, Julie's fall can nevertheless be read in the context of the storm to represent her only incomplete renunciation, which is hinted at in other ways as well. Rousseau's storm echoes in the description of the flooded landscape shortly before Werther's death (letter of December 12, 98–99) and Werther's Charlotte is often associated with water in the novel. Water is, however, a danger not to her but to Werther, and remains a subordinate motif in the characterization of nature.[26] But in *Die Wahlverwandtschaften* repetitious water imagery becomes the objectification of passion: water is contained only by precarious dams, while its inviting surface covers dangerous shallows and depths—where Charlotte and the Captain run aground and where Charlotte and Eduard's child eventually drowns. Fear of death by water dominates the novel: even before Ottilie's arrival and the enlargement of the lake, preparations are made to revive victims of drowning. Ottilie's death, like Julie's, follows from the fall of a child into the lake. The reader coming to Rousseau from *Die Wahlverwandtschaften* would have to read Julie's death as the result of her recognition that she has failed truly to renounce her lover. Goethe's more explicit allegory of water transforms the inchoate innerness of Rousseau's figures into what, following the water image, reader's now call psychological depth. In Rousseau this implicit psychological depth is equated with moral depths that his depiction glosses over. Goethe's struggles to sort out the moral discrepancies in Rousseau have led him to an allegory of psychological depth.

Die Wahlverwandtschaften is thus not only a reckoning with *Werther*, but a reckoning with Rousseau—with his influential novel, with his moral and even more his epistemological significance for us all. I am inclined to agree with Starobinski that it took a Freud to think the *sentiments* of Rousseau, but Goethe's crucial role in mediating the development must not be overlooked. Goethe thought of himself as an artist, not as a thinker, and his role was precisely to translate Rousseau's implied *sentiments* into the visible images then further translated by the psychology of the nineteenth century into the psychoanalytic discourse generally identified with Freud. Such are the images identified here as allegory. Succeeding chapters will demonstrate how Goethe adapted the traditional techniques of allegory for a new psychological purpose in drama and prose of the 1780s and 1790s, and how that language spread from him to his fellow Romantics. On that basis it will then be possible to demonstrate how and why *Die Wahlverwandtschaften* has become the paradigmatic German psychological novel.

CHAPTER 3

Goethe Contra Rousseau
on Social Responsibility

Both Goethe and Rousseau framed their versions of the subject in terms not only of passion, explored in the previous chapter, but also in terms of the individual's place in society. Renaissance man though he was, Goethe did not write essays in political theory and cannot be compared directly to Rousseau in that respect. Rather, his response to Rousseau's social thought can be read first in the conversation his novel of education, *Wilhelm Meisters Lehrjahre* (1796; *Wilhelm Meister's Apprenticeship*), conducts with *Émile, ou De l'éducation* (1762; *Emile, or On Education*), and second in his use of the *Reveries* in *Faust*, part 1 (1808). Between *Werther* and *Die Wahlverwandtschaften* Goethe only rarely expressed himself explicitly about Rousseau, but in these two major works of the 1790s it is possible to trace the shifts in his attitude, and the trajectory is telling. The first step is his enthusiasm for the pedagogical views laid down in *Emile*, expressed primarily in his participation in educating Charlotte von Stein's son Fritz. By the time of *Wilhelm Meisters Lehrjahre*, which takes on not only Rousseau's pedagogy but also his social theory, enthusiasm has shifted to critique. The tension between individual and society that appeared as solipsism in *Werther* appears in the context of education as, increasingly, egoism. The social critique becomes more severe with the completion of part 1 of *Faust* in the last years of the 1790s and first years of the new century. In effect, then, Goethe spent the late 1780s and especially the 1790s working through the social implications of Rousseau's new subject.

Though *Werther* and *Die Wahlverwandtschaften* treat selves in closed worlds, society in a test tube, as the chemical title of the second novel implies, nevertheless both Goethe and Rousseau knew that selves exist in societies; the more complicated that self was, the more important and difficult it became to integrate it into society. John Locke's *Some Thoughts Concerning Education* (1693) already posited a self not rationally preformed, but inscribed onto the blank slate of the infant mind. Rousseau, it might be said, wanted to peer into that blankness, and so the exploding interest in education in the late eighteenth century, fueled in part by *Emile*, also expresses an exploding interest in the unconscious or irrational self. Education, *Bildung*, thus became another important space of Goethe's encounter with Rousseau. But the world to which youth of the late eighteenth century were being educated was also oppressively political as the French Revolution loomed ever more threateningly, and Rousseau was one of its most influential harbingers. Thus Goethe's ambivalence toward Rousseau had to extend also into the political sphere, and that aspect appears most clearly in the first part of *Faust*, which frames the great political meltdown of the Revolution and the Terror: the Gretchen tragedy was drafted in the mid-1770s, while almost the entire remainder of part 1 that surrounds it was composed between 1797 and 1801. It also frames the composition of *Wilhelm Meisters Lehrjahre*, which took place between 1777 and 1796. In these two most important of his works, Goethe explores his ambivalence toward Rousseau's social views, so that Rousseau was the crucial subtext for his social and educational thinking in the 1790s.[1] While Goethe does not address politics directly in either of these texts, his position on Rousseau's devastating importance for the French Revolution turns out to be very close to that of Hannah Arendt in *The Human Condition*, a text that in turn will illuminate the reading of *Faust* offered here.

Education: *Wilhelm Meister* and *Emile*

Goethe's interest in Rousseau's child-rearing principles dates to his Sturm und Drang period: by 1775 he was personally acquainted with two of the three leading German language pedagogues of his day, Johann Bernhard Basedow (1724–90, with whom he traveled in 1774) and Johann Heinrich Campe (1746–1818, tutor of the Humboldt brothers; Goethe met him in 1776). The two ran a school in Dessau, the Philanthropinum, which was organized on the principles of *Emile*. The third, Johann Heinrich Pestalozzi (1746–1827), also strongly influenced by Rousseau, was known to Goethe by reputation, though not as early as the other two. Goethe himself was notorious for living back-to-nature principles from *Emile*, such as bathing naked outdoors in winter from his tiny garden house outside the city walls. His correspondence with Charlotte von Stein included effusions on Rousseau and occasionally copies of particular texts.[2] In 1775 Goethe met a disciple of Rousseau in Zurich, Heinrich Julius von Lindau (1754–76), who had become a hermit and adopted a foster child named Peter. After making Goethe promise to care for Peter, should anything happen to him, Lindau left to fight in the American Revolution (with the Hessian troops) the following year and died in New York. Several months later Peter arrived on Goethe's doorstep and joined the household, such as it was, until he became so intolerable that Goethe sent him off to learn to be a hunter. While all this was going on, Goethe's close friend Friedrich Heinrich Jacobi (1743–1819) was sending his difficult son Georg to be educated by the notorious Rousseau enthusiast Princess Adelheid Amalia Gallitzin (1748–1806), who was raising her own children according to the precepts of *Emile*. (Goethe first met her personally in 1785.)

He tried to live *Emile* more directly in his virtual adoption of Charlotte von Stein's youngest son, Fritz, whom he frequently took on trips with him, and at last, in 1783, took into his house to live with him and be educated.[3] Following the model of close, lifelong friendship propounded by Rousseau as the ideal relationship between tutor and child in *Emile*, Goethe intended that Fritz should learn by doing, and the two were close friends. When in the garden house they slept in the same room. At one point he even wrote to Charlotte that he had Fritz reading the *Confessions* aloud to him (June 5, 1782; WA 4.5:336). When Goethe fled Weimar for Italy in 1786 he left Fritz in the care of his personal servant, Philipp Seidel, until Charlotte realized four months later that Goethe had decamped for the long term and brought Fritz back under her own roof. Goethe's flight was not from Fritz, with whom he remained in lifelong contact, but from his unsatisfactory professional and emotional situation in Weimar. Indeed, his educational experiment had become by that point the brightest part of his relation to Charlotte.

Goethe's biographers tend to regard his pedagogical efforts as failures, not only with Peter and Fritz, but also with his own son, August.[4] The issue at hand, however, is not to judge the quality of Goethe's pedagogical efforts, but to consider their provenance and how they reflect on his attitudes toward Rousseau. A good example in this context is Fritz's departure from Weimar. The Duke Karl August sought to train officials and artists for his own court, and Fritz shared his largesse. After his studies in Jena and Hamburg, Fritz received an appointment and salary in 1794 to broaden himself with travel and a year as volunteer in the Prussian civil service, while the position of tutor to the crown prince was held for him. In 1796 he requested his dismissal from Weimar in order to take up a career in Prussia. The duke accused Fritz of "egoism," which he blamed (to Charlotte) on Goethe's pedagogy.[5] Nicholas Boyle points to the underlying problem: Karl August thought Fritz owed him personal and feudal loyalty, while Fritz's Goethean/Rousseauist upbringing made him see himself as an "individual" responsible above all to himself. In effect, the conflict is that between the old and new regimes. And as Boyle argues, "Goethe was an expert at concealing his own modernity beneath the feudal forms, but because it was always ultimately his personal choice to adopt them he was . . . as much a Revolutionary as any of his contemporaries" (457). Goethe, Boyle suggests, knowingly opted to hide his Rousseauist individualism under the forms of the feudal court when he decided to settle in Weimar; Fritz, however, was not up to the masquerade or had not even been made aware of its necessity. Goethe himself may not have been aware of the complexity of his own role in the days when he was bringing up Fritz; indeed, the experience in hands-on education combined with his abrupt escape from his Weimar connections must have enabled him to recognize it, for masquerade as a form of selfhood came to the fore in the dramas he completed in Italy, as the second part of this book will show.

First, however, there are Goethe's views on education and "egoism" to consider, and the fundamental text for them is *Wilhelm Meisters Lehrjahre*, the paradigmatic bildungsroman of European literature. It marries the picaresque plot as it had developed in *Tom Jones* to the intensity of the epistolary novel of passion.[6] Its hero wanders his way from youth to maturity through a series of love relationships (named, in succession, Mariane, Philine, Mignon, the Countess, Therese, Natalie) that mark his development from a dilettantish love for poetry and especially theater to mature participation in the affairs of life and society, and from rich bourgeois to marriage into a noble family that is itself moving beyond class (a reasonable ideal for the Goethe of the 1790s, who had only accepted his patent of nobility because it made social protocol at the Weimar court flow more smoothly). Since Goethe began *Wilhelm Meisters Lehrjahre* in 1777, when he was clearly committed to Rousseauist pedagogy, and rewrote it in the 1790s after he returned to Weimar from Italy with substantial distance on these experiences, it can be read as his probing of Rousseau's attitudes toward self and society. The *Lehrjahre* narrates its hero's liberation from the paternalistic small society represented by his father and brother-in-law; he leaves both for the larger, aristocratic world. The novel rethinks not only the flight of Werther, but also that of Goethe from his father and of Fritz from Karl August, with Weimar now the small world to be escaped. Escaping from his inheritance is the egoistical act of the individual. That is why the grandfather's art collection, Wilhelm's lost but regained inheritance, plays such an important role in the *Lehrjahre*. Wilhelm's father built a fancy but cold new house with the cash realized from selling *his* father's art collection, of which Wilhelm treasured sentimental, childish memories. At the end Wilhelm reencounters the collection at the castle of his ideal woman and (on the last page) fiancée, Natalie, whose uncle had bought it from Wilhelm's father. But the inheritance Wilhelm recovers is, as a collection of significant older paintings, now recognized as the general inheritance of a civilized society, no longer the personal possession of an individual ancestor. Thus the novel extends egoism to the more general sense of self and world. Accordingly Wilhelm finds many father figures along his way, the most important of whom is an Abbé, a spiritual father by profession, who transforms the church in the novel into a metaphor for the institution of society. The final version of the metaphor is the so-called Society of the Tower (Turmgesellschaft) into which Wilhelm's new circle of noble friends initiate him late in the novel—a society that binds not only individual men into a society, but also men who will live in all different nations into one larger society of mutual support. Because its followers are to disperse around the world, the tower is, with Goethe's typical irony, the Tower of Babel, but without its negative effects. This biblical allusion transforms Goethe's educated men into modernized missionaries—not of a specific religion but of human community—and thus realizes the social integration toward which Rousseau's *Emile* only gestures.

While it is not customary to compare *Emile* and the *Lehrjahre*, there are obvious similarities.[7] Not only do both works thematize education, but Goethe follows Rousseau in extolling the natural innocence of childhood as a necessary developmental stage. Goethe's title word "apprenticeship" appears in book 2 of *Emile*, and in such fashion as to define Goethe's novel: "We are not only apprentice workers, we are apprentice men, and apprenticeship in this latter trade is harder and longer than in the former one" (Nous ne sommes pas seulement apprentifs ouvriers, nous sommes apprentifs hommes, et l'apprentissage de ce dernier métier est plus pénible et plus long que l'autre).[8] Beyond this and numerous other allusions, there are generic connections: Rousseau has written a treatise, but organized it as a life history punctuated by repeated analogies to drama and capped by a brief romance. Although it discusses the infancy and childhood of the tutee at length, the treatise only comes alive and goes into detail as Emile approaches puberty. The complication and ex-

citement, such as they are, come with his maturing and courtship. Goethe's
novel drops the preparations and follows its hero from his first tentative steps
into adulthood to his engagement. Rousseau's analogies to theater become
thematic, as for example, when Wilhelm performs the title role of *Hamlet*.
Both narratives are interrupted by lengthy "confessions" shortly after the
midpoint—in Goethe the "Confessions of a Beautiful Soul," and in Rousseau
the "Confession of Faith of the Savoyard Vicar." Finally, both works end with the
unusual gesture of deferral—no sooner is the young couple engaged than the
bridegroom is dismissed on an extended journey of further education. And
just here Rousseau uses the apprenticeship image for the second time, as he
tells Emile he must serve an apprenticeship not only to life, but also to passion (*ŒC* 4:818; Bloom 445). The dictum grounds Goethe's sequel, *Wilhelm
Meisters Wanderjahre* (1821; revised version, 1829; *Wilhelm Meisters Journeyman
Years*), which is devoted to studies in passion.

Nevertheless, the differences are crucial. To be sure, Goethe adopts Rousseau's model of education through hands-on contact with the world. His Wilhelm is never shown in a schoolroom; like Emile all the characters subject to
the pedagogical efforts of the Society of the Tower learn by doing and erring.
But Rousseau's tutor functions as the daily companion and trusted best friend
for life of the tutee, whereas in Goethe tutors give way to kindly strangers
who mysteriously appear and disappear in various disguises and turn out to be
directed by a Catholic cleric—an aspect of the novel of intrigue that persisted
into gothic fiction. In the *Wanderjahre* the differences are greater yet. The tu-
tees all learn a trade, like Emile, and Emile's chosen trade, carpentry, is given
pride of place in Goethe's opening chapter. But carpentry appears there as the
trade of St. Joseph, who models his life in virtually every detail on that of the
foster father of Jesus—hardly what Rousseau had in mind. The teachers in
the Pedagogic Province later in the novel appear as an abstract trinity variously
referred to as "the three" or as "the superiors." Given Goethe's well-known
reservations about religious orthodoxy, the references sound parodistic and
suggest that Goethe's attitude toward education had become almost sardonic.[9]

The difference between Goethe's and Rousseau's novels goes to the heart
of Rousseau's paranoia, an aspect Goethe seems not to have thought about in
the 1770s. Rousseau's education is focused above all on maintaining control of
the tutee. Infants already use their crying to control adults and must be kept
rigidly in hand (even though they mustn't be swaddled), and Emile must be
subjected to similar control, lest he control his teacher. Rousseau warns insis-
tently that a single mistake and all will be lost, a single revelation to Emile of

how he is being manipulated and the tutor will lose Emile's trust and his own control forever. Especially the last book makes clear into what private depths the manipulation penetrates: what Emile thinks is the chance discovery of the perfect wife has been orchestrated step by step behind the scenes. To be sure, Wilhelm enters, in his wanderings, into relationships mostly with siblings of his future fiancée, but that trick is played by the narrator on the reader, not by the teacher on his pupil. Both Goethe and Rousseau use the motif of puppets to represent the issue of control, but only in Goethe does anyone ever drop a puppet. Thus in large and small ways, Goethe undoes the totalitarian authoritarianism of Rousseau's educational system and exposes the underlying paradox in *Emile* that only a rigidly controlled upbringing can train the ideal responsible citizen of a republic.

Rousseau's need for control derives from his primary, still stoic, pedagogical goal: happiness based on learning to subject passion to the control of reason. Rousseau's interior self must submit to the same strict control as the passions it superseded. *Wilhelm Meister*, by contrast, has no interest in educating its hero to happiness. Characters incapable of strong passion are of little interest to the hero, to his mysterious tutors, or, indeed, to the narrator. Wilhelm has much to learn from the attractive actress Philine, for example, who is more or less the embodiment of free love, but little from the Melinas, whose marriage Wilhelm had facilitated when he thought they wanted to run off to be actors; when they turn out to lack talent, imagination, and Romantic artistic commitment, Wilhelm quickly outgrows them and they remain subsidiary members of the metaphoric family he accumulates around himself. The tensions that lead to the closing engagement of Wilhelm and Natalie are anything but the tentative, idyllic love affair played out in *Emile*. Instead, Wilhelm's primary emotion in the last book is "vexation" (*Verdruss*), and the most gothic and most passionate of the embedded narratives (the imaginative waif Mignon's parentage) comes in this last book. Both Goethe and Rousseau seek to understand and elucidate the human heart, but *Wilhelm Meister* does not, like *Emile*, seek to control it. By validating the passionate and irrational aspects of his characters' lives, Goethe lays bare the moral tangle that Rousseau's emphasis on control simply represses.

But if the mature individual is not to be an object of rigid control, how does one educate him to become a responsible member of society? With its lifelong one-on-one tutoring, Rousseau's system is hopelessly inefficient. At the same time, *Wilhelm Meister* can seem hopelessly desultory; the sporadic discussion about the relative roles of fate and chance remains vague, and the

Society of the Tower's actual contribution to Wilhelm's education is much debated.[10] Goethe spurns control and leaves education up to nature. The results of nature left to itself can be magnificent, as Goethe's own studies of plant morphology in the 1790s often suggest. But nature is in Goethe amoral; it can hardly be an agent of moral socialization, as *Faust*, which Goethe took up again the year after he finished *Wilhelm Meister*, makes clear—or normally seems to. Indeed, one hardly thinks of *Faust* as a theory of socialization; it has often been seen rather as the triumph of the antisocial. Nevertheless, the drama turns on a pact, a contract, a motif that Locke and Rousseau had made synonymous with the basis of society. *Emile* rests on a contract between the father and the tutor of the child; *Faust* rests on a series of contracts—most obviously between Faust and Mephistopheles and between the Lord and Mephistopheles, as well as in the established institutions that bind Margarete to her community. *Faust*, then, is the place to look for the continuation of Goethe's critique.

Revolution: *Faust* and the *Reveries*

Initially, Goethe's tension with Rousseau appears in his deviation from the traditional Faustian pact. Instead of bargaining for twenty-four years of diabolical service, Goethe's Faust signs his bet that the devil will never be able to satisfy him with the cry, "Let us plunge into the rush of time" (Stürzen wir uns in das Rauschen der Zeit).[11] For him time represents the world into which he will escape from his narrow gothic study and his imprisoning consciousness. The language of Faust's pact reverses a line from the climax of the fifth of the *Reveries of the Solitary Walker*. There Rousseau dreams of drifting on a boat in a moment of pure consciousness without content and laments, "Among our liveliest joys there is scarcely a moment to which our hearts might truly say: I wish this moment would last forever" (A peine est-il dans nos plus vives jouissances un instant où le cœur puisse véritablement nous dire: *Je voudrois que cet instant durât toujours*).[12] Goethe's Faust transforms the lament over human submission to temporality into an explicit affirmation of it: the condition that would lose Faust his bet with the devil reads, "if I should ever say to the moment, 'Tarry, thou art so fair'" (1699–1700; Werd' ich zum Augenblicke sagen: / Verweile doch! du bist so schön!). Both Faust and Rousseau's *promeneur* lament the incapacity of life to satisfy their emotional appetites; yet while Rousseau imagines the state of happiness in a boat rocking masterless on the lake, Faust embraces the protean world that drives him to desperation. Rousseau withdraws into pure self-consciousness; Goethe prefers striving and engagement with a natural world in constant motion.[13]

Both opposed positions are taken to be paradigmatically Romantic, and both have been subject to a long tradition of critique, Rousseau's for its paranoid reclusiveness, Goethe's for its immoral imperialism. Paranoia is a ubiquitous feature of the gothic mode, while energetic expansiveness corresponds to the typical Romantic drive to transcendence. Together they constitute the Romantic dialectic of expansion and contraction, of ecstatic affirmation and irony. The difference is that Goethe comprehends both sides of this dialectic and that he uses Rousseau as the starting point for it. Faust begins part I (in the scene "Night") as precisely the self-contained subject (imprisoned in his narrow study) that Rousseau's *Reveries* articulated so emphatically. Goethe concurs with Rousseau's diagnosis of the situation of the subject, but does not allow his hero to imitate the wanderer and renounce his identity in the fog of subjectivity. Beginning in the 1790s, when he wrote the pact scene and completed *Faust*, part I, Goethe names the Rousseauist hesitation to engage the world "care" (*Sorge*) a development that culminates in Faust's blinding by a character with that name in act 5 of part 2. But already in *Die Wahlverwandtschaften*, Ottilie, blind to the moral consequences of her love for Eduard, floats helplessly on the lake after she has lost both her oars and Eduard's baby—in exactly the desirable situation for Rousseau's solitary wanderer. Although both Goethe and Rousseau have been subjected to ethical critique for their supposed blindness to society, this discussion demonstrates that Goethe himself exercised similar critique of Rousseau; he pits activity against the blindness of pure self-consciousness, yet his Faust is also morally blind. Rousseau appears in the formulation of the pact because Goethe is still pursuing the problem defined by him of settling the truly developed individual in society.

Hannah Arendt's critique of Rousseau in *The Human Condition* as the first theorist of intimacy illuminates Goethe's tense relationship to Rousseau in the pact scene. According to her, the true public realm was represented by the Greek polis, where free men could contend in the practice of politics. By the eighteenth century, however, this space had been displaced by a totalitarian extension of the patriarchal family that Arendt calls "society," for her an entirely negative development. Rousseau, however, set the self against society by making the human heart the refuge of individuality in what she calls the first theory of intimacy (38–39). This "discovery of intimacy" and its concomitant

hatred of society made Rousseau a hero—for the Romantics as well as for Arendt, but it went, in her eyes, dangerously far. It is one thing to deny society,
a largely negative construct, but quite another to exclude the vitalistic, almost
divine power of nature (that is, the larger context in which human life is an-
chored, what *Faust* calls "the great world"), as Rousseau does, for example, in
the *Reveries*. Arendt actually blames Rousseau for making "world alienation"
the "hallmark of the modern age" (254). Her use of "world" here corresponds
exactly to Goethe's in *Faust*, a natural physical space that is frequently ordered
by some human or divine mind. For Arendt Rousseau's "intimacy" spelled the
death of politics as for Faust it denied human action.[14]

Whereas Rousseau rejects society in favor of drifting alone on the lake,
the Faustian pact—despite the verbal echoes—strives for engagement, however painful it may be. If engagement with society is the equivalent of a pact
with the devil for Rousseau, then, one might say, Goethe really agrees with
Rousseau—society is of the devil. But for Goethe that is not a problem, for
society is part of the world, and the world, including all of nature, constitutes
for Goethe the realm of reality, everything that is not the ideal. And precisely
this world, the earth, is identified by the God of the "Prologue in Heaven" as
the realm of Mephistopheles. Goethe's devil has all the spirits of nature at his
command as well as all of society. Goethe does not accept Rousseau's binaries
of society and nature, control and passion, and hence Faust does not have the
option of isolating himself from the world to botanize, Rousseau's single activity in the *Reveries*. To be sure, Faust tests communing with nature briefly in
the scene "Forest and Cavern," but then leaves his sylvan grove to seduce Margarete—not because Mephistopheles tempts him, but rather because the devil
convinces him that his isolation achieves nothing and his gesture is therefore
futile. To withdraw from interaction with the world is to be dead; to be alive
and be part of time is to accept violence and change.

This equivalence between the power of time and that of nature belongs,
however, to the new meaning taken on by the term "revolution" at the end
of the eighteenth century, when it acquired an aura of natural inevitability in
the rhetoric of the French revolutionaries—whether as natural or as historical
necessity.[15] That same language characterizes all of Goethe's discussion of the
Revolution—it is a storm, a thunderstorm, a "Naturphänomen" that strikes
blindly and unavoidably. When Faust says, as he enters into his pact with
Mephistopheles, "Let us cast ourselves into the rush of time" (1754; Stürzen
wir uns in das Rauschen der Zeit), when he describes himself as the raging
torrent that will destroy Margarete (3350), he is not simply being Promet-

hean. He is speaking the language of the contemporary political violence that Goethe watched anxiously from the German periphery. In this sense Faust's pact is a fundamental political statement. The disagreement with Rousseau is more revolutionary, more political than Rousseau's own rejection of society. Goethe cannot accept turning one's back on society because it is defective or in turmoil. The issue is not whether or not one likes or agrees with the shifting tenets of the Revolution. It is simply whether or not one intends to help steer the boat to shore and pick up the pieces. Rousseau, of course, was dead twelve years before the Revolution began, but Goethe was hardly alone in European history in understanding that coming to terms with Rousseau equated to coming to terms with the Revolution.

The other great pact in the play, the bet struck between the Lord and Mephistopheles in the "Prologue in Heaven," also turns on the revolutionary influence of Rousseau, this time on its moral-psychological aspects. In his insistence that striving outweighs erring, the Lord stands closer to Rousseau than Mephistopheles does. In the *Confessions* Rousseau replaces the extensive social control of *Emile* with good intentions, which he allows to trump bad deeds. Feeling outweighs moral judgment. The Lord's often-quoted lines in *Faust* "Man ever errs, as long as he strives" (317; Es irrt der Mensch, solang' er strebt) and "A good man in his dark urges is still aware of the proper path" (328–29; Ein guter Mensch in seinem dunklen Drange / Ist sich des rechten Weges wohl bewußt) approach the extreme subjectivity Rousseau defends in the *Confessions* or in the *Reveries*. This Lord cares less about the deeds Faust will perform on earth than whether his intentions will remain true enough to his origin, his *Urquell* (324), and whether He will eventually feel like leading him to clarity (309; "in die Klarheit führen"). All the Lord seems to demand for salvation is striving, fulfilling one's natural development, and Faust's salvation at the end of part 2 shows as much. Not only has Faust there pronounced the fatal words of his bet with Mephistopheles, but he has been responsible for several murders, enforced his views on innocent recalcitrants, and grown wealthy from open piracy. Nevertheless angels wrest his soul from Mephistopheles' devils and carry it onward in the wake of the Mater Gloriosa and the forgiving soul of Margarete. Like Rousseau's, Faust's good intentions have sufficed.

Once again, Rousseau's binarisms are too simple. It remains to the devil Mephistopheles to speak for the traditional moral order of good and evil, to claim that concepts like temptation, sin, and fall are relevant to human life. It is hard not to sympathize with Mephistopheles' disappointment in act 5 of

part 2, after angels have ludicrously cheated the devil of his prey by pelting
him with burning roses, the more so as Goethe's commitment to legal order is
well known, as is his sometimes painful submission of his own better feelings
to his responsibility for carrying out the law as a member of the Weimar privy
council.[16] So Mephistopheles represents a point of view in the "Prologue in
Heaven" at least as legitimate for Goethe, perhaps more legitimate, than the
Rousseauist solipsism of good intentions represented by the Lord.

To be sure, the Lord's position is not quite so simple. By replacing feeling with nature in the Lord's language, Goethe shifts the focus. The Lord's
model for the innate goodness of man is nature: for him, Faust is a young
tree that will eventually blossom and bear fruit (310–11), the "living beauty"
(345; lebendig reiche Schöne) that brings joy to the hearts of all who watch
the Lord's spectacle. The striving that leads Faust into error is the unfolding
and development of his very nature as a human being. While Goethe criticizes
the rigid social control of *Emile* in the *Lehrjahre*, here in *Faust* he implies that
Rousseau's blindness to nature transforms his confidence in the human heart
into dangerous solipsism. The complicated morality of the scene turns on a
profound ambivalence toward Rousseau's incapacity to recognize the ethical
consequences of his new psychology. God or devil, control or licentiousness,
withdrawal or destruction, self or society—both pacts in *Faust* are based on
Rousseauist binarisms, and the plot develops from Goethe's dissatisfaction
with the terms.

Not until the end of the Gretchen tragedy does Goethe overcome the
problem. For if Rousseau is at the heart of the choices Faust must make, the
same can be said, perhaps more surprisingly, for Margarete. The crucial moment for this reading comes at the end of the scene "At the Well," where
Margarete's pregnancy is first mentioned. After listening to a neighbor gossip
about the punishment in store for another girl who is pregnant out of wedlock,
Margarete regrets her own former readiness to scold others and concludes,

> And now I myself am the sinner!
> But—everything that drove me to it,
> God, was so good, ah, was so dear! (3583–86)

> (Und bin nun selbst der Sünde bloß!
> Doch—alles, was dazu mich trieb,
> Gott! war so gut! ach war so lieb!)

Here in a nutshell is the same paradox propounded in the "Prologue in Heaven." On the one hand are the scolding (devilish) demands of right and wrong in human society, and on the other what her own heart tells her is "dear" and "good," what leads her to invoke God. God is here on the side of what led her into temptation, not on the one that punishes sin. Her repentance in the cathedral scene is dictated by an evil spirit. And while the voice from above that announces her salvation at the very end of part I seems to be that of God, only Faust's refusal to embrace her makes her actually turn to God. Her real faith in the last scene is in her lover, who brought her out of her imprisoning home into time and into the creative cycle of nature; this is the faith the play seems to reward at the end rather than her belated and unconvincing return to a God who plays second fiddle to Faust.[17] Margarete does not founder on the competing demands of Rousseauist subjectivity and the social order now precisely because her intentions outweigh her deeds. Then she can be rescued by a deus ex machina.

Once again, Hannah Arendt's critique of Rousseau illuminates what Goethe is up to. The discovery of intimacy she attributed to Rousseau is, with its focus on the heart, the social version of the problematic subjectivity under discussion here, and it spelled for her the death of politics by placing social feeling, that is, compassion, above the political values of competition and action—what she called "freedom." Margarete's first glimmer of the tragic conflict in which she is enmeshed in "At the Well" is bound to her rising sense of compassion; in the earlier part of this scene, conscious of her own guilt, she tries to express compassion for the other pregnant girl. For Arendt, compassion drove the French Revolution off track from creating a new space of freedom, as the American Revolution did, and instead allowed the social question, the poverty of the masses, to come to the forefront. Because society, that pernicious extension of the private economic realm, displaced any real politics from the public realm, there arose a persistent paradigm of revolution in which the social question, compassion, resulted in the rise of tyranny rather than of freedom. That is the central argument of *On Revolution*. Arendt's argument is in fact an effective reading of *Faust*: if Faust were to take pity on Margarete's innocence and let her be, or, in the dungeon, kiss her and comfort her as she desired, he would remain in a prison equivalent to that in which he began the play. It would turn him away from engagement in the world. Small wonder, then, that Goethe turns at the end of both parts of *Faust* to some notion of salvation; there can be only a transcendent solution to the paradox he saw so clearly.

What Arendt sees as the failure of nineteenth century European revolutions, Goethe sees as the central problem in *Faust:* the tension between competing revolutionary demands—the imperative of nature to complete self-development and the imperative of society to renunciation of self in favor of harmony and order. The mandate to self-development is a subjectivity as yet untouched by imagination or reflection, hence devoid even of compassion. It is imposed on Faust by the Lord in the "Prologue" and articulated in the two pacts with Mephistopheles, who embodies the vitalistic driving force of nature. Mephistophelean restlessness is one of the revolutionary forms in *Faust.* The second, compassionate, imperative is written onto Margarete's body; the productive vitalism of nature endangers the moral and social order and leads to personal and communal dismemberment (she is decapitated, as so many Frenchmen were just about to be). Nevertheless, the play enacts how Faust and Margarete love one another, belong to each other. Both are revolutionaries, both their tragedies engage the political and psychological aspects of the revolutionary Rousseau. They also engage both meanings of revolution in the period—its association with the circling order of the cosmos and its inevitability, on the one hand, and the disruptive utopian concern for the previously invisible people (Arendt's "social question") on the other. This latter meaning was being born from the first meaning precisely in the 1790s, the decade of *Faust*, part 1. If Faust embodies the Promethean rebellion against the limitations of the human situation in order to develop the infinite potential inherent in his place in nature, Margarete embodies the tragic rebellion against the limiting safeguards of human society, which insists on the separation of private from public. And yet the poles are also reversed. Faust carries the pain of repeatedly sacrificing his own private realm to the call of the public realm, while Margarete, the martyr to society, ends up embodying the vitalistic power of nature, the eternal feminine. No wonder there are two sides to every question about the play. As this confusing, turbulent circulation of forces cannot be restricted to the limits of a single genre, it, more significantly, repeatedly crosses the boundaries of individual and social psychology. It represents not only the revolutionary environment of the play, but its revolutionary nature.

There are good reasons why Arendt is so helpful here. As a political and moral philosopher trained in and committed to the German philosophical tradition and to the emergent discipline of sociology, but writing as an exile in America after the Holocaust, she offers an especially clear-eyed view simultaneously from without and within. Symptomatically, *The Human Condition* was published first in English in 1958, then in German in 1960 (both Arendt's versions, since neither edition acknowledges a translator). Goethe was central to the German curriculum for Arendt's generation, as he had been for the psychoanalysts, and her first scholarly project after her dissertation was a biography of Rahel Varnhagen, the founder of Germany's Goethe cult; the biography reveals detailed familiarity with Goethe's work on Arendt's part. In *The Human Condition*, at least in the English version, Arendt talks less about Goethe than about Rousseau but even a cursory examination of her rhetoric reveals that it is saturated with the language of German classicism, and particularly with that of *Faust*. Themes such as the governing role of antiquity as an ideal, the epistemological necessity for aesthetic recapitulation of history, the nature of history as unremitting struggle are central to the ideology of both *The Human Condition* and *Faust*. Arendt's three types of work—labor, work, and action—can be found everywhere in *Faust*. Most important, the language of the fleeting moment and the deed, *Faust's* governing concepts, appear repeatedly in Arendt, especially as she reaches the apex of her hierarchy of work, or at crucial moments of the argument, such as when she connects Jesus' love of goodness to Plato's love of wisdom, saying, "Attempts to bring into being that which can never survive the fleeting moment of the deed itself have never been lacking and have always led into absurdity" (75).

In fact, Arendt's phenomenology of work corresponds closely to the kinds of work represented in *Faust*. Lowest on Arendt's scale is labor, the effort that gathers and processes the products of nature for human consumption, by slaves and/or women, within the private household; in *Faust* this corresponds to the constant digging in the earth—sometimes farming, sometimes mining, sometimes digging Faust's grave—that is consistently the work of nature spirits and always under the supervision of Mephistopheles. Next in Arendt's hierarchy is work in the sense of fabrication, that is, the production of tools and objects by artisans and artists, the class she designates *homo faber*. These buildings, furniture, tools, ornaments, and works of art furnish the world and, to a large extent, determine us. In *Faust* this work, crafting of the gold and treasure recovered from repeated descents into the depths, is done by both nature spirits and humans. Faust himself, most notably, translates, creates stage settings, and stages masques, both for the imperial court and for himself (with Helena). In this respect he is the highest kind of artisan in Arendt's system, a poet. The best kind of work for Arendt is what she calls "action." Her ideal of action derives from her idealized version of the Greek polis, as Goethe's ideal of beauty in *Faust* derives from the great texts of Athenian democracy. "Action" for Arendt is democratic (arising from competition among equals) political action in the public sphere. It includes both heroic acts (feats of war or daring) and also language, both of which reveal the self to others and establish it in human remembrance. As work in the public sphere, action creates human public life. Her vocabulary around this concept in her German version of the text is the same that surrounds "deed" at the heart of *Faust*. Its closest correspondence in *Faust* is the community Faust creates at the end of part 2 on the land he has reclaimed from the seashore.

In effect, *Faust* should be understood as a major subtext of Arendt's analysis of the human condition in modernity. Like the psychoanalysts she conceptualizes and theorizes what Goethe has represented poetically in absence of the sociological and psychological discourses available to her. And thereby she brings to light an ethical trajectory that is otherwise difficult to see in *Faust*. The play has been most commonly read with focus on the individual—and I do not quarrel with such a reading. Faust trapped in his narrow gothic chamber seeking unity with the great Other outside, however one might identify it in more specific terms, is surely a modern interior self. But this focus on the individual leads to a moral quagmire as the play insists on the one hand that self-development requires complete participation in the vitality and instability of nature and yet equally firmly insists on the validity of the human social order, which amoral nature constantly violates. Goethe's response to the dilemma is his usual one—his hero's path oscillates between destructive moments of vitalist activity and moments of recognition of limits, but all the while progresses steadily to increasingly "higher" forms of activity. This is the spiral familiar from his botanical studies.

With regard to work, the play moves up Arendt's hierarchy from labor to work to action, and from "natural" to human agents. More important, the relationship of work to the word Faust so haughtily rejects in his opening monologue develops from an individual one to a social one. Here are the steps: Faust rejects words as empty in his first monologue, but when he translates the Bible after his Easter walk he translates "logos" successively as "word," "sense," "power," "deed." In the remainder of part 1 he gradually learns to respect the word in the sequence of plays within the play staged by Mephistopheles, and in part 2 he himself becomes the stager of such plays, and the creator of their settings simply by the exercise of his own poetic words (rising sun in the first scene, the setting for his marriage to Helena in act 3). The son he sires with the Helena he has himself created has long been recognized as a figure for Lord Byron, and through him for European poetry. But his name (Euphorion, "high spirits") points beyond his aesthetic significance to his psychological and social significance: in his engagement in the fundamental activities of society, love and war, he represents the entire human condition in a single human life, a microcosm of human society. Faust's final land drainage project is an action that both constitutes a human community and can be remembered by it for as long as the community endures.[18] Whether Faust's dying vision is fully realized or not, the play has already acknowledged the new human community that occupies Faust's reclaimed land and Faust can triumph, "The master's word, it alone has power . . . one mind's enough to guide a thousand hands" (11501–10; Des Herren Wort, es gibt allein Gewicht . . . Genügt ein Geist für tausend Hände). Word has become deed, both the highest human achievement and a specifically human achievement. In this respect, Arendt's progression from domestic labor to society-building action identifies the process of socialization *Faust* achieves.[19] Goethe thus rectified Rousseau's radical subjectivity, the "world alienation" made visible in the Faust trapped in a narrow gothic room, by showing that the Faustian process of engulfing and reprojecting the Other in order to know it makes both the self and the Other social, a part of history.

In effect, then, I have argued that Arendt's *Human Condition* is the theory of socialization that *Faust* was not yet ready to be, that Arendt conceptualizes Goethe's implicit attempt to rethink Rousseau's theory of socialization in *Emile*. This argument offers not only some hints as to why Faust's path from labor to action, from individual to social action is so long and so tortuous, but also lays bare Rousseau's and Goethe's fundamental partnership in creating the social world of modernity. The revolutionary nature of *Faust* rests, in this context, on the interplay of a self not so much *newly* interiorized, but now *so* interiorized as to be inchoate, and a society that has scarcely noticed, much less come to terms with, the reversal of values its newly individualized selves—actually now citizens—implies. Despite the obvious Shakespeareanism of *Faust*, an enormous gulf separates its characters from Shakespeare's. At the beginning Faust's dissatisfaction with himself is more depression than the ambition of a Macbeth or an Othello. Faust is in the grip of emotions, not of passions, and can articulate only his vague dissatisfaction, not what he wants. Margarete's self is similarly inchoate: she can't make sense of her behavior, and the moral poles of anyone's behavior cannot be aligned with previous conceptions of nature and its relation to society. More important, the text reveals how the shift and its implications were fought out on the ground, how Goethe raised concerns about the new psychology barely articulated by Rousseau and only later articulated by philosophers and psychologists precisely because they did not yet have a language in which to articulate them. I do not wish to address the question of a causal connection between the personal and social aspects of the revolutionary shift here: Goethe and his contemporaries experienced both upheavals simultaneously. But the fact that Goethe engaged Rousseau in the shaping of his life as well as in his literary experiments justifies ignoring the causal question. Goethe saw the implications of the new self at both the individual and the social level. The continuities he established between his life and his literature testify to his view of the revolutionary nature of literature and its role in creating new ways of thinking.

PART II

Experiments in Subjectivity

THE PRECEDING CHAPTERS have discussed Goethe's efforts to come to terms with Rousseau's new subjectivity in moral terms. The three chapters in Part II address his efforts to deal with the representational problems it posed. For if the interior self is unknowable even to itself, the poet has no ready way to represent its interior dynamics. Yet how else can one represent it, since its interior dynamics are what it actually is? So effective was Goethe's solution to the problem that the central figures of his mature works seem self-evidently to have fully developed interior lives, beginning already in Friedrich Schiller's review of *Egmont* in 1788 (*Sämtliche Werke*, 5:932–42). This impression arises, I think, because Goethe's classical plays, *Wilhelm Meisters Lehrjahre*, and *Faust* all appeared in the same decade from 1787 (*Iphigenie*) to 1796 (*Wilhelm Meister*; much of *Faust*, part 1, appeared in the form of a fragment in 1790). Nevertheless, even though all had long gestations, mostly dating back to the early and mid-1770s, the order of publication allows separation into three stages that reveal distinguishable steps in representing interiority. Since *Egmont* was begun right after the publication of *Werther*, and it and the other two classical plays, *Iphigenie* and *Tasso*, were completed before Goethe returned his full attention to *Faust* and *Wilhelm Meister*, they constitute an initial stage, to be discussed in Chapter 4; the epistemological problems of the interior self are imbricated in *Faust* with Goethe's scientific thinking and reception of Kant in the eighties and nineties, so it appears as its own stage in the Chapter 5. With *Wilhelm Meister*, the beginnings of which also date to the 1770s, the return from drama to narrative prose receives separate treatment in Chapter 6. As it turns out, the detour through drama that Goethe made between *Werther* and *Wilhelm Meister* is crucial to the allegorical technique Goethe developed for representing the interior self.

CHAPTER 4

The Theatrical Self

The classical plays *Egmont*, *Iphigenie auf Tauris*, and *Torquato Tasso* all deal at bottom with how to recognize and represent identity, even though they seem quite different on the surface: *Egmont*, in prose, has a large cast and disjointed scenes and owes much to Shakespeare and English bourgeois drama of the eighteenth century, while *Iphigenie* and *Tasso*, in blank verse, have small casts and tight linear plotting and look more like Euripides in the French neoclassical mode (*Iphigenie* has a typical Euripidean prologue and even passages that evoke the tone of choral ode). Thus it is necessary to explore first how identity emerges as a theme, then how Goethe experiments with genre to generate a sense for the complexity of identity, and, finally, the techniques of dramatic projection he develops to make the complexity visible on stage.

Identity as Theme

Before entering into the analysis, consider the essential similarity of the three plays based on a brief comparative plot summary. Egmont is a public hero trying to protect his people from Spanish oppression by remaining loyal to King Philip and trying to mediate. He is both Spanish noble and Flemish populist, the one side represented by his court connections and the other by his bourgeois Flemish mistress, Klare. His effort founders on the effective planning of his major rival, the Duke of Alba, and the play ends with Egmont dreaming of his mistress as the goddess of freedom and, upon waking, leaving his dungeon to be executed, while the orchestra plays a victory symphony. Iphigenie, saved from sacrifice at Aulis to be priestess of Diana at Tauris, is pulled between her longing to return to reconcile the sins of her fathers in Greece, and King

Thoas's demand that she become his wife and civilize his barbaric subjects in Tauris. When her brother Orest arrives, Iphigenie achieves the impossible mediation between the two identities by freeing her brother of his madness induced by the Furies and by making peace between her brother and Thoas.[1] The *deus ex machina* of Euripides' play is no longer necessary as all then realize that only Iphigenie is the sister the oracle summons back to Greece and that the contested statue of Diana can remain in Tauris. Tasso also has alternate identities; they appear in the choice of profession—poet or effective diplomat-courtier, as embodied in his rival Antonio—and also in two women, both named Leonore, who compete for his affection. Tasso makes his choices in both cases so clumsily that he is abandoned by the court and descends into madness. The differences between a public and private identity appear differently in the three plays even as they gradually converge on a common method of representing it.

For each of the central figures the question of identity dominates the play. Tasso would like to be not only the gifted poet that he is, but also a polished, worldly-wise courtier, like the duke's chief diplomat Antonio. Disclosure of the identities of Iphigenie and Orest is already central to Euripides' *Iphigenia in Tauris,* but Goethe foregrounds Iphigenie's identity by having her tell the story of the House of Atreus not to the audience in the prologue, as in Euripides, but to King Thoas in order to dissuade him from marrying her. The shift makes her identity more personal, in that it is presumed to affect intimate relations with others, and something to be contested, since Thoas refuses to attribute the same importance to it that Iphigenie does. Among a swirling mass of characters who all suspect one another of varying degrees of duplicity, Egmont stands as both hero and central enigma of his play. The question of how Egmont should be judged, first posed by Schiller, has dominated critical discussion ever since, with no agreement whether he is to be praised or condemned, whether he is ambitious or self-sacrificing, political or naive, competent or incompetent.

As in *Werther* the problem of self for each of these protagonists, all initially conceived during or immediately after the writing of that novel, begins with solipsism.[2] *Egmont*, begun shortly after *Werther*, is the closest to the early model.[3] Goethe eliminated all reference to Egmont's wife and eleven children in order to make him another Werther—attractive, spontaneous, and unable to accommodate the demands of propriety or the advice of well-meaning elders. Werther defending suicide to Albert sounds remarkably like Egmont in his confrontation with the similarly named Alba in act 4.[4] Although Egmont does not die for unrequited love, he does, like Werther, enter into a voluntary, staged death in order to realize an ideal (projected onto his beloved) that cannot be fulfilled in the world. The opposition between Werther's subjectivity and the narrator's more objective view of the world remains between Egmont, committed to spontaneity and acts that he claims have no political significance, and the reasonable Wilhelm von Oranien, whose historical epithet, William the Silent, echoes in Werther's silent addressee, Wilhelm. Yet Wilhelm is not silent in this *Egmont*, nor are many other figures. The shift from epistolary novel to drama signals Goethe's concern with a more interactive notion of selfhood.

Iphigenie auf Tauris, begun a few years later and completed a few months earlier than *Egmont*, begins with similar self-involvement. Iphigenie's first word, "Forth" (*Heraus*), like Werther's first words, "How glad I am to be away" (Wie froh bin ich, dass ich weg bin), identifies the need to escape her own self. Ostensibly, of course, she wants to escape Tauris and King Thoas's desire to marry her, just as Werther wanted to escape his love entanglements with Leonore and her sister. But Tauris explicitly represents for her death: she begs Diana to rescue her from a second death.[5] And death, as her first "death" indicates, when Diana rescued her from the altar at Aulis, is the loss of consciousness, the loss of self. The next scene strengthens this impression by emphasizing interiority ("Innerstes," 67, 73) and consciousness ("Ein fröhlich selbstbewußtes Leben," 110; "selbstvergessend," 113). But the problematic opacity of her self-involvement is clear from the very beginning not just in the imagery of imprisonment and death. Iphigenie has kept her identity, which might have kept Thoas from desiring her, a secret until after the play begins. The two of them disagree about the gods' will because it seems to be accessible only through surmise (Thoas) or through the voice of the heart (Iphigenie): in either case it is buried within the opaque individual. Her own feelings in the first monologue are not fully precise. She speaks in the fourth line with "shuddering feeling" (*schauderndem Gefühl*), which seems to be related to being a foreigner ("fremd," 9). But her alienation is both stronger (*schaudernd*) and more general ("my spirit remains a stranger here"; es gewöhnt sich nicht mein Geist hierher). To be sure, she longs to return to Greece, but she has no idea what might await her there, as her first conversations with Orest and Pylades reveal, while her later inability to keep the plot to escape secret from Thoas shows that she does not know herself or what she really wants. Some of Werther's blindness has moved inward. Tasso engages in similar, perhaps slightly more sophisticated blindness. Like Werther and Iphigenie, Tasso thinks he knows the particular person he wants, here the princess Leonore, whom he idealizes and adores as Werther does Charlotte, and Tasso's descent into madness is reminiscent of Werther's descent to suicide. But almost from the beginning he has sunk into the paranoia that Werther reaches only at the end. Unable to trust those around him, Tasso increasingly forces those who love him to abandon him and thus enact the scenario they wish to deny. Like the paranoid Rousseau, he makes himself impossible and lets the others punish him rather than doing it himself. Even more than in *Werther* and the earlier plays, the plot is actually in the mind of the hero, so that the problem is yet clearer in this play that Goethe has to let his hero speak without understanding his own situation. Egmont has far more confidence in his own intuitions, tragically as it turns out, than in Wilhelm von Oranien's more accurate "Realpolitik"; Iphigenie is imprisoned on Tauris and in the lurid past of her family; Tasso spins himself deeper and deeper into his own cocoon. Like Werther and the Rousseau projected by *Faust*, they are trapped in their limited views of their own identities, each earlier in each succeeding text, so that the world recedes and becomes inaccessible and incomprehensible.

The greater isolation of the self makes it ever less accessible to those around it. The problem is explicit and central to *Egmont*. Although he appears only in the middle of the second act, Egmont's impenetrability is repeatedly discussed in the preceding scenes: in the first his officer Buyck is compared to Egmont; in the second Margarete von Parma, regent of the Low Countries, and her secretary disagree as to whether Egmont is an intriguer (Margarete's view) or whether he is open and unselfconscious.[6] When Egmont finally appears on stage he hovers between their categories of hidden intentionality and unselfconsciousness. To his own secretary in act 2 he compares himself to a sleepwalker and a charioteer, in order to assert the inaccessibility of his intentions to the world and to himself. But with his further insistence that even the provocative symbols that he has deliberately added to his livery have no meaning (HA 4:400), he reveals the incongruity of his position. And to his antagonist, the Duke of Alba in act 4 Egmont says of himself, "Not every intention is manifest, and many a man's intention can be misinterpreted" (429; Nicht jede Absicht ist offenbar, und manches Mannes Absicht ist zu mißdeuten); in effect he claims that his openness and honest intentions are too interior to be understood. At the same time he interprets King Philip's concern for religion as a screen for hidden (deliberate) intentions (429), and rejects Alba's reproaches of disloyalty on the basis of his own (i.e., inner, hidden) knowledge of himself (433). And yet just a few lines later, he gasps in amazement as Alba arrests him, crying "That was the intention?" (433; Dies war die Absicht?). This confusing conflation of intention and unconsciousness, of cabal and innocence, pushes Rousseau's hidden personality to extremes.

The poisonous effects of this personal opacity are also social. In act 3, at the center of the play, Egmont arrives to visit his beloved, Klare, wrapped in a cloak, and she complains that he is not himself, that he is cold (412). To prove that he is his "real" self, the lover of Klare, he unveils to reveal his Spanish court costume, a favor she had requested some time previously. The incident plays on the myth of Jupiter and Semele, who begs to see her lover in his divine glory, and is burnt to a cinder when he appears. The suit beneath the cloak ought to symbolize Egmont's true self, but Klare is not consumed by it. Egmont's court regalia has the force neither of divine revelation nor even of human truth. Is Egmont after all a Spanish courtier and not the champion of Flanders?[7] In the ensuing discussion of the court (413–14), Egmont admits that Margarete's suspicions about his secret intentions ("Absichten" and "Hinterhalt") are justified. In response to Klare's question, "are you Egmont" (bist du Egmont?), Egmont asserts that not this splendid public self but Klare's Egmont is the real Egmont. Yet at that very moment Klare holds in her arms the splendid "Spanish" Egmont, which was, by virtue of the symbolism of the cloak, the inner, real Egmont. As the inner and outer Egmont become indistinguishable, integrity of intention seems to evaporate.

The ambiguity comes to a head when Egmont, awaiting execution in the dungeon, asserts that Alba's real motivation is personal revenge because Egmont once defeated him in a shooting match (446–47). For the first time Egmont seeks an explanation beneath the surface of events. Until now Alba has appeared as the epitome of conscious rationality in the play—in his own, in his followers', and in Egmont's eyes. Either Egmont is wrong, or else Alba, too, does not know his own intentions. Much is at stake in this alternative. If Egmont is correct that Alba acts out of petty jealousy, his death would lose its significance as a sacrifice for freedom and the stage direction calling for a victory symphony would seem grotesquely ironic. Furthermore, the play opens with a shooting match won by Egmont's officer, Buyck: if that scene was already a symbolic enactment of the repressed previous match between Egmont and Alba that drives the action of the play, then Egmont's accusation must be taken seriously, and the political superstructure of freedom in the play is meaningless. But if the first scene does not prefigure the accusation, if the accusation is random, the play makes us run the risk of overinterpreting, of seeking too much intentionality, as Egmont earlier accused everyone else of doing with regard to himself. The question is no longer what kind of self Egmont is, but why it is important to know whether or not Rousseau's hidden self exists and how to weigh its moral implications.

More rapidly than in *Egmont* the tension between two kinds of moral being in the world inherited by *Iphigenie auf Tauris* from Euripides—humanity versus the barbarism of vengeance (for Orest) and human sacrifice (for Iphigenie)—mutates into a tension between an outer and an inner self with the concomitant problem of opacity. Orest remains fully aware of what goes on in his soul and is cured of the madness caused by his matricide through the rational agency of his sister's serenity, her sympathetic questioning, and finally her revelation of her own identity. The key to the process is her ability to tease from him an admission of his own identity, which he has chosen to hide. He reveals this hidden inner, though not subconscious, self with explicit invocation of the truth just at the center of the play (lines 1080–81, out of 2,174 total), saying "let there be / Truth between us!" (zwischen uns / Sei Wahrheit!) in a moment exactly parallel to Egmont's central revelation of his "real" self to Klare. Orest's truth precipitates Iphigenie's revelation of her identity and Orest's own swoon, in which he is accepted among his dead relatives and from which he awakens permanently cured. Unlike in *Egmont*, bringing truth to light here heals both personal and social entities.

Egmont's self-revelation to Klare leads somehow to Klare appearing in his dream as the goddess of freedom; in *Iphigenie* a similar extreme development of the female protagonist takes place, and this development is so much more important that Iphigenie becomes the main protagonist. Corresponding to Orest's madness is Iphigenie's anxiety at the beginning of the play—her vague feelings of discomfort, alienation, an evident fear of matrimony, feeling dead. But revealing her identity does not achieve the same effect as it does for Orest. When she reveals it to Thoas in act 1, he simply isn't interested. In act 3 Orest is more interested, but his acknowledgment of her still does not free her to act with confidence. By the end of the play her alienation from her previously absent brother and from Thoas, whom she now accepts as a friend, is overcome and she sets out joyously for "home." While no single individual cajoles, calms, and heals her as she does Orest, nevertheless the word "truth" figures just as crucially for her as for Orest. As in Euripides' version of the play, Goethe's Orest and Pylades arrive in Tauris believing that the oracle has commanded them to bring the Taurians' statue of Apollo's sister, Diana, back to Greece, and so Iphigenie must help them steal it. Goethe's Iphigenie cannot deny her essential (inner) humanity, however, and, declaring herself the vessel of divine truth, reveals the plot to Thoas (lines 1918–19). Yet a further dose of truth becomes the final agent of reconciliation, when Orest figures out that the real command of the oracle (like the real Egmont), was for Orest to fetch his sister Iphigenie, not Apollo's sister, the statue of Diana, which can remain in Tauris. In the healing of Orest, truth was identity, now truth involves unpredictable behavior and the need for reinterpretation. The rift between truth and identity marks *Iphigenie's* new psychological depth.

The play relocates truth from the mouths of the gods to the human heart—"They speak only through our hearts to us" (494: Sie reden nur durch unser Herz zu uns), Iphigenie tells Thoas. Thus truth is no longer metaphysical but psychological, not universal but individual. The tension between universal and individual truth, however, leads directly to the moral issue that Rousseau represented for Goethe. The play seems to deal with the problem simply by superimposing universal and individual truth at the center. Orest reveals his identity to Iphigenie, saying "let there be / Truth between us!" (1080–81; zwischen uns / Sei Wahrheit!) and Iphigenie reveals the plot to steal the statue of Diana with "make Truth / glorious through me!" (1918–19; verherrlicht / Durch mich die Wahrheit!). The enjambment leading to the mid-line exclamation marks the parallelism. On the other hand, the large, glorious, social truth that the oracle really intended Orest to fetch not a statue but Iphigenie to purify the House of Atreus is identified not with the word for truth, but simply as the elimination of an error (*Irrtum*). "Truth!" characterizes the moral truth, the truth-telling that corrects deliberate lies. Telling the truth is not only revealing facts, revealing the future, or correctly interpreting the voice of the gods; the more important truth is the individual moral dimension, which comes from control over what is within. The more important truth addresses the Rousseau problem. Goethe's later critique of the play as "most devilishly humane" (ganz verteufelt human)[8] suggests that he soon came to see the inadequacy of the gesture, and, in fact, *Tasso*, the last play in this sequence, simply stops worrying about different kinds of truth, takes the need to control the inner self as a given, and skips directly to the question of representing it.

Identity and Genre

The first stylistic technique to create such opaque character depth is genre mixing—in *Egmont*, of neoclassical tragedy and bourgeois sentimental tragedy. The play's subtitle, "Trauerspiel" (tragedy), and its dramatis personae of aristocrats, officers, and functionaries arranged in rank from highest to low-est are typical of eighteenth-century neoclassical political tragedy. But half-way through the list, the political protagonists (Margarete von Parma, Count Egmont [Prince of Gaure], Wilhelm von Oranien, the Duke of Alba, Fer-dinand [the latter's son], secretaries, and officers) give way to the bourgeois heroine Klare, her mother, and her second lover, Brackenburg, to signal the more novelistic, Rousseauist realm of sentimental tragedy. In the political plot Egmont intrigues between the Low Countries and its intolerant Spanish over-lord Philip II; in the sentimental one he pursues a love affair with the ingenue Klare, whom he will of course never marry. The play segregates its neoclassical and sentimental tragedy casts into separate scenes; only Egmont appears with all the characters, and he claims, significantly, to be two different people—the public one, "a morose, reserved, cold Egmont who must control himself, smile and nod on demand" (415; ein verdrießlicher, steifer, kalter Egmont, der an sich halten, bald dieses, bald jenes Gesicht machen muß), and the private one, who is "calm, open, happy, loved and known by the best of hearts" (415; ruhig, offen, glücklich, geliebt und gekannt von dem besten Herzen), Klare's Egmont. Thus the plots define themselves in terms of different notions of selfhood and dramatic character.

In the neoclassical plot the characters intrigue about the fates of nations, while the bourgeois characters focus on their private emotional worlds. Because the characters in the political tragedy live in history, there can be for them no acts without implications, while in the sentimental tragedy, history impinges only from the outside on a self that exists and feels independently of what is going on around it—a self like Klare's whose songs emerge unconsciously and whose love exists without regard to the future.[9] Effective operation in history requires the ability to plan and to analyze action, to hide one's own intentions and anticipate how others will do the same; but no such constraints operate in the sentimental plot, where everything turns on the constant expression of emotion and where all interiority is externalized as in *Werther*. As a result the political plot operates with an inner self distinctly different from the visible surface, while the sentimental plot deals with a self totally open to view. Both distinguish public from private, but they mean different things by it. In the neoclassical plot, where all action is effectively public, public action is nor-mally intrigue and private refers to frank discussions with the confidant(e). But in the sentimental plot, where all action is by definition private, "public" means conscious or intentional and "private" means unconscious.

The cast seems to divide readily into intriguers and innocents, and the difference corresponds largely to rank, even among the characters common to neoclassical political plots. Thus the highest ranking figures—Margarete von Parma, the Duke of Alba, and Wilhelm von Oranien—are the most sophisticated schemers and the best interpreters of other people's schemes. Usually in neoclassical tragedy the villains are the schemers, but only the Duke of Alba, associated with Spanish oppression, is a villain here. The other two are associated with moderation and freedom of conscience respectively. While Klare and her rejected bourgeois lover Brackenburg are the obvious innocents in the play, there are two other innocents among the neoclassical hangers-on. Margarete's secretary, Machiavell, despite the contrary symbolism of his name, believes completely in Egmont's supposed spontaneity and lack of intentionality, while Margarete sees his deeper schemes. Meanwhile Alba's illegitimate son Ferdinand is being trained to succeed his father as a wily servant of the king; like illegitimate sons in Shakespeare (such as the Bastard in *King John*, Edmund in *King Lear*), he is to make a place for himself by his wits and eventually outshine his legitimate brothers. Yet late in the play he comes to Egmont, already condemned to death by Alba, and declares that Egmont has always been his beloved role model, in effect his true father. The cross-contamination between the plots thus lends all the characters a certain doubleness, and neither social connections nor genre effectively determine transparency of character. The resulting mélange of deliberate and not fully conscious intentions, of hypocrisy and frankness, of reasoned action and spontaneous expressions of feeling, generates the play's impression of psychological depth.

Iphigenie operates with a similar technique, but more abstractly. What is manifested as two different casts in *Egmont* appears here only in the two siblings who undergo parallel cures that proceed in different generic and rhetorical terms. Orest's cure is, in the terms of Cyrus Hamlin, "mythological," that is, it comes about by engaging increasingly with the myth on which the play is based, even though Goethe deviates from the myth in making the Furies entirely internal to Orest, and therefore psychological rather than moral instances.[10] Goethe also deviates in making Orest's cure complete from the third act on, unlike Euripides' Orestes or his many successors in eighteenth-century drama and opera. Goethe's Orest recovers from the guilt of matricide through a forgiving encounter with the shades of his ancestors. The encounter is only imagined, in effect a Freudian *Wunschtraum*. But its real significance is elucidated by his encounter with his real sister. And once elucidated, his troublesome symptoms disappear. The mechanisms are remote from Freud, but the prototype of curing through dream interpretation is established. Nevertheless there is an important reservation to this apparent modernity. The motif of the dream cure entered the Iphigenia in Tauris plot via eighteenth-century Orlando operas, where Orlando's madness is cured—under the guidance of a wise sorcerer or sorceress—by a dreamed descent into the underworld.[11] And behind Orlando's dreamed descents lie the literal descents of the many operatic Orpheus figures of the seventeenth and eighteenth centuries, who descend to the underworld to heal the loss of the beloved Eurydice. Orest's dream cure thus draws on two myths, those of Orestes and Orpheus, and it further draws on a tradition in opera that had begun to use staged dreams to represent the mechanics of interiorized psychological change. Goethe has added to this modality of myth and opera only the interpretive act of the curer.

Iphigenie's cure goes much further along this path, so that it is no longer mythic but almost naturalistic. Since it takes place over the course of the whole play, it not only frames Orest's cure but is also the overreaching subject. It is obvious that, with the Furies invisible, Orest suffers from what would today be called neurosis; but the focus on Iphigenie's purity and humanity tends to obscure the fact that she suffers from the same neurosis. Since her illness is less evident, the reader must diagnose it with more care and move beyond the mythological language that characterizes Orest's situation to a conceptual interpretation. Tradition reports the trauma Iphigenie suffered: she was almost slain at the altar in Aulis. She avoided the traumatic moment by fainting, and awoke in Tauris, where she is expected to do unto others what was almost done to her. She protects herself by persuading the king to stop sacrificing strangers. Such is her situation at the beginning of the play. But the play presents the information in a different order. Her opening monologue offers only a description of the symptoms: she is homesick, alienated, depressed. When Arkas raises the issue of human sacrifice in the second scene, Iphigenie articulates her objections in the general terms of Enlightenment humanity. Then Thoas persuades her to break her repressive silence about her past and she recites the history of her family's crimes, ending with a minimal description of her own role: "They dragged me to the altar and dedicated / My head to the goddess.—She was reconciled" (lines 425–26; Sie rissen mich vor den Altar und weihten / Der Göttin dieses Haupt.—Sie war versöhnt). Iphigenie's feelings at that moment are elided in the dash. Her prayer to Diana in the next scene brings up the sore point—she refers to the rescuing clouds of the goddess, then prays "keep my hands from blood" (549; enthalte von Blut meine Hände!)—without going into detail. After she reveals her identity to Orest, the most accurate description she can give of herself is as the sacrifice, although still in relatively gentle terms: "The goddess / Tore me from the altar" (1218–19; Vom Altar / Riß mich die Göttin weg). By now, the diagnosis is clear: an inability to act that results from the fear that all action is murder— the "curse" that lies upon her entire family. In Tauris the only action open to her has been human sacrifice: the analysis shows that her task symbolizes all human action in her world, that is, in her psyche.

But diagnosis is still not cure. In act 4 Iphigenie continues to be troubled with "worry upon worry" (1411; Sorg' auf Sorge). Embracing her brother felt like the rescuing arms of the goddess (1511 ff.), but the crucial moment of trauma still has not been addressed. Only in the last act, having progressed from seeing herself as priestess to seeing herself as Agamemnon's daughter (1822), does she finally articulate the real reason for her refusal to practice human sacrifice by reconstructing the traumatic moment:

> I trembled before the altar itself,
> And solemnly did early death close about
> The kneeling one: the knife already quivered,
> To pierce the living breast;
> My inmost self reeled in horror,
> My eyes went dark, and—I found myself in safety. (1846–51)

> (Ich habe vorm Altare selbst gezittert,
> Und feierlich umgab der frühe Tod
> Die Knieende: das Messer zuckte schon,
> Den lebensvollen Busen zu durchbohren;
> Mein Innerstes entsetzte wirbelnd sich,
> Mein Auge brach, und—ich fand mich gerettet.)

Now she can find in the depths of her own soul (1885) the power to save herself and to perform a heroic deed (1892; "unerhörte Tat"). Werther never escapes his entrapment in himself to act in the world, and Egmont leaves his prison to act only symbolically. But Iphigenie henceforth directs the action: she keeps the men under control and requires Thoas to release her. Her repeated tale of the sins of her ancestors does not just represent Goethe's appropriation of various classical texts nor a failure to get the play beyond exposition. It is not Orest's operatic dream cure, but a talking cure. By telling and retelling her story Iphigenie can finally identify the crucial memory whose denial—one is already tempted to use the term "repression"—has imprisoned her. Like the later Freudian talking cure, it excavates the past and validates Freud's recognition that fundamental psychic situations were described in literary texts going back to the Greeks. But in fact, it is more correct to say that the juxtaposition of the older mythic and operatic cure of Orest to Iphigenie's completely secular self-analysis makes possible Freud's insight about the psychological depths of great literature; indeed, only the linkage between the two makes the mythic representation of depth psychology legible as such.

The centrality of Iphigenie's talking cure to the plot explains why the play is so narrative, as well as so concerned with identifying the true inner voice, and in turn illuminates the apparent lack of action in *Tasso*. Tasso is not cured in his play (twice the length of *Iphigenie*, which cures two characters), but that is certainly not for want of extensive discussion and evaluation of his talents, virtues, and character defects, and not for want of adjurations to change himself. Like Werther both he and his interlocutors are entirely preoccupied with his talents and personality. Contrasted to this novelistic talkiness are the restrained stage actions of neoclassical drama. The real climax is Tasso's effort to kiss the princess Leonore, who represents for him the unreachable ideal;[12] kissing her equates to Werther's climactic breach of decorum when he kisses Charlotte. The act, such as it is, leads Tasso to madness, as it leads Werther to suicide. Typically in neoclassical drama action takes place offstage, as it does in *Iphigenie*. Both plays contain a few ritual embraces and a ritual—and sinful— drawing of swords, but in *Iphigenie* all kinds of fighting goes on offstage. In *Tasso*, however, virtually nothing happens offstage either. The introspection of the sentimental novel displaces the mythic narration and even the reserved action of neoclassical drama to entirely foreground the hero's interiority.

Identity and Allegory

In addition to exploiting multiple genres, Goethe develops in these plays a special kind of allegory based on parallel characters. Tasso, like Werther before him, projects his ideal onto a beloved woman; this is already a complex psychological process, but one hardly new to Goethe. But in *Die Wahlverwandtschaften* the central constellation of characters has already been seen to function as a single composite individual. In this group each character, with the identical root "ott" in his or her name, exists as an individual but also as a part of a full self—as the rational or irrational part, as the masculine or feminine part. Unlike in the personification allegory typical of European religious drama, these figures in Goethe do not represent a single characteristic or quality like Faith, Hope, or Understanding. Instead they function as autonomous characters while still not being quite whole. The chemical metaphor on which the novel's title and central conceit rest is precisely that human relationships are always composite; but individuals also become composite in this novel. In the three classical plays under discussion here, Goethe's earliest experiments with this technique become visible.

The process is easiest to identify in *Egmont*, in which a third group of characters, not traditional to either the political or the bourgeois tragedy, namely, various citizens of Brussels, populate the occasional mob scenes to which Shakespeare's *Julius Caesar* inspired Goethe. The shooting match in the first scene involves a lively group of minor characters who seem to have their own individuality, which, however, becomes increasingly problematic. Their successive toasts to the political protagonists—King Philip, Egmont, Margarete, Oranien—outline the political situation, and thus immediately point beyond individuals to situation. The first two citizens of Brussels, Soest and Jetter, have their own names as well as social functions (shopkeeper, tailor). The timid Jetter, subject to spontaneous feelings, songs, and visions (375, 395), has the most clearly defined character of the citizens; but he is a tailor, and tailors are proverbially timid. The other two citizens, Zimmermann and Seifensieder, are named only from their social function (carpenter and soapmaker). The individuality of name is undermined, and with it the particularity of character.

The scene soon escalates into an alternative, projective mode of characterization. Buyck, the soldier who wins the shooting contest, resembles his master Egmont—he shoots like him, he has learned from him, he is splendid and easygoing like him. In effect, he stands in for Egmont. Furthermore, Soest, who would have won the contest had Buyck not barged in, also prefigures Egmont: he is defeated by a professional soldier who, like Alba later, interferes with questionable right in a civilian situation. Like Egmont, Soest cooperates in his own defeat, and like Alba, Buyck ignores local customs once he has won—"I'm foreign and your king, and I have no respect for your laws and traditions" (371; Ich bin fremd und König, und achte Eure Gesetze und Herkommen nicht), he says, to which Jetter responds, "You're worse than the Spaniard" (Du bist ärger als der Spanier). Thus Buyck represents both Egmont and Alba, the most opposed figures in the play. These individuals are for all practical purposes not themselves at all, but represent other, "major" characters who will appear later, and they can represent different ones from one moment to the next. This kind of characterization belongs less to political tragedy than to allegorical drama, where signification is more important than individuality of character. The ending of the scene specifically marks its nature, because opera was the one surviving mode of such allegorical drama in the eighteenth century. Schiller criticized *Egmont* in his review for what he called its sudden somersault into opera at the end, and this criticism has echoed through the years. The externalized mode of characterization here is typical of opera and all allegorical drama, and it undercuts any assumption that *Egmont* works with consistent, realistic characters.

At first confined to the mob scenes earlier in the play, this form of dramatic representation emerges in the last act as a solution to the indeterminacy of identity. Alba's son Ferdinand visits Egmont in the prison to confess that he admires Egmont more than he does his father. Egmont's unselfconscious attractiveness has triumphed over Alba's planning after all, but so privately, literally hidden in a dungeon, that the world will never see it. Ferdinand has left the political plot behind and turned the prison into another outpost of the sentimental, indoor plot, in which it is unacceptable for Klare to set foot out of doors, and showing herself at the window draggs her into Egmont's political fate. From the interiority of the sentimental plot neither Klare nor Ferdinand can translate devotion to Egmont into effective rescue. An unbridgeable generic gap divides their devotion to him and the freedom he represents from realizing their ideal of freedom in the world.

To prevent the sentimental plot from making the political one completely invisible, Goethe turns to the projective characterization typical of the early Shakespearean scenes. Despite the subjectivity of their love, Ferdinand's, like Klare's, is inspired by Egmont's exterior, indeed, by the tales and reports of the hero's valor. Because they love not some inner, private Egmont, but the hero of song and story, what had appeared too subjective to be visible turns out to be entirely a matter of public and aesthetic representation. The final dream sequence renders the innermost self of Egmont not only visible to the audience but even into an instrument of effective political action. Egmont dreams (his unconscious self speaks) about Klare (again presumably the private self of the sentimental plot). But this expression of his most private self reveals the goddess of freedom, a public figure who seems to herald coming wars of liberation—public events. Furthermore, the dream inspires Egmont to treat his departure from the dungeon, which takes place without an audience, as a public event, a blow in the cause of freedom (for which there is no historical justification), a gesture to be celebrated in a final victory symphony. If Egmont has finally found his "true" self, that self is the warrior who has been invisible until now. From the beginning of the play Egmont is repeatedly described as the great victor of Gravelingen and others have been made to represent him as such; but he himself has never once appeared on stage in that role. Now, at the end, he takes on the role described and played by Buyck in the first scene, popularized in ballads and broadsides, and becomes the public symbol, an externalized self.

In 1829 Goethe ended his autobiography with Egmont's often quoted self-analysis in terms of the category "demonic," a theory of selfhood developed and revised over the course of his life:[13] "A person thinks he conducts his own life, makes his own decisions; and yet his innermost self is drawn ineluctably to its destiny" (451; Es glaubt der Mensch, sein Leben zu leiten, sich selbst zu führen; und sein Innerstes wird unwiderstehlich nach seinem Schicksale gezogen). The *Innerstes*—the inner unconscious self of the sentimental plot—is drawn to its destiny (*Schicksal*)—its public visible meaning in the neoclassical plot.[14] Egmont's most effective self is, finally, the example of the public's dream of freedom. The inner self has meaning only in what it is seen to represent. The play thus ends by combining the opposition of public and private and of two kinds of dramatic character into the third type adumbrated by the Shakespearean and operatic first scene of the play.

Egmont ends with a projective or theatrical version of selfhood, in the sense that the momentary, contextual effect of the representation is more significant than some abiding inner identity, whether intentional or unconscious, which is inaccessible, undesirable, and ineffective in this play. It surrounds a central theatrical self with people who use the period's dominant rhetorics of the political (intriguing) or the sentimental (spontaneous) interior self. As a result, Goethe's contemporaries and many of his succeeding readers failed to see that he was raising questions about intentionality. Friedrich Schiller's adaptation of *Egmont* for a performance in Weimar in 1796 is a paradigmatic misreading of the play into political drama with consistent character motivation; Schiller eliminated most of the language of intentionality and interpretation, including the entire role of Margarete von Parma, the character who reflects most extensively on reading. Egmont appears earlier, less as the object of analysis and more as the consistently motivated center of a coherent plot.[15] Schiller's Alba is present but masked when Egmont is condemned to death, and when Egmont accuses Alba of seeking personal revenge (about the shooting match) rather than political order, he tears the mask from Alba's face. No longer is Alba's personal motivation an ambiguous factor in the plot, but the simple clear explanation for all the action. Finally, Schiller eliminated the public vision of Klare as Freedom from the stage and had Egmont narrate what thus becomes an entirely private and subjective dream.[16] This reduction of the public self to an unequivocal emanation of a legible private self shows that Goethe's ruminations on representing an unknowable self escaped even his most sympathetic contemporary colleague.

Egmont advances toward what would become a dialectical solution to Rousseau's paradox of an inner self in search of total transparency. *Werther* was understood to glorify and elaborate Rousseau's search for it, so much so that Goethe's critique of the excessive subjectivity he saw there went unnoticed in the first version. Egmont's rhetorical self corrects and withdraws from the intentional self embodied in Werther, yet maintains the same striving toward transparency. There is nothing Egmont wants more than to be *known*, particularly by Klare. Indeed he achieves his full identity, he says, only when he is known by her (415). Werther, of course, also wants to be known by Charlotte, but what he wants her to know, his love for her, is a truth that is unacceptable and therefore blocked. Furthermore, while Werther's beloved is the idealized eternal feminine, a scarcely disguised virgin mother, Egmont's is an androgyne, a woman who would also like to be a man. Klare has more in common with Iphigenie, who feels constricted in her woman's role, with Natalie, the Amazon of *Wilhelm Meisters Lehrjahre* (and Mignon and others in the same novel), and with some of the odder (and also androgynous) figures in *Faust*, part 2, like Homunculus. Indeterminacy of form is clearly related, in the cases of Natalie, Mignon, and Homunculus, to their capacity to represent something other, higher, than themselves—in other words, to their capacity to be transparent. Klare's capacity to represent explains Egmont's willingness to give her up to Ferdinand: the essence she represents can be translated into or out of her form. Werther, on the other hand, idealizes Charlotte but cannot then separate the woman from his projection, and thus loses himself when he loses her. Translatability, the arbitrary and therefore fluid relation between representation and representing object, between significance and sign, is the new element in *Egmont*. In this sense Rousseau's transparency has effectively become the theatricality, the ability to represent implicit in the projective allegory at the end of *Egmont*. By connecting the moral issue and the generic issue *Egmont* offers an escape from Rousseau's paradox and thus represents the first step in Goethe's transmutation of Rousseauist subjectivity into a romantic self.

Iphigenie reflects openly on the theatrical representation of innerness arrived at in *Egmont*. For much of the play interior truth is less accessible to the characters than to the audience. The audience knows the myth and therefore knows Iphigenie's trauma even though she has repressed it. The Furies offer an obvious language both for Orest's conscience and for the psychological torments of the family curse/neurosis that keeps him from being able to act. Iphigenie points to precisely this use of the myth when she frees herself for an "unheard-of deed" (1892; unerhörten Tat):

> What remains to me to defend my inmost self?
> Must I appeal to the goddess for a wonder?
> Is there no power in the depths of my soul? (1883–85)

> (Was bleibt mir nun, mein Innres zu verteid'gen?
> Ruf' ich die Göttin um ein Wunder an?
> Ist keine Kraft in meiner Seele Tiefen?)

The power within her soul and the miraculous intervention of the goddess become the same thing—or almost.

With Orest's cure, myth slid toward opera. To be sure, Goethe's *Iphigenie* does not call for the elaborate staging of opera; its fantastic passions and its operatic descent into the underworld are only narrated, not staged. But the narrations in fact evoke the memory of the kind of staging still normal in opera (Christoph Willibald Gluck's *Iphigénie en Tauride*, with its ballet of the Furies, debuted in 1779, the same year as Goethe's play) and thus provide a visual dimension that goes beyond narration. Furthermore, the siblings undergo parallel cures, one more mythological, externalized, the other more verbal, interiorized. One represents the other. Or better, their parallelism connects two discourses, that of mythology and the emergent one of interiority, and shows how the one can be used to represent the other.

This issue becomes explicit in the last act. The play lacks stage directions, so it is not clear if the statue of Diana is ever to be seen on stage; however, the statue is conspicuously absent when it becomes the center of discussion at the end. In its absence the audience and characters are asked to identify Iphigenie with Diana and then separate the two images. Like the Goethean symbol, the statue is and is not the same as Iphigenie. The act of representation is now explicit—Iphigenie's truth, her inmost self (*Innres*), is suddenly represented by a statue; to be fully understood her self must be externalized, indeed allegorized, onto the figure of the goddess, which is, however, consistently identified as an image. If Egmont becomes the hero of ballad and broadside, Iphigenie's identity is best represented at the end by the statue of Diana, a role she has grown into, and both are mediated by the allegorical dramaturgy of opera.

In *Tasso* the exteriorization of identity is more complicated, because the plot does not allow Goethe the crutch of mythology. So he turns first to traditional allegorical forms. The whole play takes place within the confines of a garden: when Tasso steals a kiss from the princess, Leonore von Este, and is subsequently condemned, the enactment of the Fall is easy to read. Goethe turns not only to morality play, however, but also to the allegorical technique of court masque in the first scene, where the princess and her confidante crown busts of Virgil and Ariosto—a gesture Goethe himself considered a cliché of court masque (*Wilhelm Meisters Lehrjahre*, book 3, chapter 6). Here the action, however, does not so much honor the figures crowned, but rather reveals the inner identities of the women who carry it out: the noble princess crowns the sublime Virgil; the sociable Leonore Sanvitale, the frivolous Ariosto. The characters also operate in the tradition of court masque. Despite their historical names, they are only a step away from the personification allegories that still characterized Goethe's own court masques. They form a carefully arranged quincunx with Tasso in the center. To the one side are Duke Alfons and his minister Antonio Montecatino, to the other the Princess Leonore von Este and her friend Leonore Sanvitale, Countess of Scandiano. The pairs are separated by their gender difference, but symmetrical in the distinction of upper and middle court rank on each side. The identity of names on the one side and of the initial *A* on the other make the formal arrangement take precedence over individuality of character. And in fact, on each side one character embodies an association with the ideal and with art (the princess and Alfons, who are also siblings), while the other embodies rather the engagement with practical reality (Antonio and Leonore, the plotters). Each side taken as a whole constitutes a complete personality that balances the two drives; the female side is only distinguished from the male side by its greater emotional intensity. In the first scene of *Egmont* Buyck combined within himself foreshadowings of both Egmont and Alba; here the different modes of being are permanently separated into different figures. Tasso must in effect choose between the two Leonores. Because of their historical exteriors the distinction is much harder to see than that between the personified pleasure and virtue normally offered to the heroes of masque: they represent less moral alternatives than two ways of knowing the world that are both in effect parts of himself. The intense language and gentle, almost ritualized pageantry reveal a self that can represent itself, if at all, only in gesture and language rather than in interaction with the world.

Apart from *Faust*, which is sui generis and must be considered separately, Goethe's two further classical plays show how such allegorical representation of the self settled in. *Die natürliche Tochter* (*The Natural Daughter*, 1804) validates this reading of *Tasso*: there the characters are identified only by their social functions except for the heroine, whose given name, Eugenie, is obviously a speaking name ("well-born"). Interiorized subjectivity is represented allegorically and as social role. More compelling for our context is the unfinished *Pandora* (first act written in 1807–8, just before Goethe turned his full attention to *Die Wahlverwandtschaften*), which is not only about the social function of art and beauty, but also an allegory of identity. With its symmetrical protagonists Prometheus and Epimetheus, thinking beforehand and thinking afterward—looking forward and backward—it evokes precisely what Carl Gustav Carus in his treatise on psychology, *Psyche*, later identified as one of the first stirrings of the subconscious and then as the awakening of consciousness.[17] Here the two brothers have lived estranged from one another; the play represents their moment of mutual discovery. In effect, the two brothers begin the play in a kind of preconscious state. Epimetheus is out of touch with the passing of time: awake all night and able to sleep only at dawn, he thinks constantly of Pandora, the wife he has lost. His brother, by contrast, is so taken up with making things in the real world that he is unconscious of anything else around him or of any time but the present. Only after the play begins does each brother learn that his child loves the child of the other and thereby first come to consciousness of his true complementary relationship to the other. The first act features a dream of Epimetheus in which his daughter Elpore (Hope), whose nature is always to say "yes," appears to him with the morning star on her forehead and assures Epimetheus that Pandora will return to him. Compared to the dream of Egmont, the Freudian function of dream as wish fulfillment is much more explicit. The dream occurs at the very end of *Egmont*, but in *Pandora* it is a first step. After the dream Epimetheus's hope gives way to a new conflict, now between the lovers. But this Hegelian division consequent on the awakening of consciousness leads to a new synthesis, a higher level of conscious being: it appears as a sequence of fire, a plunge into the water, from which the hero is miraculously reborn ("ein Anadyomen," HA 5, line 1027) and, as Bacchus, the god of wine who joins fire and water into firewater, marries the heroine. The opening scene of *Faust*, part 2, elaborates this allegorical dawn onstage at greater length and more explicitly as Faust awakens and reconstitutes his consciousness of the world with the coming of day.[18] Similarly the finale of act 1 of *Pandora* anticipates that of the "Classical

Walpurgis Night" (act 2) of *Faust*, part 2, where each of the two elements is prepared for and celebrated at length, and where the allusion to birth from the sea as the rebirth of Venus from the waves is elaborated at length in the thematics of Galatea.[19] Thus the "Classical Walpurgis Night" interprets what was still only implicit, not fully conscious, in *Pandora*—dreams as representation of the not-yet-conscious. The process Goethe works through is the identical process to the coming to consciousness the texts reveal. In this sense his allegories of creativity in *Faust* are equally allegories of identity.

These increasingly allegorical dramas can now be understood as useful laboratories for investigating the nature of identity, for struggling with Rousseau and the problems of the new consciousness. Above all, dramatic allegory offered a straightforward way to represent interiority outside of the self, and thereby to allow the subconscious self to become visible to an audience even as it remained unacknowledged as part of the self by the subject. But the need for allegory threatened to drive Goethe back out of the genre. The secularization of European culture had undermined the religious framework on which allegory in drama was based, so that it had become increasingly unacceptable on the stage in Goethe's day. The kind of *Festspiel* represented by *Pandora* was hopelessly old-fashioned; scholars today still remain embarrassed by it and by the court masques Goethe continued to write.[20] Furthermore, Goethe's attention shifted with increasing intensity to science in the 1780s. He completed his classical dramas and published his collected works at the end of the decade precisely because he considered his literary career essentially over. Nevertheless, it resumed with astonishing vigor in the second half of the 1790s—with a return to prose narrative, to lyric poetry, and to *Faust*. In fact *Faust* is really the last viable product of the allegorical dramatic tradition that extended back to the late Middle Ages. Its peculiar blend of allegory and Goethe's new scientific epistemology, as well as its centrality to his oeuvre, make it the next obvious site for examining dramatic allegory as a psychological tool for Goethe.

CHAPTER 5

The Scientific Self: Identity in *Faust*

Faust has already appeared in these pages as a document of Goethe's engagement with the problematic morality generated by Rousseau's interior self. Now, in the wake of the epistemological problems raised in the classical dramas and Goethe's initial struggles to represent interiority, it is time to consider the representational issues in *Faust*, which was first published in 1790 as a fragment, then elaborated during the 1790s into *Faust*, part 1 (published in 1808). As the drama that engaged him for the remainder of his life, it is perhaps not surprisingly a summa of Goethe's thinking about representing interiority in drama. Because the second part of the play, mostly written in the 1820s and published only in 1832, unfolds and elaborates ideas implicit in the first part, it reflects a further development and clarification. Hence it is appropriate to discuss both parts together at this point. Furthermore, both parts bring the same new factor into play in thinking about knowing the hidden inner self, namely Goethe's thinking about scientific method, which in the 1790s was almost obsessive. For precisely in the period when he was coming to terms with Rousseau and interior identity, he was also coming to terms with Kant's philosophy and with his strong commitment to scientific investigation. His most important essays on science date from the 1790s, so that the drama of Faust the scholar qua scientist is central to our topic. At issue here are the connections Goethe establishes in this text between theatrical representation and his scientific epistemology.

Questions surrounding Faust's identity have always been central to the Faust legend: the Faust of the chapbook is, after all, a sinner who barters his soul for knowledge. One way to think of the modernity of *Faust* is to say that Goethe substitutes interiorized identity for soul, and self-knowledge for knowledge in the traditional schema. The problems raised by Rousseau's interiorized identity in *Faust*, part 1, have already been discussed: the issue is not inability to know the moral code, but the relationship between epistemology and morality, between knowledge and action. But Goethe takes the problem a large step beyond Rousseau, for the connection of human striving to the eternal motion of nature in *Faust* ties the essential ineffability of the interior self to the ineffability of the cosmos (or, in Kantian terms, the ineffability of the transcendental ego to that of the thing in itself). Faust faces a double dilemma—to know the unknowable self and to know unknowable nature. If science is the way of knowing nature, and theater, as the last chapter implies, of knowing the self, Faust needs them both.

The transition from the third to the fourth act of *Faust*, part 2, reveals how deeply the problem of identity in this tragedy of knowledge remained imbricated with science. In act 3 Faust marries Helen of Troy in what is essentially a play within the play whose actors, props, and costumes are elaborately assembled before the eyes of the audience. At the end of the act, Helena dissolves in Faust's embrace and her dress becomes a cloud that carries him away from Greece. Mephistopheles in the meantime removes the mask he has worn during the act to reveal that Faust's entire affair with Helena has been pure theater. At the beginning of act 4, the cloud deposits Faust at the top of the Alps and withdraws eastward, looking ever more like a recumbent goddess, or even Helena, as it goes. Then a different cloud, a wispy high one, appears that Faust readily identifies with Margarete, his ideal beloved in an almost equally theatrical experience from part 1.[1] The descriptions of the billowing cumulus cloud associated with Helena and the cirrus that represents Margarete derive from the cloud classification system of Luke Howard (1772–1864) still basically in use today.[2] Goethe deploys it to represent the two women whom Faust has cast to represent his own ideals, and thus, in a certain sense, his own self. The prominently located cloud imagery thus connects identity both to science and to theater. Because they change shape so freely and are so difficult to describe objectively, clouds are a particularly good image for connecting problems of identity and objective knowledge. By linking the clouds to Faust's two beloveds, Goethe pushes the basic problem to the extreme: both identity and phenomenon—that is, both subject and object—are unstable.[3] How can an unstable observer ever establish objective knowledge of an unstable phenomenon, and thus what kind of knowledge is theatrical knowledge of identity?

Identity is central to Goethe's epistemology. Normally since the seventeenth century experimental method has been oriented toward validating a hypothesis, but for Goethe the fundamental problem was the role of the observer or, in the Kantian terminology of the time, the problem of the subject and the object. In these terms there could be no accurate perception of the object, the other, unless the mediation of the subject, the observing self, could be taken into account. In *Faust* also the search for knowledge turns out really to be the search for knowledge of the self and its relation to the other, or of the subject and its relation to the object. As Faust learns, achieving knowledge of the subject is anything but trivial: it takes a long lifetime and about 12,000 lines of difficult poetry to learn that a self exists only in the present and is thus always in flux, always unstable. But the problem of the observing subject is also the familiar moral question Rousseau's *Reveries* had raised for Goethe in *Faust*; when the observer acts, he does not reflect, because his intentions are unknown and unknowable. Thus the many hours Goethe devoted to the epistemology of science in the 1790s, exactly the period in which he otherwise struggled to come to terms with Rousseau's new version of interiority, invite reflection on how his essays on scientific method are part of this struggle. Because part 2 of *Faust* elaborates and interprets so much material that is only implicit in part 1, its connections between representation and perception provide the last, clearest view of what Goethe actually decided he had meant after the dust had settled.

Just when Goethe was expanding the Faust fragment of 1790 into *Faust*, part 1, he was rejoicing in a new harmonious interrelation of his two deepest interests in life, art and science. In a late essay on the influence of Kantian philosophy (1817), Goethe attributes his "especially happy decade" (höchst frohe Lebensepoche) of the 1790s to the appearance of Kant's *Kritik der Urteilskraft* (*Critique of Judgment*), because it treated art and science together as mutually illuminating phenomena,[4] and in *Faust* Goethe makes art the equivalent path to science by which the self can gain knowledge of the ineffable truth or other. In the language of an essay of 1792, "Der Versuch als Vermittler von Objekt und Subjekt" (The Experiment as Mediator Between Object and Subject), to know an object means "to grasp the infinite" (10–11; das Unendliche zu begreifen), "to recognize the powers of Nature" (11; die Kräfte der Natur zu erkennen). Faust uses the identical wording: he justifies his pact with Mephistopheles at the end of the second study scene by his need to access the infinite ("das Unendliche," line 1815), and sees "powers of Nature" (438; die Kräfte der Natur) in the sign of the Macrocosm. As late as 1817 the thought of Kant brought Goethe the essayist back to such Faustian language as "eternally creative Nature" (immer schaffende Natur).[5]

The basic problem for scientific knowledge, according to "The Experiment as Mediator," is to escape the use of one's self as the measure of all things ("als Menschen die Dinge in Bezug auf sich [zu] betrachte[n]," 10). Goethe's term in the essay is *Entäußerung*, renunciation, or, literally, removal of one's self to the outside. Faust's problem at the beginning of the play is in fact "removal to the outside": he begins the play imprisoned in a narrow Gothic study from which he is desperate to escape literally. At the same time he longs to escape metaphorically from his past and present identity as a scholar dependent on words. It is the same situation as in "The Experiment as Mediator," but now expressed theatrically. Thus far the parallel might seem also to evoke Rousseau's turn to botany to fill his loneliness in the *Reveries*. But "experiment" is Goethe's term for the particular process of scientific observation that mediates between subject and object. The scientist's mission is to observe, not to force phenomena into systems nor to prove ideas invented by the observer. Too much subjectivity causes the investigator to draw arbitrary and often unwarranted connections among phenomena and to become too attached to hypotheses (his objection to Newton's theory of light, 15–16). Nevertheless, too much objectivity can reduce scientific knowledge to a mere collection of isolated facts. "Experiment," in Goethe's terms, establishes connections among facts by multiplying and varying the conditions of observation; such pluralism allows the observer to escape the limits of his own subjectivity (12, 18). As a result, major discoveries are made not by individuals, but by collectivities or by an age, as the accumulation of individual perceptions and observations reveals a pattern implicit in them.[6] Science is not essentially the work of the paranoid hermit, of extreme interiority, but leads back into the community.

For the individual observer, experiment means repeating observations under varied circumstances to create what Goethe calls an *Erfahrung* ("experience," in the sense of something learned), a slice of knowledge that consists of many subsidiary ones. Such knowledge is then of a higher order ("der höheren Art," 18). But an *Erfahrung* is still not full knowledge of what Goethe calls a pure phenomenon; this, like a Kantian thing in itself, can never be known through direct perception of its entirety; the insight of *Erfahrung* is as much as observation can achieve. Thus in "Erfahrung und Wissenschaft" (Experience and Science), another unpublished draft of 1798, Goethe summarizes his method for establishing the pure phenomenon, the thing itself as best it can be known, as follows:

> *The pure phenomenon* . . . emerges as the final result of all observations and experiments. It can never be isolated; instead it *reveals*

itself in a regular series of appearances. In order to *represent* it, the human mind stabilizes the empirical fluctuation, excludes random variation, separates out impurities, untangles confusions, indeed dis-covers (un-covers) the unknown. (25; emphasis mine)

(*Das reine Phänomen* steht nun zuletzt als Resultat aller Erfahrungen und Versuche da. Es kann niemals isoliert sein, sondern es *zeigt sich in einer stetigen Folge der Erscheinungen.* Um es *darzustellen* bestimmt der menschliche Geist das empirisch Wankende, schließt das Zufällige aus, sondert das Unreine, entwickelt das Verworrene, ja entdeckt das Unbekannte.)

This method developed into Goethe's discipline of morphology and forms and constitutes the model for his epistemology.

But as the cloud monologue suggests, a self can also be a phenomenon, a subject is an object to another subject. The phenomenon Faust studies is the colorful rainbow that represents human life in the famous image at the beginning of part 2. The scientific discipline that Goethe took up with greatest enthusiasm in the early 1790s was the study of color that lead to his anti-Newtonian *Farbenlehre* (Theory of Color). The mutual imbrication of observer and phenomenon is especially strong in the perception of color—indeed this was Goethe's lasting contribution to the field. He objected to the extreme subjectivity of Newton's theory: by isolating a single ray of light the observer had substituted an artificial situation for the occurrence of color in nature. Here, too, the Rousseauist problematic drives Goethe's interest and perhaps explains the extraordinary passion with which he pursued his antisubjective position. In any case, the presence of specifically theatrical vocabulary in this passage—"reveals itself" (zeigt sich), "in a regular series of appearances" (in einer stetigen Folge der Erscheinungen; think "scenes"), "represent" (*darzustellen*)—corresponds to the fact that *Faust*, also, is organized according to this definition of scientific experimentation; it consists of a series of repeated experiences from varied perspectives as Faust takes on a series of roles. In effect, then, the scientific formulation abstracts from the plurality of identity implied by the exteriorization of parts of the self in *Iphigenie*, where the problem of the heroine is represented both in herself and her brother, and in *Tasso*, where selves appear divided into two, or even four. What there appeared as exteriorization has now taken on a kind of objective existence that can be observed and then reintegrated into a fuller notion of the self that exists as an *Erfahrung*.

The experimental process is easy to follow in *Faust*. At first the observing self seems to be a secure concept. The self is stable in time and knowable through memory, which easily recovers childhood and other states of mind long past for the poets in "Dedication" and the "Prelude on the Stage," and for Faust himself when he hears the Easter chorus in "Night." Furthermore, as the Lord says in the "Prologue in Heaven," the self has an essential core (*Urquell*) that cannot be dislodged by any machinations of the devil. Faust speaks confidently of an identity grounded in an internal sense of himself, most explicitly to Margarete, when he says, "Feeling is everything" (3456; Gefühl ist alles).[7] He wants to believe that the same is true for nature also, whose inner core, causes, and effects he seeks to know in the first paragraph of his opening monologue (382–84). Nature—the object—however, proves less accessible to knowledge than the self, as Faust quickly learns when the Earth Spirit rejects him. Indeed, the archangels in the "Prologue in Heaven" make clear that God and his works are "incomprehensible" (*unbegreiflich*) and "unfathomable"(*unergründlich*); in the final "Chorus Mysticus" of part 2 they are still "ineffable" (*unzulänglich*) and "indescribable" (*unbeschreiblich*). The problem in *Faust* seems to be knowledge of the object, not of the subject.

Nevertheless, the self quickly becomes problematic. Already in his first scene ("Night"), Faust has to question his identity—"Am I a god?" (439; Bin ich ein Gott?), he asks of the Macrocosm, and when the Earth Spirit rejects him he can only ask whom he then resembles (515).[8] By the end of the following scene Faust has two souls pulling him in opposite directions, one heavenward and one into the world (1112). The development is more than temporary, for in the next scene his "better soul" (1180; beßre Seele) awakens as he translates the Bible. As he makes the pact, Faust reverts (as he will frequently) to the rhetoric of an interiorized core self—"And I will partake of the lot of all mankind / In my innermost self" (1770–71; Und was der ganzen Menschheit zugeteilt ist, / Will ich in meinem innern Selbst genießen). But this self is about to dissolve into the world because Faust continues, "And thus expand my own self to that of all mankind" (1772; Und so mein eigen Selbst zu [der ganzen Menschheit] Selbst erweitern). The pact requires, furthermore, that Faust renounce all stability in time: he is never to ask to tarry a while. When Faust first recognizes the two souls within himself, he calls for a mediator "between earth and heaven" (1119; zwischen Erd' und Himmel) to heal the rift, and in response there appears the black poodle who turns out to be Mephistopheles. Mephistopheles, as poodle and as pact-maker, is the sign of Faust's discombobulated identity.

And indeed Mephistopheles disrupts Faust's sense of self ever further. He removes him from his familiar academic setting, has him dress in unfamiliar clothing, brings him first to what Faust considers the unsuitable gaiety of Auerbach's Tavern, and, finally, rejuvenates him in the witch's kitchen. Mephistopheles transforms Faust from a passionate lover of knowledge into a lover of flesh: he changes his identity. Faust acknowledges as much when his encounter with the innocent Margarete makes him cry, "Pitiful Faust! I no longer recognize you" (2720; Armsel'ger Faust! ich kenne dich nicht mehr). When he withdraws from her in "Forest and Cavern," the spirit of Nature grants him two revelations. The first insight, into the breast of Nature, is his brotherhood with all beings and spirits of forest, air, and water (3223–27); his identity is dispersed into nature. The second is insight into himself (3232–33). But Faust scarcely recovers his identity thereby, for in the next line he describes these revelations within his breast as "Secret, deep wonders" (3234; Geheime tiefe Wunder). This is not a self whose essence Faust knows, but one that must be revealed and that evokes amazement—it is evidently new and unexpected. By the end of part 1 the sincere Faust for whom feeling was everything has become an ordinary street brawler, the seducer and abandoner of an innocent woman, and an outlaw. When Margarete recognizes him in prison, it is amazing that she can say so positively, "It's you" (Du bist's); she does, however, immediately add, "I can scarcely believe it"(4510; ich glaub es kaum). Her line cites the recognition scene of Tamino and Pamina, who have never seen each other before, in Mozart's *Magic Flute*. Evoking the almost silly song-and-dance routine from Mozart's wildly popular opera emphasizes how topical, and therefore how important, uncertain identity is here. As Faust tries to drag Margarete from the dungeon and refuses to kiss her, her confidence in his identity dissolves completely. Readers have always been puzzled by her calling him "Heinrich" (Henry), a name for Faust used only once before the final scene in part 1 (also by Margarete) and used nowhere else previously in the Faust tradition; Goethe probably chose the alias to emphasize his hero's lack of special or stable identity—by becoming all of humanity he has become any Tom, Dick, or, in this case, Harry.[9]

No one else has a readily graspable identity in part 1 either. When an innocent student comes to Faust for advice, Mephistopheles makes his head spin, and in "Auerbach's Tavern" he renders the drinkers unable to recognize one another. He invents the death of Frau Marthe's husband and then leads her through a labyrinth of feelings about him, until at last he reveals her total lack of core by drawing her affections onto himself. Margarete's brother Valentin has no identity of his own—if his sister is dishonored, then his life is destroyed. Margarete is the most important of these examples. In her very first line she denies the identity of "Fair young lady" (2605; schönes Fräulein) that Faust first offers her, as she says, "I'm neither fair nor a lady" (2607; Bin weder Fräulein, weder schön). There is no indication that she ever comprehends how he has projected his own ideal onto her. The spectator recognizes it when Faust describes her in her room; he makes clear that he sees in her the entire cosmos, the order of Nature, a representation of the absolute knowledge he seeks. But she, as she says explicitly, is unable to comprehend what he sees in her (3216). Margarete is in effect really two people, one for Faust and one for herself. For Faust, her tragic destruction results from his attempt to possess the ideal in literal terms; in the same way he will destroy the shade of Helena he conjures up in act 1 of part 2 simply by embracing it. But for Margarete, her tragedy is the typical bourgeois seduction tragedy of the eighteenth century. She puts on the jewels Faust offers with excitement and, in "At the Well," is unable to find her way back into the self she was before she met him. At the end of part 1 Mephistopheles claims she is condemned, while a voice from above asserts she is saved. There is a strong temptation to give the salvation voice priority, as most Faust operas do, but nothing in the text of *Faust*, part 1, indicates that one voice is right and the other wrong—the last word is Margarete's desperate call, "Heinrich." The contradicting claims correspond to the duality of her identity. Goethe has thought through yet again the impact of the seducer on the bourgeois family—first in *Werther*, then in *Egmont*, and now here. The ending for the woman becomes ever darker as the moral implications of the hero's exaggerated subjectivity become ever clearer.

One might argue that the characters are all in some sense the puppets of Mephistopheles, but even his identity is not firmly fixed. Playing the devil is his assigned role, not his essence, for the Lord identifies him in the "Prologue in Heaven" as his assistant who "must function as devil" (343; muß als Teufel schaffen). Faust asks after his essence when Mephistopheles first manifests himself in "Study." Mephistopheles has already changed his outward identity several times (from poodle to hippopotamus to elephant to scholar), so it is clear that physical form says nothing about essence. Even so, Faust should know better, as Mephistopheles implies, because he has also already acknowledged the inadequacy of words, so you can't tell somebody about your essence. Mephistopheles then identifies himself to Faust with a riddle, that he is "a part of that power that would always do evil and always does good" (1335–36; Ein Teil von jener Kraft, / Die stets das Böse will, und stets das Gute schafft). The riddle presupposes a dialectical universe in which all phenomena are denied only to give birth to some new version of them; identity in this universe is always impermanent. Mephistopheles' riddle also presupposes a divided self in which will and deed are always at odds.[10] For Mephistopheles, as for Faust, there can be no action with self-knowledge. As a poodle he can cross the magic sign on Faust's threshold to enter the room, but as a scholar with higher intellectual faculties, he cannot cross it again to leave. In part 2 the devil's gender becomes unstable (female as Greed in act 1 and Phorkyas in 2 and 3, homosexual in his relations with the angels in act 5), and Goethe considered saving him. If even the devil can be worthy of salvation, what is there to hold on to? With typical sardonic irony Mephistopheles declares identity to be imponderable: "When all's said and done, you are what you are" (1806; Du bist am Ende was du bist). It takes patient experimentation in part 2, twenty years later, to establish the order that underlies this apparent chaos.

In the first scene of part 2 Ariel symbolically restores Faust's shattered identity by sprinkling him with the waters of Lethe; the remainder of part 2 enacts the cure at greater length and with greater complexity in an extended, almost psychoanalytic, allegory of identity. In fact, the waters of Lethe do not cure Faust; they make him forget, indeed, one might say, they repress the disastrous effects of the disunity of his identity. In place of his individual disunity this radical discontinuity between surface and depth appears translated onto the court of the Emperor in act 1. The court, the Emperor, and all the courtiers are in a state of chaos or fragmentation due to the sorry state of the Emperor's finances. But money belongs to a network of images in the play—including gold, fire, wine, sunlight—that has been associated from early in part 1 with the absolute, with truth. In part 1 it hovered consistently above Faust in some version of a divine realm, but now for the first time it is located in the depths of the earth, which are interpreted to be the depths of the past, of the cultural imagination and of Faust's own imagination. In order to produce his dumb show of Paris and Helena Faust descends, as the stage direction specifies, to the depths, to find the mysterious Mothers. His personal origin is oddly pluralized to become the origin of culture, so that the Mothers represent the subconscious, the unknown depths of the self.

In part 1 Faust talked about himself as divided and confused; in part 2 he is often actually represented in triplicate. In act 1 he appears in the carnival masque between Boy Charioteer, his idealizing soul or self that wants to fly upward, and Mephistopheles dressed as Greed, the self that holds fast to the gold that comes from beneath the earth. This trio actually appears for the first time on the way to the Walpurgis Night late in part 1, where Faust climbs the mountain between a flighty will-o'-the-wisp and Mephistopheles (again), who calls his attention to the gold of Mammon in the mountain. The two outer figures appear again in the "Walpurgis Night's Dream" as Shakespeare's two nature spirits, delicate Ariel and mischievous Puck. In the "Classical Walpurgis Night" in act 2 of part 2, the whole trio appears yet again with Faust and Mephistopheles in their accustomed places, and Homunculus as the flighty imaginative side of Faust. This dispersion of the self, by objectifying its separate parts, makes it more visible, and therefore legible, to the reader, if not to Faust himself. It is the technique of the classical plays, now writ large by virtue of its stability through the wanderings of part 2.

As paradigms of human beauty the shades of Paris and Helena that Faust brings back from the Mothers enable the psychic and social integration so sorely needed; accordingly, their arrival tames an audience that has been most unruly during the carnival masque into something approaching a community of spectators.[11] By focusing Faust's striving on Helena they also provide him with a language for the object that Ariel's gift of forgetting in the first scene of part 2 had rendered temporarily nameless. In acts 2 and 3 the descent to the Mothers from act 1 is reenacted as a more elaborate descent into Faust's own past and subconscious (when he is brought back unconscious to his own study from part 1) and further yet into the historical depths of European culture when he descends with Mephistopheles and Homunculus to the Classical Walpurgis Night. This detour to the depths results in extraordinary moments of synthesis or psychic integration, the most obvious of which are the marriage of fire and water at the end of act 2 with Galatea and Homunculus (not surprisingly, act 2 has provided an especially rich quarry for Jungian psychoanalysis), and the union of Faust and Helena in act 3. The nonmythological Mothers displace the mythological ancestors of Orest's cure in *Iphigenie* to register the further development of the motif. To the extent that they represent the memory of the European tradition, they are Memory, mother of the Muses, exactly the place where myth turns into allegory.

By the beginning of act 4 Faust's identity seems on the way to reintegration. Without anguish he watches the cloud that represents Helena recede into the depths of memory, and welcomes the returning consciousness of Margarete and his striving of part 1. Here for the first time Faust finally seems able to read the objectifications of himself. He now proceeds without wavering to his final stages of achievement, striving and insight—building dikes for settlers to lead a free and productive existence of eternal striving and creation in act 5. Two additional motifs signal his return to a stable identity: the inner light that shines when Care blinds him ("But inside me bright light shines" [11500; Allein im Innern leuchtet helles Licht]) and his revitalized faith in the once-rejected word, which now, far from empty, "is all that carries weight" (11502; gibt allein Gewicht). And yet, as already noted, billowing clouds seem an odd metaphor for a stable identity, while scholars still cannot agree whether Faust's final acts are to be understood triumphantly or with bitter irony. The stability of Faust's reintegrated identity still remains in question, indeed has become less dependable than ever in the last part of the play.

The process of recurrent destabilization is largely driven by theatricality, the primary mode of representing the world in *Faust*. The "Prelude on the Stage" and "Prologue in Heaven" each transform what follows them into plays within the play, so that, as so typical in the seventeenth century, "all the world's a stage, / And all the men and women merely players" (*As You Like It* 2.7.139–40). The "Walpurgis Night's Dream" is a play staged within the play; so is the masque in act 1 (in which Faust performs), so is the creation and destruction of Seismos's mountain in act 2—like the "Walpurgis Night's Dream" it turns out to be nothing but illusion. To enter the realm of the Mothers, Faust must take on a theatrical "stance" (*Attitüde*), and the Helena he brings back performs on a stage set up in a knightly hall. The tragedy of Margarete as well as the Helena sequence are both plays within the play (Helena is actually an opera within the play); Faust dons his costume in "Witch's Kitchen" for the first and in the "Classical Walpurgis Night" for the second. "Witch's Kitchen" itself contains the play of the apes, while "Auerbach's Tavern" contains both musical performances and the drinkers acting out a little play at Mephistopheles' behest. Mephistopheles functions at different times as maestro, producer, director, and increasingly, in part 2, actor. Marthe and even Margarete play their little roles at Mephisto's direction, Valentin proudly dies "as a soldier" (3775; als Soldat)—in his chosen role—and even the rat in Mephistopheles' song in "Auerbach's Tavern" plays a role—"as if she were in love" (2132; als hätte sie Lieb' im Leibe) is the refrain. In order to experience all that is open to humanity, Faust must play all the possible roles. Accordingly, all the shifts of identity chronicled above are also changes of costume—in part 1 Faust changes to the clothing first of a gentleman, then of a youthful lover; in part 2 his roles as wise man, Plutus, imperial treasurer, medieval prince, Renaissance knight, elderly landowner all call for different outfits. And the roles are endless, if one takes account of the parodic or collateral versions of Faust the striver, like the student, the Emperor, the Baccalaureus, Boy Charioteer,

Homunculus, Lynkeus, Euphorion. Apparently, theater is inherently unstable: the first line of "Dedication" calls for "wavering forms" (schwankende Gestalten) to emerge from the poet's own yellowed manuscript. And Faust is all too aware that theater is only metaphor, for he rejects the sign of the Macrocosm as "just a play" (454; Schauspiel nur) and tells Wagner life is nothing but a "ranting tragedy" (583; Haupt- und Staatsaktion). At the same time Wagner takes his master's genuine ranting for declamation of Greek tragedy. The prominence of the play motif everywhere, but especially in the prologues, shows that however hostile Faust may be to theatricality and to words, he will have to learn that roles are his only access to truth, just as the audience learns that the play is its only access to truth (the message of the last chorus). And this is precisely what Mephistopheles, clown that he is, has to teach him. Faust wins his way through to a "stable" identity by accepting that no identity is permanent. Only conceived as a series of roles can the subject exist in the flux of temporality. In a typical Romantic paradox, theatricality offers stability precisely because it is so unstable.

Yet theatricality is, ultimately, only a metaphor in the play: its meaning for the subject/object problem, however, can be clarified through the use of mirror and reflection, less prevalent, but precisely for that reason more readable, images of identity in the play. The mirror is an obvious symbol of subjectivity for the nineteenth century and later, but in fact mirrors tended just about until Goethe's day to reflect the world more than the individual self, as, for example, in the well-known painting by Petrus Christus, *A Goldsmith in His Shop*, of 1449, where the mirror reflects the street outside (Figure 1). When the mirror does reflect the self, then it signifies vanity, as in Bernardo Strozzi's *Vanitas (The Old Coquette)* of 1637 (Figure 2), or self-examination, as in "Prudence" in Cesare Ripa's *Iconologia*. It most commonly reflects truth, although a magic mirror may very occasionally reflect an enchantment or distortion of the devil.[12] Thus in *Faust*, part 1, the sea is a "Spiegelflut" (700; mirror-flood) that attracts Faust to new worlds, and, in the vanity mode, Frau Marthe, mother of all vices, invites Margarete to come to her to parade before the mirror in her jewelry (2888). Reflection in "Night" catches both aspects simultaneously: when Faust is rejected by the Earth Spirit, he laments,

> I, reflection of the Godhead, who thought myself already
> So near to the mirror of eternal truth
> Rejoiced in my heavenly glory and clarity (614–16)

Figure 1. *A Goldsmith in His Shop, Possibly Saint Eligius*, by Petrus Christus. The Metropolitan Museum of Art, Robert Lehman Collection, 1975 (1975.1.110). Image © The Metropolitan Museum of Art.

(Ich, Ebenbild der Gottheit, das sich schon
Ganz nah gedünkt dem Spiegel ew'ger Wahrheit,
Sein selbst genoß in Himmelsglanz und Klarheit)

The capacity of the mirror to reflect eternal truth is distorted by the unwarranted substitution of Faust's self in place of the Godhead.[13] Thus the two older meanings of the motif barely raise the subject/object problem.

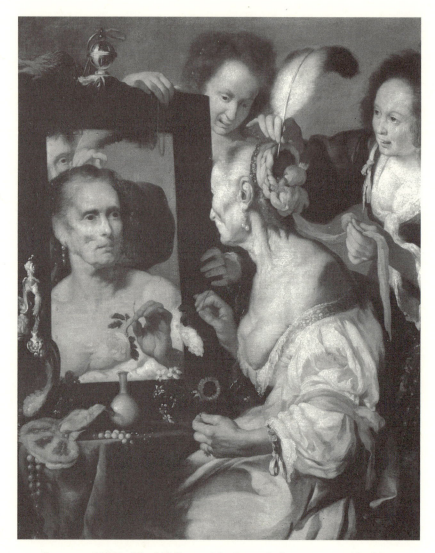

FIGURE 2. *Vanitas (The Old Coquette)*, by Bernardo Strozzi, ca. 1637. Pushkin Museum of Fine Arts, Moscow. Image Heritage Images.

But when the mirror actually appears on stage as a symbol, something new happens. When Margarete finds the first casket of jewels, she puts on a necklace and steps up to the mirror. She indulges in vanity for only two lines ("If only the earrings were mine! / You look so different in them" [2796–97;

Wenn nur die Ohrring' meine wären! / Man sieht doch gleich ganz anders drein]), then quickly shifts to an almost mystical incantation of gold:

For gold contend,
On gold depend
All things. Poor us! (2801–3)

(Nach Golde drängt,
Am Golde hängt
Doch alles. Ach wir Armen!)

She sees in the mirror not herself but the heightened self she could be with the addition of gold. Part 2 makes amply clear that gold is the equivalent of the light of the sun, ineffable truth. Margarete thus sees herself idealized. The point is even more obvious when Faust stands before the magic mirror in "Witch's Kitchen." He doesn't see himself in the mirror either; instead he sees a recumbent Venus. One would expect from a magic mirror and from Mephistopheles' predictions that the figure would awaken his lust, but it arouses rather his sense of the ideal, for he addresses the figure in the same language he uses to address the sign of the Macrocosm. Like Margarete Faust does not indulge in vanity (self-satisfaction), but sees in the mirror a projection of his imagination, the very ideal he is about to project onto Margarete. In each case what is seen in the mirror is less a self as is, than an imagined role to be played, in both cases by Margarete. The fact that Faust projects his ideal identity across the gender boundary emphasizes even more the importance of imagination in generating identities that are in truth roles.

In part 2 reflection becomes a more objective form of knowledge. The paradigmatic formulation comes, like all paradigms for part 2, in the first scene, "Charming Landscape," when the glittering stars are reflected ("sich spiegelnd," 4646) in the lake. The phrase might first appear to be a traditional Renaissance personification of the stars as the eyes of heaven. But nature is already personified in this scene, in the nature spirits who sing this line to Faust; the stars are only the natural objects they describe. Reflection is of the object by the object—no subjects involved, just as in the late poem "Dämmrung senkte sich von oben" (Dusk Descended from on High), where "Blacker still the darkness grown / Reflects within the lake's deep skies" (HA 1:389; Schwarz-vertiefte Finsternisse / Widerspiegelnd ruht der See). Mephistopheles peers about him in the "Classical Walpurgis Night," and the indecency reflected ("sich . . . spiegelt," 7085) in his eyes almost overwhelms him, as the sunrise almost did Faust at the beginning of part 2. The subject has apparently no engagement in this process; instead the reflection penetrates the viewer from outside of his self. The Emperor sees himself reflected in a Counter-Emperor (10407): only then, he says, does he "feel"—not "imagine"—his own potential greatness. The small shift in rhetoric is telling. Reflection is now, as so often in late Goethe, a state of being.

At the same time, the mirror is no longer glass, but water.[14] Water is already reflective in part 1, but in part 2 its role is foregrounded more explicitly. The paradigmatic moment, again, is the rainbow in "Charming Landscape" at the very beginning: its colorful *Abglanz*, reflection and refraction simultaneously, represents all human life. In act 2 Faust has two visions of Leda and the swan: as the conception of Helena they represent his deepest-rooted desire—his subconscious, perhaps his inmost identity. Both feature the surface of the water, which reflects the beauty of the mother of Helena (6912, 7284). In the first, completely subconscious vision, a dream, the water is described as crystal, but in the second description this last remnant of the mirror's former artificial character falls away. Homunculus must live in a crystal vial because, he says, he is artificial (6884); hence the process of mirroring in the water has become, by contrast, completely natural. The reflective surface of the water is invoked twice when the members of the Greek chorus dissolve into nature at the end of act 3 and explicitly renounce all claim to human identity (9999 and 10010). Mirrors began in *Faust* as objects before which figures are costumed for their roles; they end as the site at which role dissolves into nature.

The cloud monologue in act 4 is the culmination of the motif, the final manifestation of identity reflected in water. Now the water is barely even water, but water vapor, and the clouds, unstable in shape as they now are, reflect "fleeting days' great meaning" (10054; flücht'ger Tage großen Sinn). They represent, of course, the memory of Helena, whose robe turned into these very clouds at the end of the preceding scene. They exist objectively in the play; they are connected objectively with Helena. Faust need supply no subjective component to give them meaning. And yet, subject to temporality in their constant changes of shape, they also represent—reflect—the profound significance of human history. If the mirror began as the solid otherness of the world in contrast to the self, that objective other has become now completely fluid. If the self is unstable, so is the nature in which it mirrors itself. Both are unstable, because both exist only in time. Goethe follows Kant in seeing art and nature as equivalent categories; so Goethe's mirror image shows that self and world must also be seen as equivalent or at least analogous categories—both are fluid enough to exist in time, and both nevertheless are capable of mirroring something more permanent than themselves. While both the water and the self have depths, what can be known of them is only what lies on the surface. Thus in a closely related image, when Goethe's fisherman sinks into the water at the end of his poem ("Der Fischer"), his fate must remain unknown. All that can be said is that he was never seen again. Whatever permanence and stability either the world or the self has, it is ineffable and can only be comprehended from the summation of the different temporary manifestations. With this insight, Goethe's experimental method and his notion of identity as a series of theatrical roles come together.

Faust's monologue at the beginning of act 4 introduces the last of his transformations. Right after this speech he identifies the seashore as the venue for what turns out to be his last adventure, his final act of striving to drain swamps and provide land for a free and active people. It is not a more important, culminating, or more typical adventure than any of the others, but yet another in the series of roles Faust has played. For it to be superior or definitive would not be in the spirit either of *Faust*'s theatricality or of Goethe's scientific method. As researcher in *Faust* Goethe lays before us a series of *Erfahrungen*. They are all equivalent, but laid out next to each other, they reveal the underlying pattern, the natural law. Faust's divided and unstable identity appears to be integrated, and the theatricality of part 1 begins to appear more objective in part 2—not because anything becomes more real, but because more and more figures in the repeated reflections of stage and mirror render the pattern that is the natural law ever more visible. Thus Margarete, Helena, Galatea, and all the rest have crossed the stage before that anticlimactic mystification, the "eternal feminine," is spoken. The articulation of such profound and ineffable truths cannot help but seem simultaneously banal and esoteric. Natural laws, like theatrical roles, must be *angeschaut*, to use Goethe's word, must be seen, to be believed.

Identity is thus equivalent to natural law, or the subject to the object. Or is it? Surely it defeats the purpose to be so reductive. The elimination of the self, *Entäußerung*, as a scientific term reduces the observer to an unthinking eye. This is the reflexive self-contemplation at which the mirror imagery in part 2 arrives. But in the theater *Entäußerung* means to take on a role in the world; it means to create exteriority, to make the ineffable concretely visible, to give it body: Homunculus in search of a body to house his spark of life is the paradigmatic example of the process of theatricality. The true self, like the thing in itself, is the equivalent of natural law, but the focus of the two discourses is different. Experiment gazes inward toward what remains constant as the phenomenon is observed from different points of view, while theatricality makes whatever is constant in the self visible to the spectator in a series of roles. Experiment is epistemological; theatricality is representational. Theatricality and experiment in *Faust* are thus reciprocal and complementary processes, as identity and natural law, subject and object are reciprocal and complementary phenomena.

This, Goethe's last word on Rousseau, is also, as in the classical plays, well on the way to Freud. What appear as plays within the play in *Faust* have already appeared in more rudimentary form in *Iphigenie* and *Egmont* as explicit dreams—Orest's dream of reconciliation with his ancestors, Egmont's dream of Klare as the goddess Freedom. In *Faust* the language of dream is never far from such representations. Nineteenth-century opera composers filled the later parts of the Gretchen tragedy with dreamlike ballets, but Goethe himself has his trio of Faust, Mephistopheles, and a will-o'-the-wisp speak of entering the realm of dreams as they climb the Brocken to the Walpurgis Night (3871). The scene, like much of the end of *Faust*, part 1, operates like a bad dream, and the fantastic illogical masque that forms its anticlimax is explicitly titled "Walpurgis Night's Dream." The obvious allusion to Shakespeare's *A Midsummer Night's Dream* hammers home the connection between theatricality and the dreams of the self. The "Classical Walpurgis Night" in part 2 plays more and more on this idea: Faust is unconscious at the beginning of the act, and Stuart Atkins, one of *Faust*'s greatest readers, has argued he remains unconscious until the end of act 3.[15] Faust dreams twice in act 2 of the conception of Helena, the encounter of Leda with the swan. Both dreams are described at length, the first in Faust's chamber and the second on the banks of a river, a setting that matches the content of the dream. The encounter is then reenacted at the end of the marine procession that closes act 2 as Homunculus pours out his flame at the feet of Galatea in the water. As soon as one substitutes for "theatricality" "dream," the increasingly frequent title for theatricals in *Faust*, we are most of the way to psychoanalysis.

CHAPTER 6

The Narrative Self

Faust is not only Goethe's most sophisticated dramatic allegory, achieved after the coherent cosmos on which allegory depends had passed, and managed by sheer force of individual genius, but it also remains unclassifiable for our essentially secular culture today and tends to be received as epic as much as drama.[1] Since narrative allegory has had a different history from allegory in drama and has been tied less closely to specific religious structures, the ambiguous genre of *Faust* reveals the implicit connection to Goethe's use of dramatic allegory in his later novels, where the allegory is less open, more mysterious, and therefore more appropriate to the invisible self that drives the action.

When Goethe began writing prose narrative again in the 1790s, he returned to *Wilhelm Meisters Lehrjahre*, the major fragment he did not complete for the collected edition of his works and the novel that put self-development on the map for the European nineteenth century. Unlike previous analysis of the content and nature of Wilhelm's development, the matter of many substantial books, this discussion focuses specifically on Goethe's exploratory representations of interiority.[2] Werther had known at every moment what he thought and felt, while the addressee of his effusions, Wilhelm, remained silent. The Wilhelm of the *Lehrjahre* is no political hero like his namesake in *Egmont*, but he does already in the first of the novel's eight books learn not to express his feelings, whether in poetry or to his confidant Werner, a name strikingly similar in sound to "Werther." His subsequent occasional letters reflect and evaluate but do not examine innermost feelings. Although neither novel makes any claim about the identity of its Wilhelms, now the quiet figure is the hero.[3] This Wilhelm becomes increasingly a listener to the feelings of others—in the sequel, *Wilhelm Meisters Wanderjahre*, listening is his primary activity—and yet his unarticulated emotional development is the subject of the novel. In order to understand the specific contribution of narrative to representing selfhood, the argument builds on the themes that already organized the previous two chapters: first, the genre mixing used in the classical dramas emerges here as an organizing tension between drama and narrative; second, the allegorical representation of selfhood through the combination of the projective allegory of the classical dramas with the experimental version of identity and incipient morphology discussed in the previous chapter, and, finally, the novel's terminology and analysis of psychological categories, a phenomenon that finally begins to emerge clearly in this text.

The novel is difficult to describe to those who haven't read it, because it is so complex and tightly organized beneath its casual picaresque surface. The maturation of its ironically named hero, Wilhelm Meister (master), takes place in two main strands. In the first, he overcomes his youthful passion for the stage to join a mixed-class (aristocratic and bourgeois) community of men, called the Society of the Tower (Turmgesellschaft) and led by Wilhelm's ego ideal, Lothario, and his tutor, the Abbé. Their goal is to develop and administer their lands responsibly for the benefit of society in different parts of Europe, so that they can offer each other mutual support in a world of revolution. The second strand is a series of love affairs culminating in Wilhelm's engagement to the ideal woman, Lothario's sister Natalie, on the last page. All this comes to pass as Wilhelm wanders aimlessly from his paternal home via various adventures on stage (he performs the title role in *Hamlet* among other things) to the castle of Natalie; the two places are, however, secretly connected by an art collection, which once belonged to Wilhelm's grandfather and now belongs to Natalie. Along the way Wilhelm collects, like Dorothy in *The Wizard of Oz*, companions—a virtual family composed of a mysterious harper, a strange child who can communicate only through music (Mignon), and later a beautiful boy who turns out to be his own son by his first mistress, the actress Mariane, from whom he was separated by a misunderstanding. His larger circle includes a whole theater company (Laertes, Philine, the Melinas) that he adopts, then finally, the family of Lothario—Friedrich, Natalie, the Countess, and Lothario (siblings), their aunt, known as the "Beautiful Soul," a great uncle, and the family tutor, the Abbé. Only gradually in the course of the novel do their names and relationships become clear to the reader and to Wilhelm.

Theater and Narrative

As if speaking directly to Goethe's dramas, the opening of the novel undertakes to overcome theatricality as the essential mode of being. The first sentence, "The play lasted a very long time" (Das Schauspiel dauerte sehr lange),[4] emerges as an allegorical program, as the innate theatricality of the novel's world unfolds. The characters appear only as the roles that constitute the typical cast of comedy—pretty girl in disguise (the actress Mariane), old servant (Barbara), competing lovers (Wilhelm and a coarse merchant named Norberg, who remains offstage)—with the elderly servant, the first "on stage," trying to control the staging; the action proceeds via two dramatic entrances, as Mariane and then Wilhelm arrive. Elements of costume are enumerated (muslin, cotton, scarves, ribbons are laid out on the table, while Mariane enters with plumed hat and sword), but they only take on individuality, their specific colors (white vest and red uniform), in the last paragraph of the chapter when the lovers embrace. Mariane rebels against Barbara's efforts to make her reject the naive Wilhelm for the wealthy Norberg with the rhetoric of individual identity: until Norberg returns to town, she says, "I shall be my own self" (will ich mein sein) and dispose of "my entire self" (10; Dieses ganze Mein). For her, individual identity is the opposite of the conventional dramatic roles. But theatricality still dominates and even the narrator sounds like a drama reviewer with his suppositions about motives, his exclamation points, and his evaluative opening assertion that the play was (overly) long. Yet the detectable presence of the narrator establishes narration as an alternative to drama, so that Mariane's efforts to free herself from Barbara's plan for her align innerness and narration against theatrical identity.

The structure of the plot fits this pattern. In the first half of the novel Wilhelm progresses through puppet play, childishly staged romance, and folk drama to contemporary popular theater and allegorical tributes to visiting dignitaries; in each case, however, preparing the theatrical externals takes priority over both text and dramatic expression.[5] His encounters with the works of Shakespeare and two mysteriously internal characters, the sensitive acrobatic waif Mignon and her unnamed protector, the Harper, mark a turning point. Wilhelm joins a troupe of professional actors, and the dramas now invoked, Shakespeare's *Hamlet* (in a neoclassical adaptation by Wilhelm) and Lessing's *Emilia Galotti*, have become sophisticated, neoclassical, and character oriented. In books 4 and 5 Wilhelm analyzes the central characters of both plays before planning costumes and sets, although these latter still engage his serious attention in the first of the productions. Book 6, devoted to the introspective memoir of the "Beautiful Soul" (schöne Seele) marks another turning point: Wilhelm breaks emotionally with the stage and turns his attention to selfhood in the world. He becomes more attentive to the attitudes of the people around him, more sensitive to the moral implications of his behavior; he becomes a father rather than a son; he enters (or at least foresees entering) an existence conditioned by economic and political considerations. The stages of the journey are marked by Shakespeare, who became for Goethe the epic, unstageable dramatist (cf. his essay "Shakespeare und kein Ende" [Shakespeare Yet Again, 1815 and 1826]) and then the *schöne Seele*, who represents herself exclusively by narrative rather than performance. In the last book the hidden interiority of Mignon and the Harper, only hinted at through their earlier performances, is also at last revealed and explained, now by recourse to a narrative about them read aloud.

The trajectory from theater to narrative and selfhood in the world is inherent in Goethe's odd choice of the rake Lothario, brother of Wilhelm's ideal beloved and eventual fiancée Natalie, as the model male figure in the novel. Lothario takes his name from the seductive villain of Nicholas Rowe's popular tragedy *The Fair Penitent* of 1703, the figure whose name rapidly became synonymous in English with "seducer."[6] Eighteenth-century dramas and novels were preoccupied with rakes, seducers, kidnappers, and the efforts of women to protect themselves from them. But as the century proceeded the novel rapidly became the dominant form, and, especially in England, drama receded. In novels where the rake is not the villain—Henry Fielding's *Tom Jones* (1749) is the obvious example—the rake merges with the picaro to grow up, to marry, and to administer his estates responsibly. This is the model to which Goethe turns as his novel moves away from theater. Goethe's original title was *Wilhelm Meisters theatralische Sendung* (Wilhelm Meister's Theatrical Mission). The change from "mission" to "apprenticeship" suggests that Wilhelm's maturation will not be achieved in the orderly, didactic fashion of drama, but will follow Rousseau's educational precept of learning by doing. But unlike Rousseau's Emile, who is most certainly not a rake, Wilhelm wanders without the constant presence of a totalitarian tutor. His apprenticeship is, rather, picaresque.

Although *Emile* is to a large extent about how to keep a child from turning into a rake, the opposition is important. The rake's problem is lack of emotional stability: his affections slide from one object to the next and, like Werther, he is at the mercy of every passing feeling, in eighteenth-century terms, being too "sensible" (*empfindsam*).[7] Or, too subjective: a rake's feelings drift, exactly like Rousseau's solitary wanderer rocking in his boat. This kind of subjectivity is associated in the *Lehrjahre* not only with the theater, but with many forms of art. Goethe finished the novel in daily intellectual exchange with Friedrich Schiller, who had just published his *On the Aesthetic Education of Man in a Series of Letters* (*Über die ästhetische Erziehung des Menschen in einer Reihe von Briefen*) in 1794–95. For Schiller art raised people to the state of reason by creating in them an aesthetic mood, a state of infinite determinability or fixability (*Bestimmbarkeit*). For Goethe such infinite openness had to sound remarkably like the state of Rousseau's wanderer. The *Lehrjahre* moves away instead not just from theater, but from the aesthetic state, away from art, as Novalis angrily meant when he called the novel a "Candide against poetry" (*Schriften* 646).

Yet the theater and the aesthetic are not simply a detour to be overcome. The excessive innerness of characters like Mignon, the Harper, the passionate actress Aurelie (a former beloved of Lothario), and the Beautiful Soul are at least as problematic as Wilhelm's theatrical aberration; characters named for Narcissus appear only near the beginnings of life stories (Wilhelm's when he adopts Mignon in book 2, the fiancé in book 6 whom the Beautiful Soul outgrows). Natalie's castle, where the action climaxes, is a veritable temple of art where important events like Mignon's funeral are marked with stylized ceremonies that engage all the performing arts, including role playing and the dramatic revealing gesture (when Mignon's tattoo is revealed). A place from which the "coarse" details of reality seem to ban themselves (sexy Philine refuses to accompany her lover Friedrich [Natalie's younger brother] because she is pregnant), the castle becomes the scene of the most operatically dramatic occurrences in the entire novel—the Harper's suicide and the tale of his incestuous love. It is also, like the theatrical world of the earlier parts of the novel, a place of costuming, where Mignon dresses as an angel. While the characters wait for the couples to sort themselves out at the end after painful complications, they engage in idle dialogues that carefully avoid uncomfortable realities: their humane manners are in fact a higher form of theater. It takes, finally, the clownish Friedrich, the character who has remained closest to the stage, to cut the Gordian knot and make the reticent Natalie admit that she loves Wilhelm so as to bring about the traditional theatrical happy end with the "right" couple newly engaged. At the beginning of the novel Wilhelm has nostalgic memories of his grandfather's art collection, which he sorted by his ability to identify with the figures pictured. At the end he reencounters the collection in Natalie's castle, where he is better able to appreciate the aesthetic merits of the pictures. Like subject and object, the theatrical and the real must interact.

Because the picaresque novel ends like a stage comedy, the representation of the dialectic of theatrical exteriority and interiority is equally a dialectic of drama and narrative. Wilhelm's insistence in the novel's last lines that he does not deserve Natalie, that he is like Saul who went in search of his father's she-asses and found a kingdom, emphasizes the picaresque nature of the plot. At the same time, none of the characters can really talk to each other: the resolution comes about in a series of narrations, which include the extended novella of Mignon's ancestry from an incestuous affair between the Harper and his sister Sperata (reading the *text* drives the Harper to suicide) and Friedrich's reports of what Natalie told the Abbé behind closed doors—"offstage." While the content of the plot is as dramatic as they come, its form is narrative. Apparently the increased interiority of the character mix has driven Goethe beyond drama, at least at this stage of the representational tools at his disposal. Or, more accurately, the refined techniques for representing interiority developed in the dramas enable Goethe to return to his abandoned narrative and make it work.

Morphology and Allegory

Curiously, representing interiority requires more space than drama normally allows—*Faust* is surely the exception that proves the rule. The projection of interiors onto multiple dramatic characters in the classical plays in effect opened up the space of Werther's constricted interior, as *Faust* allowed its hero to escape from his narrow gothic chamber, the prison house of the self. In the dramas it was fruitful to understand characters as parts of the main character, and in *Faust* as versions or alternate perspectives of him. But in the *Lehrjahre*, written in the first flush of Goethe's morphological discoveries, the process takes on a characteristic dynamic that demands the spaciousness of narrative.[8] By "morphology," Goethe meant studying biology in the fashion described in the previous chapter for discovering the natural law underlying each group of phenomena. He established the existence of the intermaxillary bone in humans, for example, by examining large numbers of mammalian skulls, drawing his observations more and more carefully as the skulls approached the form of humans, so that he was able to identify the suture that revealed the bone's vestigial existence in the human jaw; the underlying natural law was that all mammals had such a bone and thus that humans are continuous with the rest of creation. Hellmut Ammerlahn recommends thinking of character development in the *Lehrjahre* as a tendency toward form in the morphological sense, that "the figures that twine around the central development are to varying degrees parts of Wilhelm himself" (die um diese zentrale Metamorphose sich herumrankenden Gestalten in verschiedenen Gradverhältnissen Teile [Wilhelms] selbst sind).[9] The model for Ammerlahn, obviously, is Goethe's description of the metamorphosis of plants, with its spiral (*herumrankenden*) development around a center (Wilhelm) driven by the alternating contraction and expansion of organs. What follows extends this insight systematically to read the characters in the novel as sets of morphological series with regard to different aspects of Wilhelm's development.

Wilhelm's choices in life are, to begin with, personified in pairs of opposed women: before the novel starts he has written a poem personifying the choice between business and art as that between an old and a young woman, who appear then as the mercenary Barbara and lovely Mariane in the first chapter. At the same time, Wilhelm is pulled between his mother and the life represented by the two women of the theater. As is typical for the novel, it is difficult to decide if Wilhelm's mother is a foil to Barbara (the good mother versus the bad mother) or to Mariane (the old woman versus the young one): the series is already dynamic and its figures evolving. Later pairs include a generously amoral actress named Philine and the mysterious, self-contained Mignon, introduced together in repeated alternation in the long fourth chapter of book 2: they roughly embody free love versus single-minded devotion. In book 3, they are varied and moderated in the Baroness and the Countess (who is also a foil for Philine and her more ideal sister Natalie). The more single-minded Aurelie, angrily unable to forget her former lover, Lothario, appears in book 4, first as an alternative to the Countess and then as a consistent opponent of Philine. The patience of the Beautiful Soul (book 6) during illness and her attitude toward men reverse Aurelie's passion. In the last two books Therese, Lothario's fiancée, and Natalie then emerge as the rational and spiritual ideals. The figures who represent intense passion become less romantic and more rigid as one succeeds the next, while flexibility in one's choice of love object becomes more acceptable, more understandable, less rakish. Business and art return at the end as Therese and Natalie, Lothario's fiancée and sister respectively, best of friends and both loved by Wilhelm. What began as simple oppositions—business and art, faithfulness and rakishness—end as possibilities rather than alternatives, names for a scale rather than absolutes, positions that mean different things in different temporal contexts, goals that can coexist. The novel's move from the rather ordinary Mariane through a series

of reversals to the ideal Natalie, taken as the single entity the "eternal feminine," reveals the driving tension of metamorphosis familiar from Goethe's
biological essays, "polarity and enhancement" (Polarität und Steigerung).
In effect, then, Wilhelm's development and maturation, his change in attitudes and values, his discovery of who and what he really is, is represented
not through the narrator's insight and interpretation, but through the same
kind of projection onto other characters observed in the classical plays and in
Faust. Next to descriptions of Wilhelm's moods and interior monologues the
novel makes visible with the techniques of dramatic allegory the psychosocial
maturation Wilhelm undergoes.[10]

Parallel transformations of traditional images redefine the nature of interiority. Fire, for example, begins as a traditional metaphor for passion and
even involves the clichéd dramatic gesture of burning letters. Starting in book
3 several real fires emerge from the plot, and it is only in retrospect, when the
sultry passions of both Mignon and Philine burst into flame after the *Hamlet*
performance with the buildings around them, that their association with the
disorderly lives of the actors becomes clear. At the same time, Wilhelm's ability
to douse the fires reflects his increasing care for those around him. Thereafter,
accompanying Natalie's rise to dominance in the last few books, fire refers
exclusively to the flame-like experience of insight (Beautiful Soul, 369; and
Wilhelm, 428), already anticipated in the halo of light Wilhelm saw around
Natalie's head at their first encounter in book 4. In book 7 Wilhelm sees a
rainbow on his way to Lothario's castle, then dreams of Natalie joining fire
and water, a pairing familiar to any reader of *Faust.* In *Faust* the rainbow is fire
and water, and the pairing signifies the connection of self-knowledge to understanding one's place in the cosmos and subjection to time. The Renaissance
image of passion now signifies recognition of the self's deepest needs.

Similarly, the early part of the novel opposes wealth to creativity, as in
Wilhelm's poem about the hag Business and a beautiful muse. In book 4 the
oppositions join inextricably in a purse of gold coins sent to Wilhelm by the
Countess, whom he has served as poet and also embraced. He is told to regard
it not as wealth, but as the equivalent of a precious gift (such as the ring the
countess has already given him) enhanced by the purse, crocheted by the lady
herself; the gold is a "substitute" (*Ersatz*) for Wilhelm's time, and appropriate
precisely because he is not pure "mind" (*Geist*); he should only regard it as
a "magic wand" (*Zauberstab*), an instrument of creative transformation, to
preserve his memory of the Countess (204). The women's creativity, evidenced
in the textile/text that encloses the creative power of the gold transfers their

creativity to Wilhelm. They are his muses, in effect, but they work with the means of business. Concern with money throughout the novel connects this significant purse to Wilhelm's marriage to Natalie, who embodies the combination of aristocratic good taste with constructive work in the world. The apparently real purse and the somewhat prosy conversation it unleashes can thus be read like one of the mystifying allegories in *Faust*, part 2, even though it hardly feels like one. The real and logical context of discussion obstruct the appearance of allegory, but, cut off from the context, the image functions as a coded language of mental creativity. Such language generates surfaces that, by bursting the bounds of the real world of the novel and reflecting something above them, imply hidden depth.

The names of the characters serve this elaborated allegory in more nuanced fashion than in the plays to mark Wilhelm's progress along the spiral of development familiar from the morphology of plants. It seems obvious that the two men named Narziß (book 2, book 6) are self-involved without realizing it, as Wilhelm is at the beginning of the novel, while characters named Philine and Philo each teach their friends about love. It is equally clear that Wilhelm is indeed fortunate in his son Felix, that Aurelie, who leads Wilhelm to Lothario, in fact represents a dawn for him, and Natalie a rebirth. Natalie's sister, the Countess, has no proper name, for, especially when she appears in her shining jewels at the end of book 3, she represents the "shimmering appearance" (schöner Schein) that characterizes aristocracy at that point in the novel. And her aunt appears only as "the Beautiful Soul." Only when their physical and spiritual beauty are joined in Natalie does a properly significant name emerge. Classes of names also have meaning. Men Wilhelm admires (all characterized by charisma and a form of achievement-focused rationality that borders on amorality and cynicism) have names ending in *o*—Jarno, Serlo, Lothario. The hierarchy among them, as with the other patterns in the book, corresponds to where they appear.[11] Another group of characters have names beginning in *M*—Mariane, Mignon, Melina, Madame Melina, Lothario's former beloved Margarete, and in book 1 alone, Wilhelm's "Muse," his "Mutter," and his beloved "Marionetten."[12] All the *M*'s belong to the early stages of Wilhelm's (or Lothario's) careers in love, and the women in the group are all particularly lovable and particularly capable of passionate love that is not primarily selfish (this is true even of Madame Melina in book 1 and in her farewell from Wilhelm in book 7). The more self-involved Aurelie and Lydie have names beginning with other letters, as do the women who are to become related to Wilhelm by marriage from whom he must henceforth keep his distance—Therese, Philine—and of course Natalie, whose initial N ties her, however, in a sort of impure alliteration, to the first group. Furthermore, the initial letter of "Wilhelm" and his alter ego "Werner" is an inverted M. Thus Melina, in whom Wilhelm sees himself mirrored in book 2, reverses not only Wilhelm's situation by wanting to abandon the theater, but his initial as well. On first reading, the names in the novel seem more realistic than significant, but in fact they have become, in effect, hieroglyphics.

An Emerging Terminology
of Psychological Representation

Goethe's morphology of character makes character markers external, data to be entered in charts (see note 10). His scientific method requires the observer to intuit (*anschauen*) from them the law of development, the dynamic, that underlies the sequence. But at the same time, the obvious external markers of identity (gender, class, nation) are called into question. What kind of law can be intuited from signs whose stability is so uncertain? By posing this question, the novel points to something crucial to identity beneath the surface of all these signs that cannot be, as yet anyhow, read through them. Goethe has found a way to represent the inchoateness of character, precisely through his narrative methodology of ordering natural phenomena beneath the eye of the observer. At the same time, he introduces in this text a taxonomy of psychological representation that has become the norm for representing character. The overlaps between the following survey and the previous discussion reveal how the new terminology reorders insights developed from different lines of thinking and thus how creatively Goethe reorganized our psychic landscape.

Mental Illness

The most thematic motif is mental illness. The madness of the Harper is explained in terms of an Oedipal family romance, since he defied his father and married his sister. A parallel narrative in slightly less explicit terms is the memoir of the Beautiful Soul, whose close early attachment to her father leads to a celibate life of frequent illness, largely cut off from the world.[13] Therese and her father form a less destructive father-daughter dyad that can finally be normalized by the Abbé's discovery that she is not the daughter of her father's unloving wife. This morphological series represents ultimately Wilhelm's only moderately dysfunctional relationship with his father, in which the transition from unloving father to loving fatherly Abbé normalizes his situation and heals him of what Freud was to call his Oedipus complex. The situation is not conceptualized in the novel, but rather imagined, narrated, and imaged in the ubiquitous wounds inflicted upon Wilhelm, and by him upon others.[14] Wilhelm's healing proceeds through several steps. He begins by acting out his rebellion against his father by neglecting his business tasks for the theater, then enacts it on the stage in *Hamlet*, and ends by reading and hearing written narratives about projections of himself. Whereas Iphigenie cures herself by telling her story, which is of course a well-known narrative in the European tradition, the cure in the *Lehrjare* becomes less one of talking than of narrative.

Projection

The *Lehrjahre* provides a virtual anatomy of projection, a process already observed in the plays. Having formed his plan to elope with Mariane and join a theater, Wilhelm arrives in book 1, chapter 13, to collect a debt from a household where the daughter has run off with an actor. Wilhelm is embarrassed to be so prophetically scolded for his own plan, but, watching the young woman defend herself, he imagines Mariane in her place and "placed an even better speech in her mouth" (51; versetzte ihr noch schönere Worte in den Mund); in bed that night he develops an entire novel about what he would do in Melina's place (55). The process soon proceeds beyond parallels (a technique already familiar from *Werther*) and imaginative substitutions. Wilhelm soon tries to pour his own fire into the Melinas—which he continues to do for much of the novel—and also transfers "the entire wealth of his feelings onto Mariane" (57; den ganzen Reichtum seines Gefühls auf [Mariane]). But it is not only Wilhelm who projects, for the story of the Melinas is the projection of the narrator, not entirely of Wilhelm. Indeed, Wilhelm feels sympathy for the girl's father before he does for the runaways. Neither he nor the narrator calls attention to the possible feelings of Wilhelm's own father for the time when Wilhelm will have run off with an actress, but Wilhelm's qualms in book 5 about his father suggest that his sympathy for Madame Melina's father also stands in for unarticulated feelings about his own. Projection of feelings and situations onto another now differs from the performance of one's own or someone else's identity. The focus shifts from the enactment to the interior of the projector behind the actor, be it Wilhelm as aspiring writer or Wilhelm as represented by the narrator of the novel.

Nevertheless, the novel also includes a metamorphic series that traces the shift of projection from the theater to narrative. This episode with the Melinas is characterized as a "play" (49; *Schauspiel*). A comic posse that brings them to the bailiff is twice characterized with the adjective *unförmlich* (47–48), the word used for Wilhelm's clump of wax when he first betrays his devotion to the puppet play of Jonathan and David. The characters—"elderly bailiff" (alter Amtmann), "clerk" (Aktuarius), "the girl" (das Mädchen), "the young man" (der junge Mensch) (50–51)—are types, and the action is "what tends to happen only in novels and comedies" (52; was nur in Romanen und Komödien vorzugehen pflegt). The broadening to include novels in this sentence is key. When Friedrich later fights a duel, with Philine's newest flame, a groom, Wilhelm organizes, indeed, stages, it to protect the foolish boy. Both the narrator and Wilhelm recognize the events as a "performance" (140–41; *Darstellung*) of Wilhelm's own jealousy of the groom. Wilhelm describes Shakespeare's characters as crystal clocks whose internal workings, "Räder- und Federwerk," are always visible (192). In the staging of *Hamlet*, it becomes clear to the reader and eventually, through Jarno, also to Wilhelm, how all of the actors in his troupe play themselves, not as the willed projection of an identity, but unwittingly, so that Shakespeare has become the vehicle of narrative as well as dramatic psychological projection. Thus Wilhelm's friend, first introduced as a nameless fencer, then with the odd formula "whom we shall call Laertes for the time being" (92; den wir einstweilen Laertes nennen wollen), takes his name from the role he is to play in *Hamlet*. The easy transition from play to novel points to Shakespeare's affinity for narrative—Wilhelm encounters him by reading, and he must butcher *Hamlet* in order to stage it. So it is no surprise when Laertes frees himself from both his role and the theater to become wealthy. Yet he remains in this respect still a projection of Wilhelm, who does exactly the same. Ultimately it is hard to find a character in this novel who is not in some respect a projection of its hero. Thus the theme of theater in the novel is not just about the state of the theater or about art, as the Romantics assumed, but more basically the metaphor for the novel's discovery that figures can be made to represent parts or phases of one another.[15]

Multiplicity

It is necessary, however, to distinguish projection from the narrative's tendency to multiplicity, to ubiquitous parallels and variations on its central figures. Wilhelm and Mariane, for example, whose similarity is already marked by their inverted initial, are both innocents of good family embarked in a world they do not fully comprehend and engaging in commitments they do not understand until too late. Wilhelm and the Beautiful Soul both come from well-to-do backgrounds, Wilhelm from the urban high bourgeoisie, the Beautiful Soul from court officialdom—the two classes Goethe bridged when he went to Weimar. Both are fascinated with illness (Wilhelm with the sick prince, the Beautiful Soul with her own) and wounds, both are sober and (at least most of the time) celibate, both have bad taste in painting. More important both keep forming new relationships as they develop, encounter figures named for Narcissus, and figures named for love (Philine, Philo). Wilhelm is moved by the Beautiful Soul's memoir, learns from it perhaps, but hardly considers projecting himself into her situation or understanding her as a mirror of himself. Instead the parallels transform all the characters in this novel into nuanced variations on one another. But this formal quality points in its own way to one of the most important psychological characteristics of the novel, the perplexing multiplicity of individual identity.

The novel is emphatic that characters change in time, that a tendency to change is a natural part of one's identity. Philine's constant undependability is emblematic, but other characters keep changing unexpectedly. Mignon discovers a zither and develops "a hitherto unrecognized talent" (146; Talent, das man an ihm bisher noch nicht kannte). Possession of the costumes and props among which she found it renders Melina, too, in the next paragraph, a completely different person. At the end of book 3 both the Count and the Countess undergo abrupt conversions in consequence of unexpected intimate encounters with Wilhelm. And Wilhelm, finally, can only make sense of Hamlet's character by figuring out what he was like before the death of his father. This example reveals the underlying issue. A self is both something innate that stays constant but can be shaped or deformed as circumstances impinge upon it. The most beautiful example comes in book 7, chapter 7, where Lothario encounters a woman he had loved ten years before. He finds her, Margarete, now a mature woman together with her small daughter and a cousin, who exactly resembles the Margarete of Lothario's memory, and describes the meeting as an encounter "between past and future, as in an orange grove, where blossoms and fruit at different stages live together in the same small space" (470–71; zwischen der Vergangenheit und Zukunft, wie in einem Orangenwalde, wo in einem kleinen Bezirk Blüten und Früchte stufenweis nebeneinander leben). As a result, all identity is necessarily multiple, who we were once and who we are now.

Multiple identity develops further with the imagery of mirrors, which goes beyond the projection of desires and ideals already seen in *Faust*. The mirror helps the actor perfect his exterior: mirrors are among the first missing necessities registered when the theater company enters its inadequate housing in book 3 (159), and the last thing Wilhelm does before going on stage as Hamlet is to look in the mirror (320). In a prank that runs awry, Wilhelm is discovered disguised as the Count and seated in his dressing room; but the Count actually does not see Wilhelm, but rather his image in the mirror (190). Without noticing that there are two images of himself in the mirror, the Count takes his vision as a revelation that he must change his life. Theatrical identity (Wilhelm playing the Count) modulates into calling, indeed, into salvation, the most existential version of identity. Henceforth mirrors become essential tools to discovering one's identity—"why can't I show it to you in a mirror" (warum kann ich's Ihnen nicht im Spiegel zeigen), Aurelie cries about herself (252); Mariane steps happily before a mirror when she can say she truly belongs to herself (480); and Wilhelm stands with Felix before a mirror to make out the child's true identity (489).[16]

But finally the mirror leads beyond personal identity in the conscious sense. In his enthusiasm Wilhelm wants the actor to reflect the entire world (58), and the Beautiful Soul wants her soul to be a mirror of God (361). As Wilhelm reads the description of his own apprenticeship in the first chapter of book 8, "he saw for the first time his own image outside of himself, not a second self, as in a mirror, but a different self, as in a portrait" (505; er sah zum erstenmal sein Bild außer sich, zwar nicht, wie im Spiegel, ein zweites Selbst, sondern wie im Porträt ein anderes Selbst). The distinction is important and colors multiplicity of character in a way that became the norm for the Romantics. For the self that is not another self but an *other* self, a different self; it is uncanny. It is familiar and not familiar. The statement in this form does not sound uncanny, but the reference to portraits connects to the most theatrical and romantic motifs in the novel, which thus color it here. The first two portraits belong to the kind of antiquated theatrical homage Wilhelm so opposes, while the third (in chronological terms) is one of Wilhelm in the ill-fated Shakespearean garb in which he is wounded by robbers (referred to by Werner in book 8, chapter 1). The *Hamlet* performance heightens the romantic element, for the most effective scene is the appearance of the ghost next to his identical portrait—an element crucial to Wilhelm's conception of the scene. The motif returns to the plot when Lothario glimpses a portrait of Therese's mother in book 7, chapter 6. Neither Therese nor the reader understands at first why he flees. Then it turns out he had slept with the mother of his fiancée. Then it turns out that Therese is not the daughter of her mother. The mystery, the emotional intensity, the brush with incest, Therese's dying father unable to reveal the truth of his daughter's birth, the recovery of long-hidden true identity: these are all the stuff of gothic romance, hardly of staid *Bildung*. Then Wilhelm, more than once cast as a prince, discovers the painting of the sick prince he remembers from his childhood—now in Natalie's manor, where he is about to discover himself. Before this background Wilhelm studies the portrait of the Beautiful Soul in Natalie's castle and learns to see in it two beings, the mysterious Amazon with the halo (Natalie) and the religious aunt. The portrait blossoms into a full-fledged doppelgänger.

The motif has already been introduced with its full—ironic—panoply in book 3, when the Count takes the disguised Wilhelm for a supernatural sign that he will soon die, while his wife takes the hero equally irrationally for the bringer of her death by cancer. Natalie has actually two doubles, her aunt and her lovely younger sister, the Countess, whose handwriting is indistinguishable from Natalie's and causes Wilhelm much anguish. The sisters function for Wilhelm as romantic doubles often do—the one brings him inexpressible joy, the other guilt; they render thereby uncanny alternatives that at the beginning of the novel were matters of rational choice, like Wilhelm between business and the muse.[17] The motif reaches its most extreme form in the appearance of the Abbé through the novel—is this mysterious stranger Catholic or Protestant, one person or two, if two, why is the mysterious twin brother never present at the same time as the Abbé? All of these romanticizing mystifications generate the novel's sense of the complexity of the self.

The uncanniest aspect of multiple identity is the awareness it brings of feelings not really known to the conscious self. In the *Lehrjahre* there is a continuous network of secrets ranging from those that are explained to those that cannot be explained. Here is a list in no particular order: Who is Therese's mother? Who is Felix's father? Who is the father of Philine's child? What is the significance of Wilhelm's extremely precise dream in book 7? Who came to Wilhelm's bed in book 5? Who are the mysterious stranger(s) Wilhelm keeps meeting? Who directs his fate? What is the Turmgesellschaft? Who is

Mignon? Who is the Harper? Who is the person in the red uniform kissing Philine? Who is the Amazon? What has the Beautiful Soul to do with the narrative? Who plays Hamlet's father? Who leaves behind the veil and why? What happened to Mariane? What made the Countess dismiss Wilhelm so abruptly? The less interesting ones receive definitive answers—sometimes a name, sometimes the withholding of a name, as in the case of who played the ghost. But some lead to extended discourses or inset novellas, like the story of Therese's parentage and especially that of Mignon's. And some, in a certain sense the central one, the forces behind Wilhelm's development, are nothing but a mystification—the Turmgesellschaft is behind the plot of the novel, but what is the Turmgesellschaft? A product of youthful enthusiasm that no longer represents anything serious at all, simply a metaphor for the ties that bind the young men at the end. Behind all of these gothic secrets lies only one substantial fact—the characters with whom Wilhelm becomes enmeshed all turn out to form one family. If this is a secret, then it replaces the original Oedipal family romance with which the novel seems to begin. And if all this is secret, then the secret of life that Wilhelm learns in the novel is to know his family, to know his origins, to know himself.[18]

Self-knowledge also extends to Wilhelm's love life—he has not been preyed upon or betrayed by women like Mariane, Philine, Mignon, the Countess, but, as he realizes by the end, *he* has injured them. In the first part of the novel Wilhelm has a high opinion of his generosity and his rectitude; he is constantly promising to help others, offering a hand that is not taken. But when Aurelie slashes the hand he holds out to her, he begins to realize, and the reader begins to realize, that Wilhelm himself has unwittingly perpetrated one injury after another on the women about him. Only after he has foolishly offered his hand for the last time, to Therese, does he fully comprehend the measure of his guilt. Thus at the end he does not offer his hand to Natalie, but receives her from the hand of Friedrich: as in *Faust*, all action in the world incurs guilt. This tragedy, the horror inside the self, is, apparently, the great secret of the novel.[19]

And yet, no one would seriously call *Wilhelm Meister* a gothic novel. In fact, it is not a horror novel. Its abandoned castle is located right behind the new castle in book 3, and it is haunted not by ghosts, but by officers out for a good time. At the same time, its mysteries are not demystified by rational explanation. Instead, the explanations of the mysteries of Mignon and the Harper lead to the novel's most gothic moments. Thus Goethe is not simply out to parody the gothic as Jane Austen does in *Northanger Abbey* by reaffirming a sensible, rationalist psychology in the face of the irrational. Instead the gothic and the ordinary coexist side by side in this novel. Goethe experimented with creating psychological depth by using multiple genres simultaneously as early as *Egmont*. Here in the *Lehrjahre* the technique has reached full maturity. The multiple self rests on multiple styles and the gothic is transformed into the substance of *Bildung*.

Interiority

If Wilhelm's moral failings derive from his inattentiveness, the power of the novel derives from what is below the radar screen. Consistently throughout the novel the self is characterized as an interior space with the terms *Innerstes* (twenty-five times), *Inneres* (twenty-two times), and *innerlich* (five times); these words are used exclusively to characterize the interior of the self, never interior spaces in the novel. The Grimms' *Deutsches Wörterbuch* locates Goethe consistently among the earliest citations for forms of the word "inner" used as emotional intensifiers. It seems to go without saying that the self in this novel has an interior element, regardless of how else identity is configured. Interiority is much intensified in Mignon and the Harper, who can communicate nothing about their social or physical identities, or about their aspirations. Neither has a language for direct communication; to the extent that either has feelings that can be identified by reflection, they cannot be communicated directly to others. The language of their poems is obscure, indirect, incomplete; they operate with disconnected images rather than clear predicates. They join Wilhelm in book 2 and by book 3 are his "family," extensions of himself, so that when Jarno speaks harshly of them Wilhelm himself is hurt. The poem "Kennst du das Land" (Knowest thou the land), placed prominently at the beginning of book 3, gives the self a new depth as it gradually reveals beneath the beautiful surface of the natural paradise that is Italy first a frozen interior of marble statues and then the deadly serpents lurking in the cave beneath the route to that paradise. Only now does Shakespeare enter the novel, to illuminate the darkness of the interior spaces that Mignon and the Harper have opened up. If they are mysterious riddles, Shakespeare's plays seem to solve all riddles, as Wilhelm tells Jarno,

His people seem to be natural, and yet they are not. These most
secret and complex creations of nature behave before our eyes in his

plays as if they were clocks with face and case made of crystal; they would show the passage of time as they were designed and at the same time it would be possible to see the wheels and springs that drive them. (192)

(Seine Menschen scheinen natürliche Menschen zu sein, und sie sind es doch nicht. Diese geheimnißvollsten und zusammengesetz-testen Geschöpfe der Natur handeln vor uns in seinen Stücken, als wenn sie Uhren wären, deren Zifferblatt und Gehäuse man von Kristall gebildet hätte, sie zeigten nach ihrer Bestimmung den Lauf der Stunden an, und man kann zugleich das Räder- und Federwerk erkennen, das sie treibt.)

The mechanical interior described here evokes the mechanical nature of Mignon's movements. But if Shakespeare seems able to illuminate the interiors of his characters, does the novel do the same? The reader eventually learns the secrets of Therese's, of Mignon's, of the Harper's backgrounds, but does that explain their identities? In the case of Therese, perhaps. Her tastes seem to derive from her father and her capabilities from her real, secret, mother, the maid, rather than from her theatrical and unloving public mother. But in what sense does the romance of Mignon and the Harper explain their passion, their entrapment in their pasts? The incest on which their story turns represents their entrapment more than it explains it. The novel can only recede into a world of poetry in their case, seal Mignon off into the Hall of the Past (Saal der Vergangenheit), not really explain or illuminate their interiority. Goethe's achievement here lies in moving from a conventional interiority, where emotions are known, to Shakespeare, where only the poetic genius can render the interior comprehensible, to his own world at the end, where certain riddles can never be understood. The barrier of speechlessness that separates these characters from the others in the novel evokes the presence of the unconscious by hiding it.

Dreams

As a result, one can think of the other psychological techniques in the novel as ways to create depth of character by hiding the surface. The most obvious, indeed so obvious it scarcely needs to be discussed here, is the use of dreams.

Dreams in the novel remain partly in the Homeric tradition of messages about the future. In book 1 Wilhelm dreams about losing Mariane, and Goethe emphasizes its apparent exteriority to Wilhelm by having not Wilhelm but Mariane narrate to Barbara what Wilhelm told her about the dream (44–45). In a later extended dream description in book 7 it is again possible to see the final disposition of the characters proleptically laid out as Mariane disappears with Wilhelm's father and Natalie saves Felix's life and then leads Wilhelm off through the garden. Again, the separateness from Wilhelm is emphasized by the introduction "Remarkable dream images appeared to him toward morning" (425; Sonderbare Traumbilder erschienen ihm gegen Morgen). And yet, no serious reader of the novel would deny the psychological power and complexity of these dreams.[20] Unlike Homeric dreams, it is the experience of dreaming them more than the prophecy that evokes powerful affect in Wilhelm. He does not take them to be messages about his future; only the reader does that. Instead, the first causes him to moan in his sleep and to be relieved when Mariane awakens him. The second follows on an episode of uncontrollable weeping, as an etching of a shipwrecked father and daughter remind him of his Amazon; when he awakens to sunshine the next morning it is clear that the dream has effectively defused his overwrought feelings. For Wilhelm the dreams are performing emotional work that he is either unwilling to face, as in the first dream, or cannot quite identify, as in the second.

Inversion and Repression

Two further techniques are particularly important here, inversion and repression. Both are intended as commonsense terms, since it is too early to use them in a specifically Freudian or psychoanalytic sense; the point is to see how Goethe's patterns enabled a later more precise use of such language. Inversion extends the technique of projection in the novel. As the inversion of the letter *W* to *M* connects by identity (projection), it also hides the connection by reversal. Similarly gender inversion ambiguously hides and reveals connections; when Mignon dresses as a boy in Wilhelm's colors, it signals that she represents something inside Wilhelm of which he remains unaware. It both connects him to and disconnects him from certain feminine qualities in himself (attentiveness to others, for example) as well as to his inchoate creative talent. Mignon's disguise simultaneously covers over her similarity to Philine when she is introduced as the opposite pole. For the two are introduced together,

both have small feet, and Philine's "clatter" (*Klappern*) with her shoes on the
stairs both as she fetches Mignon and later in her relations with Serlo and
Wilhelm connect her with the wooden, puppetlike Mignon.[21] Precisely such
networks of seeming and being, of similarity and difference, evoke the sense
that everything in the novel has meaning that cannot quite be elucidated.

Wilhelm's dominant problematic emotion is, oddly, *Verdruss* (irritation,
with overtones of depression), especially but not exclusively in the last book.
It is hardly one of the traditional passions inherited via baroque tragedy from
the Middle Ages and Seneca. Wilhelm is in love, but whenever he approaches
the actions of a truly romantic or heroic lover, the novel deflates him—his
ecstasies outside Mariane's window are cut off by the banal note from Norberg
he finds in her scarf; his duel in the forest leads to a convalescence supervised
not by the beloved, but by the embarrassing Philine. Similarly he is too easygoing (*gutmütig*) to become really angry, hence his primary negative emotion
is irritable unhappiness. Wilhelm suffers from the same typically Goethean
emotion as Werther, whose *Verdruss* (again, not anger) is so extreme that it
leads to suicide. This emotion is present-oriented and appropriate to the limited, unheroic parameters of modern bourgeois existence. Thus one of the
oddest aspects of *Wilhelm Meisters Lehrjahre* is Wilhelm's lack of anxiety. He
wanders off into the world—not only fearlessly but even rashly in the case of
the robbers in book 4; he ignores all obligations to father and mother with
no visible fear of retribution and scarcely any pangs of guilt. His father dies
with no apparent concern for his son's defection, and his mother evaporates
from the novel. Only the reader feels anxiety about whether and how the real
world might retaliate in the early books of the novel, and by the middle even
the reader gives up worrying. The combination of the picaresque tradition and
the novel's concern for the integration of the individual into society results
in a new genre that seems to abolish fear. *Verdruss* is not the dread so soon to
be discovered by Kierkegaard any more than it is baroque passion. Instead,
Verdruss serves to repress the stronger emotions characteristic of Goethe's form
of narrative.

Repression otherwise appears in the novel not yet as Freudian repression,
as the unconscious refusal to know, but rather as images of intentional forgetting: Mignon with her uncontrollable passion is lowered into a sepulcher in
the Hall of the Past. Her story, her past, and that of her father the Harper are
similarly sealed off into the enclosed narrative read and created by the Abbé
from the Italian of the visiting Marchese, who has departed by the time the
story is read. Mignon's funeral has already been celebrated once, in the Abbé's

narrative, as her mother assembled the bones collected from the lakeshore and ornamented them with embroidery. Her story comes almost last in the novel, but the time line of the plot makes Mignon's second burial in the Hall of the Past effectively into a very early version of the return of the repressed. Another kind of repression that takes place in the novel is Wilhelm's turn from art to business; the process of representing in the novel changes from the representation of spirit through art to its representation through money (compare the discussion above of the purse at the beginning of book 4). As in the case of Mignon, Goethe is never content really to let the past be past (in a famous line from the dungeon scene in *Faust*); the court masque in act I of *Faust*, part 2, returns to the theme of money three decades after the *Lehrjahre* in order to uncover the creative force of intellect pushed behind the image of money in the novel.

It is probably more accurate to talk about a dialectic of memory and forgetting rather than repression.[22] The most visible expression of their importance is Lothario's encounter with Margarete in book 7, a moment of remembering that enables him to encounter the past embodied, and yet the essence of that special moment is the Faustian ability to put the past behind him and live each moment afresh. The theme of memory is summarized in a series of admonitions to remember that punctuate the novel (*Gedenke* . . . : 94, 245, 495, 540, 557). The various narratives embedded in the novel—the memoirs of the Beautiful Soul and the biographies stored in the tower—show that memory is essential to education. Yet in Natalie's realm in book 8 virtually everyone's past is neutralized. The whole company is sworn to secrecy lest the recovered Harper learn that the others know his past; and when he learns that it is known and remembered, he commits suicide. The unfortunate effects of Lothario's affair with Therese's mother are eliminated by recovering her true identity and severing her relationship to the family. Mignon is sealed away in her marble sarcophagus in the Hall of the Past. The result of Wilhelm's recovery of his grandfather's art collection at Natalie's castle is that he can stop being the sick prince of the painting and be a healthy one instead. Wilhelm, who has long sought to forget his disastrous encounter with the Countess and is now surrounded by people who know the story, can only relax when it is suppressed at the final meeting between the two at Natalie's home. He would also like to forget and have forgotten his guilt with regard to Mariane and his proposal to Therese. Small wonder that the novel ends by reversing all its injunctions to memory: "Don't remind me!" (Erinnern Sie mich nicht), Wilhelm says to Friedrich in the last paragraph; by denying that he deserves

Natalie in the last line of the book, he tries yet again to sever the connection between past and present. The function of memory in Natalie's realm is essentially Freudian: one remembers in order to deal with the troubling past—loosely, in order to be able to forget.[23]

The pattern of remembering and forgetting reveals the essential complementarity of Lothario and Natalie, Wilhelm's twin ideals. If Lothario's memory brings a momentary fulfillment, forerunner of the Faustian highest moment, Natalie offers the balm of forgetting that frees to new activity, much like the elves at the beginning of *Faust*, part 2. And yet neither simply allegorizes the one principle or the other. Lothario lives essentially only in space—"here or nowhere" (hier oder nirgends) is his characteristic phrase—while his relation to time is largely unreflected. Natalie, on the other hand, is preoccupied with time—her phrase is "never or always" (nie oder immer). Unlike Lothario's space in the novel, Natalie's is elaborately described and interpreted; it seems to be of great interest for all of the characters except for Natalie herself. In her idealized space she lives out of time, so to speak; for her love is not succession but either eternal or nonexistent. If unreflected existence needs memory, its opposite needs forgetting. About Natalie circle busily, like Chiron in *Faust*, part 2, the men—rakes—who live in time but don't want to think about it. At the center, revered by all, she tends the Hall of the Past, dwelling like Manto at the portals of the underworld (from the same scene in *Faust*), the priestess of forgetting, in whose realm the individual disappears to be reincarnated in the general.[24] And yet in spite of, or perhaps really because of, her isolation, she is the ideal revered by all, the goal of Wilhelm's inchoate striving, his calling. It is the man's calling to forget in order to move forward to his next calling, so to speak. Repression thus transforms the pathos of historicism into progress.[25]

The relevant anthropological terrain has been sketched out by Harald Weinrich.[26] While the art of memory has been cultivated since antiquity, its logical counterpart, the art of forgetting is an essentially modern phenomenon, first clearly visible when Galileo, Bacon, and Descartes restrict the role of memory in acquiring and disseminating knowledge. *Faust* becomes, in this context, a critique of the morality of the scientific scholarly enterprise, as Faust falls victim to Mephistopheles' "devilish art" of forgetting,[27] while Freud offers a theory of healing based on remembering in order to forget. In this context repression emerges as another version of the Rousseau problem. Mephistopheles and Lothario, as the proponents of forgetting and embodiments of nature and, in effect, the life force, stand to one side of the moral order in ways that are problematic but unavoidable. The tragedy of *Faust* arises from precisely the conflict they pose between nature's mandate to forget and society's need for memory.[28] But the immoral aspects of forgetting are actually pushed to the background in *Wilhelm Meister*. Whereas Faust ends forgiven by Margarete, Mariane has been forgotten for some time by the end and is there only in the positive presence of her son. What Wilhelm wants to forget, at the end, is not Mariane, but his really rather harmless encounter with Philine. The *Lehrjahre* foregrounds the healing aspects of remembering and forgetting, rather than their problematic morality. Goethe has sketched out already a strategy for dealing with the demon Rousseau had discovered.

PART III

The Language of Interiority

THE PREVIOUS CHAPTER concluded with a glossary of simple psychological terminology as it was becoming conceptualizable in *Wilhelm Meisters Lehrjahre*. The remainder of the book turns to structures and terms more obviously associated with modern depth psychology to show Goethe's approach to the other asymptote of this argument, Freud. Again, the issue is not to explain Goethe through Freud or Freud through Goethe, but to show the emergence of ways of talking about identity and the unconscious more familiar to us today in terms of two specific examples, anxiety (Chapter 7) and the uncanny (Chapter 9), and (in Chapter 8) to elaborate one clear example of the translation of the initially rationalist psychological representation of *Werther* into what we recognize as the depth psychology of the Romantic generation, a group that acknowledged the tremendous impact of Goethe's classicism, his plays and prose of the 1790s, in advance of his broader acceptance beginning only in the middle of the nineteenth century.

CHAPTER 7

Goethe's Angst

When passion was repressed and turned inward in the previous chapter, it seemed reduced in intensity: anger and guilt appeared merely as *Verdruss*. The most recognizable form of this phenomenon for children of the twentieth century is the reduction of the German *Angst* (fear of what is to come) to anxiety or "angst" as used in English, the generalized sense of insecurity coupled with ill-defined feelings of guilt modeled in the pervasive mood of Franz Kafka, Hugo von Hofmannsthal, or Edvard Munch, the often formless fear that arises with no objective external threat. The topic is hardly obvious for Goethe, whom even Harold Bloom declared free of the anxiety of influence.[1] The turbulent emotions of the young Goethe of the 1770s are too conscious, too articulated: one can speak of hysteria, perhaps, but not angst. The Olympian serenity of the classical and older Goethe, as he was understood into the last generation, may have generated a good deal of angst in his readers, but hardly in him.[2] To be sure, Goethe shared in the political anxieties of his age: he experienced the collapse of a social order widely understood to have been in place for centuries. His letters between 1790 and 1817 express almost constant worry about the political situation and its sometimes very immediate effects on him and his far-flung circle of friends. Goethe experienced angst as a debilitating concern with overwhelming circumstances, but he also struggled to transform it from an incapacity to act into constructive deed. This struggle, to be described below, reveals that his angst is actually a more general version of the paralyzing paranoia into which Rousseau collapses in the later parts of his *Confessions*. In this respect Goethe's efforts to control anxiety reflect his continuing attempts to deal with the great predecessor precisely as he identifies Rousseau's importance for modernity. Yet if Goethe experienced angst, he did not express it, unlike, for example, his freely articulated feelings of guilt for abandoning an early beloved, Friederike Brion. Hence the language and specific literary techniques that express angst point more clearly toward his linguistic contribution to expressing the unknown feelings of the inner self.

Although contemporary German usage aligns only *Angst* with fear of the indefinite or undefined, and both related terms, *Furcht* and *Sorge*, with a definable object, Goethe more commonly used the word *Sorge* for what is known today as *Angst*, or "angst."[3] *Sorge* occurs 451 times in the literary works, about three times as often as *Angst*.[4] It expresses inner anxiety that arises from within the subject;[5] the fear arising from an external cause Goethe calls *Furcht*.[6] *Sorge* results from concern about what might happen or what ought to happen; at issue is not an objective cause of fear but an imagined one. It also has a second meaning, that of "caring for" (*sorgen für*) rather than "worrying about" (*sorgen um*). There is a kind of care that leads to constructive action, but this meaning can also lead to anxiety that a responsibility will not be fulfilled or that the object of one's care might suffer. Goethe uses the word in both senses, as did Martin Heidegger in his later well-known distinction.[7] As the self-generated fear of circumstances that do not really exist or not yet exist, *Sorge* is the clearest marker for Goethe of what is now called "angst."

Sorge occurs throughout the literary works, but not equally distributed. It appears at best once or twice in early works like *Werther* and *Götz*, then with particular intensity in the 1790s and first decade of the nineteenth century.[8] Of course the Revolution and Terror in France made the 1790s an anxious decade, but Goethe's protagonists in this period encounter similar problems to those of the earlier works.[9] Werther suffers intense emotions, personal insecurity, and a threatened identity just as do Egmont, Tasso, and Faust. They are all trapped in their own interiors and their limited views of their own identities, so that the world recedes and becomes inaccessible and incomprehensible. The dramatically increased use of *Sorge* reveals not that the problems of character have changed, but that they are experienced and expressed differently in ways now to be examined—less explicitly, with less emphasis on feeling and more on imagination. As it turns out, the term *Sorge* in the 1790s is associated with developing techniques of repression, transference, and screening that enable language to represent the buried inner self.

A few examples of *Sorge* in short poems offer an overview of the process. In the 1770s emotion is something to be displayed and enjoyed: Werther, the early Faust, the speakers in Goethe's love lyrics and hymns luxuriate in their emotions and seem almost to enjoy their self-entrapment. Goethe's first poem on the topic, "Sorge" (ca. 1776), emphasizes the feeling of entrapment by ordering Sorge to go away and ends begging it to make him reasonable (HA 1: 131). Personified Sorge is supposed to help the speaker both deny his feelings and transform them into something better. In the 1790s love becomes the way to deny *Sorge*. In an unpublished elegy about a love affair in Rome, "Eines ist mir verdrießlich vor allen Dingen" (One thing specially annoys me; *verdrießlich* is the same root as Wilhelm's *Verdruss*), the speaker depends on the loyalty of his beloved to keep "lisping Care" (lispelnde Sorge) at a distance (WA 1.1:257); this Sorge that lisps like a lover is actually fear of syphilis. Since the beloved and the anxiety caused by love are similar, it seems unlikely that the personification can enable the speaker to turn his worry into saving action.[10] And in a slightly later distich, Love seems to be even worse than Sorge: "Care! she mounts your steed with you, she boards your boat; / And Amor is much pushier yet" (WA 1.1:348; Sorge! sie steiget mit dir zu Roß, sie steiget zu Schiffe; / Viel zudringlicher noch packet sich Amor uns auf). If anxiety can be dispelled, then it is surely only through the irony in the distichs, so that irony becomes the preferred tool to control angst.

A last example, "Erste Epistel" (First Epistle of 1795; WA 1.1:298) takes such irony to extremes. After weeks of living at an inn on credit, a normally carefree sponger starts to worry about his bill, but the gods scold him, because his function in life, they say, is to be Hans Ohnesorg (Hans Carefree), and his only care is never to work and never to care about the consequences. Here fantasy banishes care by fiat. The shift in technique from the elegies is significant: the outright denial of *Sorge* is accompanied by a generic shift to fable and a rhetorical focus on personification.[11] "Lisping Care" in the love elegy was already personified, but as an eighteenth-century convention that is ambiguously both abstraction and person. Now in the epistle the character is turned into the personification "Hans Ohnesorg" by the lesson he learns in the poem. *Sorge* is resisted not by reason or the will, but by the poetic manipulation of language. The resistance to *Sorge* is not conceptual, as in the previous examples, but completely rhetorical.

The classical dramas recapitulate the beginning of this trajectory. They begin with the strategy of converting anxiety (*sorgen um*) into care for others (*sorgen für*). In *Egmont* the first seven occurrences of *Sorge* all refer to subjective anxiety, but at the end, with reference to his own tragic fall, Egmont speaks rather of his care for his country, which, however, will be taken care of: "Sorge für dieses Land! doch auch dafür wird gesorgt" (HA 4:451: Care for this land! But that too will be taken care of). He not only denies anxiety about his own death, but even refuses to use the word *Sorge* about it; instead he speaks of his anxiety for his country, the proper object of his care as its ruler. The repetition "Sorge für" and "dafür wird gesorgt" underlines the change in meaning. In a simple example of transference the claim to take care of his country substitutes for, literally takes the place of, his anxiety for himself. *Iphigenie* performs a similar substitution, more deftly perhaps because the motif is secondary. Three references to *Sorge* in the play (lines 1411, 1534, 2027) evoke the paralyzing anxiety of indecision, while two (lines 1640, 2076) transform *Sorge* into a positive moral force.[12] *Tasso* divides the meanings of the word not by earlier and later usage, but by character. Duke Alfons and Antonio use the term only in the sense of caring for, but for the Princess and Tasso the word refers to their own, especially to Tasso's, anxiety. Only in the final scene does Tasso switch to the other meaning of the word as he twice offers to care for the duke's garden, even though he seems more in need of care than able to give it. One might read Tasso's failure to achieve the status of caregiver as the tragedy of the play—he fails to triumph over *Sorge*. The word is not purified or adjusted in meaning as in *Egmont* and *Iphigenie*, whose happy ends have been the object of controversy since their first publication. The serious pun that replaces "sorgen um" with "sorgen für" cannot be achieved.

In *Pandora* (1807–8) Goethe seems to have reached at least a temporary reconciliation, for the two meanings of *sorgen* can scarcely be distinguished. Epimetheus (Goethe's contribution to the myth), the after-thinker, is connected etymologically with *Sorge*, but his twin daughters, Elpore and Epimeleia (Hope and Care) undermine the old opposition. Epimeleia, as "sorgen für," loves and comforts Epimetheus during Pandora's long absence. Elpore teases him with dreams in which she can be recognized in the distance but neither grasped nor comprehended; instead of creating feelings of anxiety, however, the dreams cheer Epimetheus. As a result, the word *Sorge* is transformed. Epimetheus begins as a sleepless worrier pacing the stage at night, but as the scene proceeds he puts his worry from him and falls asleep to dream of Elpore, just as Egmont dreams of Klare as Freedom in prison. Epimeleia, by contrast, who has always cared for her father, loses the positive connotation of *Sorge* when her lover mistrusts her:

> Dear Father! Epimeleia
> Has cared for you many a day;
> Now she is burdened with cares about herself,
> And Remorse slinks in to join Care (lines 558–61)

(Teurer Vater! hat Epimeleia
Sorg' um dich getragen manche Tage;
Sorge trägt sie leider um sich selbst nun,
Und zur Sorge schleicht sich ein die Reue.)

In these lines the meaning of *Sorge* slides from "caring for" to "worry and re-morse," reversing the shift that *Egmont, Iphigenie,* and *Tasso* struggled for. But Epimetheus is also a caregiver (*Fürsorger*): the pain of Pandora's disappearance was long since distracted by his "Vatersorge" (fatherly worries, line 743) and now he cares for Epimeleia in her misery. Prometheus begins the play as a nonworrier ("Wer falle? stehe? kann ihm wenig Sorge sein" [line 299; Who falls? who stands? is little cause to worry]); but once he has rescued Epimeleia he takes an interest in her entire story. As the word *Sorge* disappears from the fragment, the caretaking becomes more general. First it belongs to the whole community, as Prometheus's men save Epimetheus's household from a fire, then to the cosmos, as Eos describes Phileros's fall, rebirth, and marriage to Epimeleia. The care of one human for another becomes that of the gods (i.e., Nature) for us. The splendid finale to the act is the harbinger of the more splendid finale planned for act 2, in which Pandora was to return and bring culture to mankind; its equivalent in *Faust,* part 2, is the triumphant marriage of fire and water at the end of the "Classical Walpurgis Night," which brings about the appearance of Helena, beauty incarnate. *Sorge* now leads via hope to creative imagination.

The three earlier plays lack the imaginative freedom that concludes *Pandora.* Still, they do experiment with more playful measures. So, after twice commanding personified Sorge to leave him alone, in his last speech in act 2 (HA 4:407) and later in his dungeon in act 5 (HA 4: 439), Egmont can sleep peacefully and dream of his beloved as the goddess Freedom. Is this an act of will, as in the previous denials of angst? Is it a Freudian wish-dream? Or is it an act of imagination? And if so, of his own or of the poet's? The outcome of the dream transforms the cause of Egmont's greatest anxiety (the execution await-ing him) into the triumph of Freedom. The operatic gesture appealed to Bee-thoven, but its explicit exteriorization of inner feeling was too arbitrary and operatic for Schiller. *Tasso* handles the problem more subtly. Here, too, the inner self is exteriorized, this time by assigning the two meanings of *Sorge* to different characters. The reasonable characters who act self-consciously, Alfons and Antonio, care for the country, while the impulsive idealists, Tasso and the Princess, suffer anxiety. The tension between the two meanings of *Sorge* is thus embodied in the action.[13] When in the last act Tasso fails to transform his constant "Sorge um" into "Sorge für" and then compares Antonio to the rock embraced by a drowning man, the stage picture of the two men hand in hand seems to show the two meanings of the word united. Of course, the unity is highly ambiguous, for the one-sided embrace cannot last and Tasso is going mad, losing all connection to reality. In this respect, the image functions like the Freudian dream image: the signifier and its opposite mean the same thing.

The simple denial of *Sorge* in the poems by means of wordplay appears in these plays as repression. In both plays the image on the stage, the equivalent of a dream, displays a moment of harmony that actually works to conceal what the protagonists do not want to know. Repression in the psychoanalytic sense requires that the conscious self not know something that is still accessible to the unconscious part of the self; it only applies to *Tasso* if the various characters are understood to represent parts of a single psyche, or perhaps two (one male, one female), the argument made above in Chapter 4, but is a more appropriate term for the dreams in *Egmont* and *Pandora*. It is still a leap from "repression," as I want to use it here, and the explicit refusal of the heroine of Heinrich von Kleist's "Marquise von O," who says, "I do *not want* to know" (Kleist: *Sämtliche Werke* 2:129; Ich *will nichts* wissen). Nevertheless, by the time of *Pandora* the repression is so complete that only the genre, *Festspiel* (festival drama), reveals that the harmonious conclusion cannot be literally true. As *Sorge* becomes something to banish, increasingly to repress, it also becomes increasingly concrete: it moves from the company of abstractions like "Klugheit" (cleverness) in the poem "Sorge," to that of Love, a familiar, even mythological figure, and ultimately becomes an allegory, an embodied personification.

The finer details of the process emerge in the less obvious projection of feelings onto landscape. In the rationalist psychology of *Werther* the protagonist himself projects feelings onto the landscape. When he is happy, the weather is good and the landscape gentle; if he is unhappy, there is a storm. In either case, he is aware that he makes the reflection take place. In the first half of the letter of August 18 late in part 1, when Werther is still calm, the rivers flow, but in the second, excited half of the letter, floods wash away whole villages. And the reason for the change is that "It has opened before my soul like a curtain drawn aside" (HA 6:52; Es hat sich vor meiner Seele wie ein Vorhang weggezogen). This clarity about the relation of landscape to inner self shifts in Goethe's autobiographical narratives beginning in the 1790s and leads the way to Romantic narratives of the mid and late 1790s, such as Ludwig Tieck's

"Der Runenberg" or "Der blonde Eckbert" (Blond Eckbert) where the landscape still reflects the protagonist's feelings, but the reason for the connection
is obscure.

The crucial text in this development is *Briefe aus der Schweiz* (Letters from
Switzerland), both parts of which were written in 1796 but not published together until 1808. Part 1, based on a journey taken with his Sturm und Drang
friends the Stolberg brothers in 1775 and introduced as a discovery among
Werther's papers, contains little specific information beyond the fact that the
group climbed the Furka and Gotthard Passes, met some attractive girls, and
visited Geneva.[14] In fact, as Goethe later reported in his autobiography (*Dichtung und Wahrheit*, part 4, books 18–19, 1833), they climbed many mountains
and met many important people, including Duke Karl August of Weimar,
Goethe's lifelong friend and patron. In the spirit of the genre mixing that has
characterized Goethe's interiorizing language, the rhetoric of the *Briefe* mixes
the style of *Werther* from the original diaries with the most sensual aspects of
the Italian Goethe. It moves rapidly from typical Sturm und Drang language
of freedom to a naive love story and then to the theme of beauty. During the
journey the speaker, presumably Werther, shifts his interest from the emotions
aroused by the landscape to the beauty first of the male then of the female
body. In order to study a beautiful naked female body, he has a procuress in
Geneva arrange a tryst. After displaying her charms the young lady teasingly
invites the speaker to bed: end of story. Far from being a fragment as it seems
to claim, the text has reached its logical conclusion; it has traveled the same
trajectory that Goethe himself had pursued from *Werther* to his Roman love
poems (*Römische Elegien*), from feelings to bodies, from insides to outsides.

Part 2 is based on a second journey made in 1779 with Duke Karl August
and first published under the title *Briefe auf einer Reise nach dem Gotthard*
(Letters from a Journey to the Gotthard) in Schiller's *Horen* in 1796. It returns
from bodies to landscape, but landscape as object rather than as source of
emotion. The *Römische Elegien* had been attacked for indecency when they
were published in 1795, so it is not surprising that Goethe held back part 1 of
the *Briefe* in 1796, and perhaps he even hoped that the sobriety of the travel
writing in part 2 would make the point about his new style without the transition from sentimentality to objectivity traced in part 1. But evidently by 1808
he had changed his mind: the joining of the two texts as *Briefe aus der Schweiz*
summarizes and highlights the move from the elaborately subjective interior
self of Goethe's first novel to what might be called his more objective form of
interiority.

For the shift does not mean that the speaker has no interior in the second part of the *Briefe*, just that it is revealed less directly, indeed, as angst. The standard narrative of eighteenth-century emotion would expect fear, since Switzerland is the paradigmatic sublime landscape. Interestingly, however, the word "sublime" (*erhaben*) appears only twice in the text and is associated in this text not with fear, but with humility and with serenity.[15] Goethe's term for his negative emotion is once again not *Angst*, but *Sorge*. On this second journey through the Alps he worries primarily about the weather, because he wants to repeat his ascents of the Furka and Gotthard Passes, but this time in winter. "Sorge" emerges as the now familiar personification to break the otherwise calm tone of his letters:

> Thus whispered Care, who mostly took over one of my ears. At the other Encouragement spoke much more reliably, reproved me for lack of faith, reminded me of the past, and called my attention to the current weather. (276)

> (So flüsterte die Sorge, die sich meistentheils des einen Ohrs bemeistert. Auf der andern Seite sprach der gute Muth mit weit zuverlässigerer Stimme, verwies mir meinen Unglauben, hielt mir das Vergangene vor und machte mich auch auf die gegenwärtigen Lufterscheinungen aufmerksam.)

The two personifications resemble the good and bad angels in a morality play, and Sorge's whispering evokes the lisping of Goethe's fear of contagion in the *Roman Elegies*. The sinister inner voice stands in striking contrast to the optimistic objectivity of his weather observations. Even though the weather is not at all threatening, his *Sorge* expands as the party crosses the Furka; there he is

> in the most barren region in the world, and in a monstrously uniform mountainous waste covered with snow, where no living soul is to be found for three hours in any direction, on both sides the great depths of labyrinthine mountains—to see there a line of men, each treading in the deep footsteps of his predecessor, and where in the whole smoothly coated distance there is nothing to see but one's own track. The depths from which one has ascended lie gray and endless in the fog behind. The clouds pass before the pale sun, fluffy

flakes drift below and draw over everything a constantly shifting veil. (290–91)

(in der ödesten Gegend der Welt, und in einer ungeheuren einförmigen schneebedeckten Gebirgs-Wüste, wo man rückwärts und vorwärts auf drei Stunden keine lebendige Seele weiß, wo man auf beiden Seiten die weiten Tiefen verschlungener Gebirge hat, eine Reihe Menschen zu sehen, deren einer in des andern tiefe Fußtapfen tritt, und wo in der ganzen glatt überzogenen Weite nichts in die Augen fällt, als die Furche die man gezogen hat. Die Tiefen, aus denen man herkommt, liegen grau und endlos in Nebel hinter einem. Die Wolken wechseln über die blasse Sonne, breitflockiger Schnee stiebt in der Tiefe und zieht über alles einen ewig beweglichen Flor.)

Now whispering Sorge generates powerful anxiety from the uncanny emptiness of the scene and its absence of visual cues. The fitful light and swirling fog simultaneously obscure and reveal depths on all sides.[16] The depths of the landscape and the whispering voice become one. This barren, uniform, smooth desert without a living soul would be the underworld, if only there were no self present to make a track in the snow and to experience fear. This gothic moment reduces the group of people to a single set of tracks and the subject to bare selfhood, pure consciousness without identity.[17]

But why should the pass occasion such anxiety, especially in the absence of any serious threat? Only ten pages later does the truth veiled by the fog begin to shimmer through. The Gotthard Pass, the ultimate goal of their journey, is the passage to Italy, the same spot where Goethe turned back four years earlier and this time again turns back to Germany. The successive descriptions of Goethe's two turnings back are telling. In part I of the *Briefe* Goethe simply remarks in passing, "Ah, I ascended the Furka, the Gotthard! I shall never forget these sublime, incomparable landscapes" (203; Ja ich habe die Furca, den Gotthard bestiegen! Diese erhabenen unvergleichlichen Naturscenen werden immer vor meinem Geiste stehen). But in the second part he reflects more calmly:

Here, we've decided, we shall stop and turn our steps homeward.
I feel very strange up here, where I spent a few days four years ago
with completely different cares, attitudes, plans and hopes, at a dif-

ferent time of year, and, with no sense of my future destiny, moved by I don't know what, turned my back on Italy and went blindly to meet my current calling. (299–300)

(Hier, ist's beschlossen, wollen wir stille stehen und uns wieder nach dem Vaterlande zuwenden. Ich komme mir sehr wunderbar hier oben vor; wo ich mich vor vier Jahren mit ganz andern Sorgen, Gesinnungen, Planen und Hoffnungen, in einer andern Jahrszeit, einige Tage aufhielt, und mein künftiges Schicksal unvorahnend durch ein ich weiß nicht was bewegt Italien den Rücken zukehrte und meiner jetzigen Bestimmung unwissend entgegen ging.)

The turn back is at least mentioned, but as a decision already taken. Both the literal and punctuational sublime evaporate. Only the words *wunderbar* and *bewegt* connect to the emotional language of the segment from part 1, while the unusual formulation *unvorahnend* (with no sense of) simultaneously affirms and denies the critical importance of the decision not to continue the journey to Italy. The text then turns away from self to extensive description of the inn, the view, and the magnificent weather. When Goethe returns decades later in *Dichtung und Wahrheit* to his decision to turn back on the first journey up the Gotthard, not only is there no detectable emotion, but the idea of going down into Italy is attributed exclusively to his companion. In place of the emotion is yet more extensive description of the landscape. The result of the decision on that first journey was Goethe's move to Weimar and, from the vantage point of 1796 (and even more from that of *Dichtung und Wahrheit*), his calling, his establishment in history, and the birth of classical German culture. The decision to interrupt yet another almost-journey to Italy and go to Weimar instead constitutes the last climax of *Dichtung und Wahrheit*. All three versions of the experience on the Gotthard avoid acknowledging the significant choice being made, and with each repetition there is less description of Goethe's emotions and more of the landscape. The great anxiety he suffered on the Furka is also absent. The Furka is a site of anxiety, and the Gotthard is a site of repression.

This formulation moves us into the territory of psychoanalysis. The anxiety being repressed is tied to whatever it was that made Goethe miss that and other opportunities to make the Italian journey that in his own and in the eyes of his father would complete his education. His return to Italy from dangerous and uncomfortable Sicily, where he had resisted blandishments to continue his journey to Greece, was also a moment of great anxiety, as will appear below, and he resisted (unsuccessfully) a second visit to Italy.[18]

Visiting Italy meant a new identity; Goethe talks repeatedly at the beginning of *Italienische Reise* (*Italian Journey*) about his rebirth. But rebirth was not necessarily so blissful as the elation of the final version would make it seem. Egmont's rebirth at the end of his play is death; Orest's rebirth in *Iphigenie* is figured as a descent to the underworld; Tasso's creativity is the spinning of a cocoon-coffin. Wilhelm Meister's transit of the Alps at the beginning of the *Wanderjahre* is figured as a death and rebirth. As Goethe wrote from Italy to his then closest confidante, Charlotte von Stein, December 20–23, 1786:

> And yet all this is more effort and worry for me than enjoyment.
> The rebirth that is remaking me from inside continues its effects,
> I expected to learn something here, but that I would have to go so
> far back, that I would have to relearn so very much never occurred
> to me. So much the better, I have submitted completely and it's not
> just my sense for art, but also my moral sense that suffers a com-
> plete renovation. (WA 4.8:101)

> (Und doch ist das alles mir mehr Mühe und Sorge als Genuß.
> Die Wiedergeburt die mich von innen heraus umarbeitet, würckt
> immer fort, ich dachte wohl hier was zu lernen, daß ich aber so weit
> in die Schule zurückgehn, daß ich so viel verlernen müßte dacht ich
> nicht. Desto lieber ist mir's, ich habe mich ganz hingegeben und es
> ist nicht allein der Kunstsinn, es ist auch der moralische der große
> Erneuerung leidet.)

Like all rebirth in Goethe, his rebirth in Italy presupposed a death, in this case a loss of identity that this passage suggests he had already anticipated. The repressed anxiety is the fear of the new, the pressure of time not toward death, as in the seventeenth century, but toward change. Only at the end of his life does Goethe articulate these threatening changes, the new political order threatened by the French Revolution, the new economic order of the end of *Faust*, part 2, and the *Wanderjahre*, and above all the increasing pace of change in the industrial world.

The projection of emotion onto landscape is furthermore not only complete, but layered: the anxiety associated with Italy is expressed in the landscape, but in the landscape at the edge of Italy, not that of Italy itself, and not through the Gotthard, the gateway to Italy, but through the previous pass, the Furka. Italy typically harbors threats to the identity in Romantic narrative. Indeed, in Joseph von Eichendorff's "Das Marmorbild" (The Marble Statue) and "Aus dem Leben eines Taugenichts" (Memoirs of a Good-for-Nothing), Italy itself is the threat, and the snow of the Alps signifies the return to the safe homeland where one's identity is secure. The curious echoes in the passage about the Furka—"Furca" (Goethe's spelling), *Furche* (track), *Furcht* (fear)— mark how the language itself has become layered. *Furche*, halfway between "Furka" and *Furcht*, contains the crucial clue. Goethe's anxiety has to do with his track, with the traces his feet mark in the snow, with the signs he can leave behind him. Traces in the snow are by nature impermanent, and in this passage his track is de-individualized as each member of the party walks in exactly the footsteps of his predecessor—a terrifying thought indeed for the star of the young genius generation. Would going to Italy make him walk in precisely the footsteps of the great classical predecessors and rob him of his individuality, of his calling (*Bahn*) as a great poet? The figure of the *Bahn* is important for the Romantics (as, for example, with Friedrich Hölderlin's "exzentrische Bahn"), as was the more abstract version of *Bestimmung*, and it reechoes in Ottilie's failure to follow her *Bahn* in *Die Wahlverwandtschaften*.[19] The signs being marked in the snow with great effort both literalize and externalize Goethe's anxiety about being a great writer; the emotion being projected onto the land- scape is visible as the traces left in the snow.[20]

The metaphor of the featureless waste settles in the same year into an image of the sea. Goethe is actually well known for not having been a poet of the sea, for not having sent any of his characters to sea, and indeed for never having made any journeys to the sea or on the sea, except for his visit to Sicily in the spring of 1787. And yet in the mid-1790s the sea becomes his compel- ling image for anxiety, or more accurately, the screen onto which he projects by choice the anxiety of his figures.[21] The stormy sea of life is an image that goes back to Greek tragedy, and the ship arriving safely in harbor is a favorite of the baroque age. *Iphigenie* and *Tasso* still draw on this convention.[22] Here is the same still, smooth emptiness of the snowfield on the Furka and the same anxiety in "Meeres Stille" (Calm at Sea, 1796):

> Deep silence rules the water,
> The sea rests motionless,
> And the boatman sees with concern
> Glassy smoothness all around.

Not a breath from no [*sic*] direction!
Dreadful silence of death!
In the monstrous distance.
Not a ripple moves. (HA 1:242)

(Tiefe Stille herrscht im Wasser,
Ohne Regung ruht das Meer,
Und bekümmert sieht der Schiffer
Glatte Fläche rings umher.
Keine Luft von keiner Seite!
Todestille fürchterlich!
In der ungeheuern Weite
Reget keine Welle sich.)

Goethe's new sea of the 1790s is dangerously and uncannily calm. The uncanniness of this surface becomes clear if one compares "Meeres Stille" to his ballad about a fisherman and a mermaid, "Der Fischer," of 1778. There a mermaid pops out of the rushing water and offers the initially calm, cool fisherman several arguments for joining her beneath the waves. Eventually his heart swells in response to her blandishments, he dives in and is "never seen again" (HA 1: 154). In the ballad's rationalist psychology all emotions can be named by the narrator and the change in the fisherman's emotions can be brought about by rational argument. The water is not uncannily calm, but it rushes and swells. Only the content of the mermaid's argument, in which she identifies the water as the fisherman's own inner emotions—she calls it his own face—points the reader toward an understanding of her, who after all rises from the depths, as the death drive, an unknown voice from within the fisherman that was suppressed by his initial apparent calm. Now in the snow passage in *Briefe aus der Schweiz* and "Meeres Stille," the surface is calm, with no meaning of its own, and the emotions of the fisherman become more complicated. Now the human subjects—Goethe and his party, in the poem only the boatman—are reduced from actors to seeing subjects, and negation is intensified ("Keine Luft von keiner Seite!"). At the same time, emotion is toned down. The longing aroused in the fisherman becomes anxiety. Only when the mood is detached from the human subject is its full power articulated; then it becomes "Todestille fürchterlich!" in a sentence fragment parallel in its ungrammaticality to the previous strong negation. The denial and terror are no longer explicitly that of the observing subject, but infect the speaker and reader as well. The emotion is explicit but also generalized, the anxiety spreads outward as if on its own in a fashion uncannily recalled by Edvard Munch's famous *Scream* a century later. The coherent allegorical narrative of "Der Fischer" is disarticulated, and therefore derationalized to the image of the motionless sea, and this image is recalled even more abstractly in the frozen waste of the Furka Pass in winter.[23]

The water's blank face is precisely its danger; a more concrete version of the swirling fog on the Furka, it is an unreadable surface over the unknown and potentially dangerous interior, the ancestor of the uncanny still ponds of Romantic narrative. Yet water is worse than the snowy wastes of the Furka; there at least it was possible to make a track and thereby recognize that one still existed; there it was still possible to be conscious. But the still water doesn't even hold a track; it is unwritten because it can hold no marks. It threatens the self, especially the self of the poet, with complete disappearance because he can leave no traces of his existence. The smooth snow on the Furka drove the poet to describe the Gotthard extensively. Now only the tiny poem stands between him and the enormous silence of unconsciousness.

The mechanism of repression attached to the image is as important as the image itself. In *Briefe aus der Schweiz*, *Sorge* is associated with language of mastery, *bemeistert*, in the passage about whispering in his ear . This sinister inner voice stands in striking contrast to the optimistic objectivity of his weather observations. Despite the similarity to morality drama already noted, this is no longer the traditional battle between passion and reason, but rather a modern one between angst and reason, between a neurotic inner self and the self connected to the reality principle. It is really a question of who will have mastery, the voice of Sorge or the self, the Ego, between two whispering voices. The issue becomes more complicated when the party crosses the Furka. After the description of the trackless waste discussed above, Goethe adds: "I am convinced that anyone who let his imagination take over even the least bit on this journey, even in absence of apparent danger, must perish from anxiety and fear" (290–91; Ich bin überzeugt, daß einer, über den auf diesem Weg seine Einbildungskraft nur einigermaßen Herr würde, hier ohne anscheinende Gefahr vor Angst und Furcht vergehen müßte). Now the word has shifted from *Sorge* to full-fledged *Angst*. And this anxiety is identified as a creation of the imagination, specifically of the uncontrolled imagination, the inner voice run wild and overpowering reason. What was the voice of personified Sorge in the earlier passage is now the imagination: imagination and angst are two sides of the same interior self. With this linkage the inner self becomes vastly more complex. It is not just a part of the self unknown to and in struggle with the rational self, not just a will in conflict with reason, but something itself characterized by seemingly opposite categories like creativity and care—a manic-depressive, a Faustian self.[24]

Goethe's most complex example of the sea image and its relation to the anxious imagination is his description of the return to Italy from Sicily, experienced in 1787 but only published in part 2 of *Italienische Reise* in 1817 (the entries for May 13 and 14, 1787; HA 11:314–21). Here the sea becomes a tool of suppression through which Goethe projects and sublimates his anxiety. The journey through Sicily had generally been anxious for Goethe: primitive conditions, difficult and slightly dangerous travel, and, most important, the temptation to go further to the promised land of Greece—a temptation he resisted as he did Italy atop the Gotthard. The word *Sorge* falls at the beginning of the journey back. The French ship on which Goethe and his companion, the painter Christoph Heinrich Kniep, have taken passage lies becalmed just outside the Bay of Naples, where it risks shipwreck on the rocks of Capri, and Goethe represents to the captain the "Mißtrauen und Sorge" (315; mistrust and anxiety) of the other passengers. The *other* passengers, he reports, had chosen this ship because, with its blank white French flag, it was safe from pirates, as those of other nations were not. Thus there are two causes for anxiety, pirates and shipwreck. Goethe claims to experience neither; instead he reflects serenely on the peaceful connotations of white cloth (315). The uncanny threatening blankness of the trackless snow and sea are now hidden behind a plethora of meanings adduced for whiteness. The sea and the snow have been reduced to a white cloth, the forerunner of the white screens on which we project today.

And now the blank white screen becomes specifically the realm of art. As the ship drifts ever further toward Capri and the passengers' fear rises, Goethe discusses with his companion how to paint the magnificent sunset, the elaborate description of which ends: "Beneath an entirely cloudless sky there sparkled the still, scarcely moving sea, which in the complete calm lay before us like a clear pond" (316; Unter einem ganz reinen wolkenlosen Himmel glänzte das ruhige, kaum bewegte Meer, das bei einer völligen Windstille endlich wie ein klarer Teich vor uns lag). Here again are the circumstances of "Meeres Stille," and even the many ponds of the Romantics. But Goethe's reflections on the beauty of the scene hide from him the anxiety that surrounds them, for he says, "These scenes so welcome to us kept us from noticing that a great disaster threatened" (317; Über diese uns so willkommenen Scenen hatten wir unbemerkt gelassen, daß uns ein großes Unheil bedrohe). Now imagination has acquired a new function; it no longer heightens the danger of anxiety, but helps to control it. Goethe finally realizes with "horror" (317; *Grauen*) that the current will wreck them on the rocks of Capri with no hope of rescue. As the other passengers voice their terror, Goethe, unable, he says, to tolerate disorder, reminds the crowd how Jesus calmed the storm at Lake Tiberias, and commands them to pray to the Holy Virgin for rescue and leave the captain in peace (318). Then, feeling seasick, Goethe goes below. An upset body stands in for upset emotions. There he lies in his bunk, he reports, despite the horror of the situation, "with a certain pleasant feeling that seemed to derive from Lake Tiberias" (319: mit einer gewissen angenehmen Empfindung, die sich vom See Tiberias herzuschreiben schien). Yet the source of his comfort is not religious, but aesthetic, for he thinks about the illustration to this passage by Matthaeus Merian the Elder, of one the greatest engravers of the seventeenth century (Figure 3)—"And the power of all sensual-moral impressions always proves itself strongest when we must rely entirely on our own resources" (319–20; Und so bewährt sich die Kraft aller sinnlich-sittlichen Eindrücke jedesmal am stärksten, wenn der Mensch ganz auf sich selbst zurückgewiesen ist). No anxiety for Goethe: quite the contrary. Just like the painting of the sunset earlier, Merian's etching replaces anxiety; art is the embodiment of the controlling/ controlled imagination ("sinnlich-sittlich"). Only the passengers with undisciplined imaginations suffer—when they must rely entirely on themselves.

This particular Merian image is itself an old-fashioned emblem of consciousness. In the Bible Jesus reproaches his followers for waking him and not believing they were safe simply because he was there. On first publication, however, the image was accompanied not by the biblical text (Matthew 8) but by a Latin quatrain and three German couplets about the storm, which Christ calms with a word in the last line. In the picture Christ sleeps peacefully in the bow while the disciples struggle against the tempest and one cautiously tries to waken him. What the image shows is not Christ/religion calming the storm, but the moment earlier. The remarkably violent waves appear only right around the ship; beyond it the water is calm and rowboats float there peacefully. For a seventeenth-century reader the image is an allegory of a self in danger because its captain, Understanding, sleeps, as in, for example, Calderón's Corpus Christi play *Los encantos de la culpa* (*The Sorceries of Sin*), where the allegory is not identical but still suggestive. Such a notion still underlies the imagery of "Der Fischer." But Goethe's boat returning from Sicily radically changes the notion of self represented by the image. For as Goethe

FIGURE 3. *The Storm at Sea*, by Matthaeus Merian (the Elder). From Reinier Anslo, *Icones biblicae . . .* (1648). Reproduced by permission of The Huntington Library, San Marino, California.

lies peacefully in the cabin, relying entirely on himself with Merian's image hovering before his inner eye, he resembles less the sleeping Christ (although the parallel doubtless did not escape Goethe) than Rousseau lying in his aimlessly floating boat in the fifth promenade of the *Reveries,* being purely conscious and perfectly happy. Why does Goethe invoke Merian here and not Rousseau? Because Merian's Christ is about to awaken and calm the storm (just as Goethe's own consciousness is not completely empty, but is fixed on Merian); he is about to perform a constructive action: he is about to transform his consciousness into moral action, to overcome the failing that so distressed Goethe in Rousseau. Jesus is about to rescue his companions from drowning, the same action that Wilhelm performs for his son at the end of the *Wanderjahre*. Repression keeps Goethe's angst from becoming Rousseau's paranoia.

This more complex version of repression underlies Faust's great confrontation with the terrifying personification of Sorge late in act 5 of *Faust*, part 2, a dramatic struggle between Faust and the allegorized consequences of his own acts and being. Sorge's connection to Faust's innermost identity is revealed in her ability to slip through the keyhole of Faust's locked door. The outcome—Faust drives her away, but she blinds him—seems at first to share in the tragic ambivalence already observed in *Tasso*. The battle against angst can never be won unequivocally. But the lesson of *Faust* is that no achievement is ever unequivocal or permanent; no moment can last. This lesson, however, applies as much to Sorge as to Faust in act 5. For blinding Faust has no effect on his identity or on his actions. Instead a new light shines within him and he hastens to realize his own visions—"What I thought, I hasten to achieve it; / The master's word alone carries weight" (11501–2; Was ich gedacht, ich eil' es zu vollbringen; / Des Herren Wort, es gibt allein Gewicht). Instead of falling prey to anxiety, Faust now sees and thinks afresh and can transform his thought into word, the original form of creation in the Bible and the creative act of the poet. The language of the passage does the same thing. The inaccessible interior still cannot be lit up, but it shines out of its own accord, no longer veiled by swirling mist or reflecting water. And so word takes on weight, it becomes concrete. Whether or not Faust's exercise of creativity has any effect in the world is irrelevant in this context; the issue is strictly the model created of a complex but healthy interior identity that can act morally, that can be conceptualized and discussed.

In this passage, the danger posed by *Sorge* is freezing time, the very thing that would cause Faust to lose his bet with Mephistopheles, a stasis already figured in the snow on the Furka. Faust's rejection of *Sorge* implies that identity, healthy human existence in the world, requires connectedness to temporality and to space. Norbert Elias's argument that time must be understood anthropologically, not metaphysically, shows where Goethe's insight leads. According to Elias, time exists only as a correlation of activities by the human mind. The capacity to think in and about time belongs, for Elias, to a very high order of civilization, which he defines as the ability to maintain a pause for reflection between the impulse to an act and its execution. To this necessary pause Elias attributes the tendency of modern philosophy (i.e., Descartes and later) to think of the self as interior and to construct both space and time as metaphysical entities (*Über die Zeit*, 102–3). *Sorge* is associated with temporality in Goethe because it is the ultimate development of interiority, and for Elias, the two are parallel philosophical phantoms. But in these terms, the effort to overcome *Sorge* in Goethe's plays is an effort to overcome interiority. Goethe probably perceived the issue as a continuation of the problem of *Werther*, where interiority is solipsism, or as a continuation of the Rousseau problem, where it is paranoia.[25] But the effort becomes increasingly anti-gothic, a battle against the ghosts of the subconscious. In creating the language in which the phenomenon of interiority can be explored, Goethe already tries to go beyond it. His eagerness to banish demons connects directly to healing, but also seems to lead beyond the entire notion of interior identity.[26]

The shift requires a rethinking of Faust as hero. In common with the Prometheus of *Pandora* and Egmont even earlier, Faust lives only in the present and acts without moral reflection. He is all Faustian "deed." Yet his encounter with absolute beauty and the Western mind analyzed in such detail in *Faust*, part 2, allies him rather to the wiser, gentler Epimetheus. This reading of the myth goes against the glorification of Prometheus in Goethe's fragment of the 1770s. Epimetheus is thus one of the new passive heroes who emerge at the end of the eighteenth century, and so is Faust, insofar as he is a combination of both brothers. Like Wilhelm Meister, like Hermann and his role model Tamino in the idyllic epic *Hermann und Dorothea* of 1797, Epimetheus thinks, indeed worries, rather than acts. Werther, Egmont, Tasso, and the Promethean half of Faust try to banish *Sorge* rather than recognizing it as part of themselves. But Wilhelm, Hermann, and Epimetheus represent the ultimate transformation of Hamlet, the worrier par excellence, who had become the century's favorite Shakespearean hero. The task of the late eighteenth century was to integrate Hamlet into the old-fashioned active hero represented in Egmont. One had to reflect, to worry, but not too much. Placing Epimetheus over Prometheus thus clarifies the earlier attempts to banish *Sorge* by trying to shift the focus from anxiety to caring for another. Now *Sorge* is something greater. It is Epimetheus's memory of beauty, it is in effect cultural memory. And its association with peaceable nonaction relates it to what Elias calls civilization (i.e., repression as it has emerged above), the capacity to delay action. For Jung the cultural memory represented in, say, the "Classical Walpurgis Night" was the stuff of the unconscious; for Freud the unconscious was personal memory, but personal memory of universally experienced patterns that had already been given shape by great works of literature (e.g., the Oedipus complex). The psychological, the social, and literary form all work in tandem here.

The issue is less the thematic outcome than the representation. In *Egmont* Freedom appeared on stage to signify and validate Egmont's triumph over *Sorge*, but in *Faust* the allegory signifies the problem, not the solution or evasion of the problem. Goethe may not have achieved full control of angst, but he has become much more confident in representing it. The spectator no longer wonders whether the apparent triumph over *Sorge* represents the fantasy of the hero or the not quite convincing fantasy of the author, as in *Egmont*, but only whether the outcome is triumph or tragedy. Only the content of the allegory is the problem, not the technique itself, as it is in *Egmont*.[27] Goethe has achieved a convincing representation of an anxiety that comes entirely from within the self. His allegory rests, of course, on a long tradition of personification going back to Senecan tragedy, in which emotions seem to be personages stalking the characters. The "lispelnde Sorge" of the suppressed Roman elegy is a clever example of such personification, and Sorge in *Faust*, part 2, is such a personification concretized in the manner of morality drama. Goethe has transformed a traditional rhetorical form to create a language for the new form of identity.

CHAPTER 8

"Es singen wohl die Nixen": *Werther* and the Romantic Tale

Goethe's adaptation of dramatic personification allegory into a tool for representing the subconscious demands precisely the readiness to read allegorically that emerged among the young Romantic generation assembled in Weimar and Jena in the second half of the 1790s (the Schlegels, Tieck, Novalis, Fichte, Schelling, Hegel), all of whom came to be near Goethe and Schiller. This readiness shows not only in their emerging defenses of allegory, but also in a new narrative style that suddenly appears in Tieck's "Der blonde Eckbert" (1797). This tale and those for which it set a paradigm reveal allegorical reading as well as writing because, as the analysis below will demonstrate, they uncover (perhaps not yet fully consciously) a subtext—indeed, a text of the unconscious or subconscious—beneath the surface of *Werther*'s rationalist psychology. What follows is the reading of *Werther* implied by the subsequent texts of the German Romantics, as well as by some of Goethe's later fairy-tale texts; their reading follows from the practices I have been discussing in Goethe's classical dramas and bildungsroman, for which the German Romantics were the initial enthusiasts. In that specialized sense, this chapter offers the first depth-psychological reading of *Werther*.

Although *Werther* was a runaway European best seller, the most typical and famous work of the Age of Sensibility, and the high point of the epistolary novel in Europe, it played a surprisingly small role in the further development of German narrative. Romantic theory and practice ignored it in favor of *Wilhelm Meister*, and, despite Goethe's continuing fame as its author, hardly a German work still in the canon today from the succeeding four decades could readily be labeled "Wertherian." The single prominent exception, Friedrich Hölderlin's *Hyperion*, is, however, more an elegiac autobiography than a novel of thwarted love and thwarted subjectivity. When the plot of *Werther* (the suicidal disappointed lover) reemerged in Biedermeier Germany, it was in cycles of poems, not primarily novels—examples are Wilhelm Müller's "Die schöne Müllerin" (The Fair Miller's Daughter) and "Die Winterreise" (Winter Journey) of 1815 and 1817, both made famous by Schubert's settings, and Heinrich Heine's parodistic poems of the 1820s in *Das Buch der Lieder* (Book of Songs, 1827). Some of the energy and skills developed to represent the interior subject in the epistolary tradition are reborn in Romantic autobiographical and meditative poetry, represented in Germany by Goethe himself and by Hölderlin, but otherwise at best fitfully in, say, Schiller and, much later, Eduard Mörike. In the lyric cycles of Wilhelm Müller, where what might be called the "Werther plot" first resurfaces, it coexists with another paradigm of the period, the dangerous mermaid, familiar from Romantic fairy tale. But if we read with Romantic eyes, opened, so to speak, by Goethe's works of the 1790s, it turns out that the Romantic mermaid paradigm is already implicit in *Werther* and that the Romantic tale is the true heir of *Werther*'s plot and psychological insight. Once the connection is identified, parallels spring to mind. *Werther* is not much longer than the longest of the Romantic tales; both involve lyrical and emotive prose otherwise foreign to German narrative; the similarities reveal that *Werther*, too, is a milestone in the European depiction not only of the subject, but also, without probably even Goethe having realized it, of depth psychology.

The argument begins from Wilhelm Müller's cycle of poems "Die schöne Müllerin," whose compelling interest for the age is best documented by Schubert's setting, in order to generate a twofold reinterpretation of *Werther*. First, at issue is not the direct representation of the hero's subjectivity—whether exaggerated or triumphantly emergent—but the disruption of the hero's connection to nature depicted in the novel. As a result, the novel suddenly looks much more like German Romantic tales such as Tieck's "Der Runenberg" (1804) or Friedrich de la Motte Fouqué's "Undine" (1811) than previously recognized. Hence, second, *Werther* then appears as the originary text of German depth-psychological narrative rather than as the climax of sensibility. Romantic tales elaborate implications of *Werther* that Goethe himself might well not have been able or willing to articulate when he wrote the novel in the early 1770s, but that became the central endeavor of his classical works of the 1780s and 1790s. These Romantic tales began to appear in 1797—in the wake of *Wilhelm Meisters Lehrjahre*, with its occasionally gothic inserts.

But the suicide plot goes back to *Werther* and marks yet another fundamental contribution the novel made to the representation of psychology.

"Die schöne Müllerin" and the Paradigms of Romantic Narrative

In the abstract, the plot of "Die schöne Müllerin" is very close to that of *Werther*. Werther's opening words, "How glad I am to be away" (Wie froh bin ich, daß ich weg bin) could well be those of Müller's miller, who begins by singing "Wandering is the miller's joy" (Das Wandern ist des Müllers Lust).[1] Each hero puts his past behind him as he enters an idyllic springtime world, inhabited by a young woman with whom the hero falls in love. The woman actually belongs to someone else—to an earlier betrothed in the case of Werther's Charlotte, to a hunter in Müller. While Werther has known of Charlotte's virtual engagement to Albert from day one, Müller's miller feels betrayed by his beloved. But it is not explicit that the girl was ever really in love with the miller, or that she did not have some earlier relationship with the hunter, since everything is seen so consistently through the eyes of the miller. About halfway through each work the surrounding world begins to seem hostile to the hero, and his alienation grows apace. Both end with suicide. This sequence, the "Werther paradigm," can be readily summarized: A nature enthusiast falls in love with a woman he cannot marry. First he idealizes her, then interprets her inaccessibility as his complete alienation from nature. Confronted with the prospect of eternal suffering caused by the indifference of a nature beyond the control of his own subjectivity, he commits suicide.

Müller's later cycle, "Die Winterreise," also set by Schubert, begins after the lover has lost his beloved, if he ever really had her. ("The girl mentioned love, the mother even marriage" [170; Das Mädchen sprach von Liebe, die Mutter gar von Eh] implies less commitment than the traveler thought he had.) The linden tree in its fifth song ("Der Lindenbaum") alludes to a particularly sentimental episode late in Goethe's novel in which Werther visits his childhood home, a small town with a memory-laden linden tree before the gates (part 2, letter of May 9). As in "Die Winterreise," the tree is associated with journeying and with failure in life. If Müller's traveler fails to commit suicide at the end of "Die Winterreise," it is surely not for lack of longing for death, but because the brook, which welcomed the unhappy miller, is now frozen solid.

Both cycles have in common with *Werther* copious projection of the hero's emotions onto the landscape—through seasonal imagery and especially through constant writing activity. *Werther* is a novel in letters, in which the hero writes down his feelings and describes the world around him, especially nature, in terms of his own feelings. In both cycles the heroes literally inscribe their emotions into the landscape by cutting names and dates into trees or into the surface of the frozen stream, and they read the babbling of the brook and the falling of the last isolated leaf from a tree as messages to them alone. "Is that what you meant?" (44, 45; War es also gemeint?), the miller keeps asking the brook. Like Werther, the heroes of Müller's cycle are solipsists. The only difference is that Goethe's novel inclines toward a critique of Werther's extreme subjectivity, while Müller and Schubert tend to romanticize it. This, then, is the Werther paradigm as it appears in later German Romanticism.

But there is another way to read "Die schöne Müllerin," by focusing on the obvious importance of the water. In the second song, "Wohin?" (Whither?), the wandering miller follows the sound of a little brook, which eventually leads him to the mill of the *schöne Müllerin*. He is attracted by the rushing sound ("I heard a brook rushing" [43; Ich hört ein Bächlein rauschen]), which awakens incomprehensible longing to follow the brook ("I don't know what came over me . . . / I had to follow it" [43; Ich weiß nicht wie mir wurde . . . / Ich mußte auch hinunter]), he knows not where. Uncertain of the brook's message ("Is that then my path? . . . You have completely / Intoxicated me with your rushing" [44; Ist das denn meine Straße? . . . Du hast mit deinem Rauschen / Mir ganz berauscht den Sinn]), he nevertheless decides to follow what he takes to be the call of nature:

Why do I speak of rushing?
That can't be rushing.
It must be the mermaids
Singing far below. (44)

(Was sag' ich denn vom Rauschen?
Das kann kein Rauschen sein.
Es singen wohl die Nixen
Tief unten ihren Reihn.)

He follows the sound of the nature spirits "downward and ever further" (43; hinunter und immer weiter), pursuing the voice of nature into the depths.

Titled with a question and punctuated with further questions, the poem turns on the miller's interpretation of his own description. One must read beneath the surface—of the water and of the text.

Small wonder the miller seems confused to arrive only at a new mill. "Is that what you meant?" (War es also gemeint?), he asks at the end of the third song and repeatedly in the fourth. When the brook does not answer his pressing questions as to what its call meant, he succumbs and uncertainly transfers his affections from the mermaids of the brook to the miller's daughter who has unexpectedly turned up in their place. Miller's daughters have none too good a reputation in literature of the period: in Goethe they lure innocent young aristocrats into the mill of love and then betray them, as we shall see below. In his tempestuous passion for the girl Müller's miller seems to drown out the music of the brook, though his questions periodically resurface (at the end of song 6, for example, or in 8). In his epistemological insecurity the young miller betrays the mermaids of the brook for the miller's daughter.

In this context the miller's death by water is more than suicide for unrequited love. After the girl abandons him (or whatever it is that happens) for the hunter, he returns to the brook, in which he ends up drowned. The mermaids have taken revenge for his betrayal, and now, in full possession, they rock him to sleep, much as the nixie Undine in Fouqué's tale weeps her beloved to death. Had the miller not betrayed the mermaids, but surrendered to them directly, he would still have drowned—but as the object of seduction, not revenge. All through the cycle the water attracts the miller downward, as if it represented some implicit death wish. The mermaids' revenge and the miller's own inchoate longing for the Other combine to the same end. The young miller is destroyed by the conflicting attractions of the supernatural and the natural for his very soul.

This version of the plot may be called the "Undine paradigm," and it pervades shorter narratives in the Romantic period, where the hero is pulled between two versions of the beloved, the one real and the other supernatural or uncannily demonic, often a mermaid. The moral or religious valence of each may be obvious or it may be unclear, and the hero may or may not commit himself to the nature spirit, but if he does, he disappears or goes mad (often the two are identical). If he commits to the mermaid and then abandons her, he must either die, lose his sanity, disappear, or all three. Thus in Fouqué's "Undine" Huldbrand von Ringstetten encounters Undine in her isolated home, forgets the lovely Bertalda, whose service he had sought to enter, and marries the mermaid. Upon their return to the city they form a close friendship with Bertalda, who turns out to be the real but lost daughter of Undine's foster parents, hence a sort of double for Undine. The three maintain an uneasy love triangle (shades of *Werther*), as Huldbrand wavers in his affection between the two women. Finally he leans definitively toward Bertalda and Undine must leave him; when he then marries Bertalda, the unfortunate mermaid must (literally) weep him to death on his wedding night. In a final Ovidian gesture she turns into a weeping spring on his grave.

The paradigm occurs at its harshest in early Romanticism. In Tieck's "Der Runenberg" Christian is torn between the ambiguous forest witch (Waldweib), incarnate both as hag of the forest and as the beautiful guardian of mountain crystals, and the gentle Elisabeth, through whom he is bound to the human community. After accepting the magic tablet of the beautiful forest witch Christian loses it and flees to the human world and Elisabeth. Drawn back to the mountains against his better judgment, he ends in apparently insane devotion to the now hideous witch. Tieck's "Der blonde Eckbert," perhaps the primal tale in this pattern, records the same basic plot. The apparent protagonist, Bertha, turns out to have been her husband Eckbert's sister and stand-in when he reenacts her marvelous journey to the wilderness paradise, and the gender distinction, like all other distinctions in the tale, has no apparent validity. In flight from the real world, Bertha has been sheltered and raised by a hideous yet pious witch, but betrays her after some seven years of happiness by returning to the human world and marrying Eckbert. After Eckbert feels compelled to confess her crime, Bertha dies, Eckbert's life collapses, and he is drawn back to the witch, who reveals his life of incest to him as he falls into madness. While neither of the supernatural women in these tales is a mermaid, it is striking that Eckbert's witch is located (on both Bertha's and his own journeys) by following the sound of a waterfall, and Christian's mountains are full of the mysterious sound of brooks murmuring in an incomprehensible language. Tieck's figures are sirens.

Other versions of the paradigm may also be vague about the specific status of the supernatural woman. E. T. A. Hoffmann, for example, makes his Serpentina in "Der goldene Topf" (The Golden Pot, 1814) a salamander (spirit of fire) rather than an undine, but she and Anselmus do go off to live in Atlantis, presumably beneath the sea, at the end. In Eichendorff's "Das Marmorbild" (The Marble Statue, 1819) the demonic female is Venus herself; nevertheless all of the hero Florio's encounters with her take place by a mysterious pond (*Weiher*). And in his related poem, "Frühlingsfahrt" (Spring Journey, 1818) in which two youths go out into the world and succumb to the opposite kinds of love, the second falls victim to the sirens singing in the waves of the spring. But Hans Christian Andersen's Little Mermaid and all the Melusines who spook through the German nineteenth century, even as late as Theodor Fontane's *Der Stechlin* (1899), make clear how persistent the underlying popularity of the mermaid motif for this figure was. The preference for mermaids over other nature spirits derives from the particular importance of flowing waters for the Romantics: they speak and one can drown in them and lose one's identity to nature. They image the classical Goethe's concerns with the instability of identity and the threat of self-loss, often, as just demonstrated in Chapter 7, in the image of water.

The valence and import of the mermaid figure are vague. Sometimes the choice between the two women appears to have religious implications, as in Eichendorff, sometimes primarily aesthetic, as in Hoffmann, or psychological, as in Tieck. But which is good and which dangerous is neither clear nor consistent. Whereas Hoffmann's Anselmus seems to find eternal happiness with his Serpentina and to be endangered by the real Veronika, Eichendorff's Florio has clearly done right in resisting Venus for the human Bianka. While Hoffmann associates the supernatural with the ideal, Eichendorff sees it as sin. But in Eichendorff's "Frühlingsfahrt" both of his "robust youths" (l. 1; rüst'ge Gesellen) seem to have made the wrong choice.[2] Müller's miller, remember, keeps questioning the meaning of the brook's babble. If it were easy to choose between the two women, none of these tales would have to be written.

Werther as Romantic Narrative

The fact that the two paradigms, "Werther" and "Undine," coexist so peacefully in "Die schöne Müllerin" raises the question of their relationship to one another. In fact, the Undine paradigm is already implicit in Goethe's first novel. The thesis must not be understood in too extreme terms: it is really implicit, not fully worked out. Goethe and his Romantic successors only later solidified the paradigm and drew the full implications from it. Indeed, it is not important whether they even recognized its origins, though the case of Wilhelm Müller shows they probably could have articulated them. *Werther* contains the inchoate underpinnings of the Romantic myth of identity.

On the very first page Werther introduces himself as a seducer and abandoner, a trifler with the affection of innocent women. This seems at first the obvious quality inherited from the eighteenth-century epistolary novel and Rousseau's *Julie* that took on increasing importance in *Wilhelm Meister* and

Faust. "Poor Leonore" apparently fell in love with him (and did who knows what to herself) while Werther trifled with her more outgoing and fascinating sister. Yet Werther did not ignore her; he admits to having nurtured her emotions (letter of May 4; HA 6:7). When he and Charlotte visit a country pastor, Werther irritates the daughter Friedericke's fiancé by taking too much interest in the young lady (July 1; p. 32); and he does the same with Albert's fiancée Charlotte as well. Yet Werther is no garden-variety gay Lothario, but a man of deep feeling whose sympathies and emotional relationships are very real to himself, at least during the moment of experience. In that respect Werther is a link between the rake of the eighteenth-century novel and the hero of the Romantic tale with a genuinely dual focus to his emotional life—a duality so strong that the two beloveds can appear as doppelgängers, as they do in Eichendorff. Werther, between Leonore and her sister on the first page of the novel, anticipates a long line of Romantic and post-Romantic heroes between their two beloveds, from Goethe's own Wilhelm Meister right down to Fontane's Stechlin between the sisters Armgard and Melusine (who effectively rights Werther's wrong by choosing the quieter sister).

But Goethe does not develop the motif of paired but opposing women explicitly. Instead his version is more like that of Wilhelm Müller. That is to say, Werther's first love is nature itself, subject of the first quarter of book 1 until Charlotte appears. As in the Romantic tales, the turn to nature is an escape; the first letter celebrates Werther's liberation by saying, "The town itself is unpleasant, but as compensation the unspeakable beauty of nature all around it" (8; Die Stadt selbst ist unangenehm, dagegen ringsumher eine unaussprechliche Schönheit der Natur). Werther flees society to recover the innocence he lost in the affair with Leonore, if not earlier; thus the neighborhood is "paradisal" (*paradiesisch*), and he devotes the entire last paragraph of the first letter to a garden of which Werther declares himself, like Adam, the master. Then he compares his feelings for nature to those for the maternal friend of his childhood (May 17; p. 12). The second letter, describing the cathedral of nature, seals the returned Werther's bond with the beloved—"then when it grows hazy before my eyes and the world all around me and the sky rest entire inside my soul like the form of a beloved" (9; wenn's dann um meine Augen dämmert, und die Welt um mich her und der Himmel ganz in meiner Seele ruhn wie die Gestalt einer Geliebten).

Such strong language of nature as the beloved is relatively rare in *Werther.* More commonly his devotion is expressed in three less poetic (but no less true) forms: in his love for common people (who normally shy away from members of the higher classes, but are drawn to Werther [May 15 and 27]), in children (also particularly drawn to Werther [e.g., May 27]), and in his efforts to draw landscape (May 26). Werther draws successfully, however, only before he meets Charlotte, mainly in the letter of May 26, where he insists that he will henceforth cleave to nature alone (p. 15). Within six weeks of meeting Charlotte he confesses that he can no longer draw (July 24), and drawing is not mentioned until almost a year later, when he has been away from Charlotte for nine months, and then only after a brief visit to the city of his birth, where he is greeted by the linden tree picked up by Wilhelm Müller, the embodiment of the innocence of nature, the pre-Charlotte life.

Werther's bond to nature centers on water in the form of a well, first introduced as a place haunted by spirits:

> I do not know whether such deceptive spirits hover in this region or whether it is the warm, heavenly fantasy in my heart that makes everything all about seem so paradisal. Just outside the village is a well, a well to which I am bound by a spell, like Melusine and her sisters. You go down a little hill and reach a vault, some twenty steps lead down to where perfectly clear water bubbles up from marble rock. The low wall that encloses it above, . . . the coolness of the spot, all that has something appealing, something eerie . . . so the patriarchal idea lives around me so intensely . . . just as beneficent spirits hover about well and springs. (May 9–10; p. 12)

> (Ich weiß nicht, ob täuschende Geister um diese Gegend schweben, oder ob die warme, himmlische Phantasie in meinem Herzen ist, die mir alles ringsumher so paradiesisch macht. Da ist gleich vor dem Orte ein Brunnen, ein Brunnen, an den ich gebannt bin wie Melusine mit ihren Schwestern.—Du gehst einen kleinen Hügel hinunter und findest dich vor einem Gewölbe, da wohl zwanzig Stufen hinabgehen, wo unten das klarste Wasser aus Marmorfelsen quillt. Die kleine Mauer, die oben umher die Einfassung macht, . . . die Kühle des Orts; das hat alles so was Anzügliches, was Schauerliches . . . so lebt die patriarchalische Idee so lebhaft um mich, . . . wie um die Brunnen und Quellen wohltätige Geister schweben.)

Werther comes to sit here for an hour every day—until he meets Charlotte, after which he neglects the beloved spot. The parallels to the wells and springs in "Undine" and to brooks in "Die schöne Müllerin," especially given the invocation of Melusine, Goethe's favorite water spirit, surely speak for themselves. Note also Werther's uncertainty: he cannot tell if the Edenic feeling is natural (projected by his own fantasy) or the supernatural effect of deceptive spirits. Like the miller's brook, the place invites one to descend down to the water, here to pass the explicit barrier of the small wall that presumably prevents accidental drownings. The effect upon him is ambiguous, both "appealing" (*anzüglich*) and "eerie" (*schauerlich*). By the end of the passage deceptive spirits have been replaced by beneficent ones, and the fairy-tale mood is gradually supplanted by allusions to the patriarchal idea of the Old Testament. Here is the epistemological uncertainty that will be writ so large for Müller's miller or for Eichendorff's Florio.

The abandoned well's revenge makes sense of two passing episodes associated with water in the novel. In the letter of July 6 Werther chances on his well while walking with Charlotte and realizes how he has neglected it. Overcome anew with its power he impulsively kisses Charlotte's younger sister Malchen; the child immediately scrubs her face in the water. Charlotte explains the act as offended innocence, but the mysterious occurrence makes more sense if the child, like the well, is understood to embody the nature Werther now realizes he has neglected in favor of Charlotte. His passing repentance, expressed in the kiss, is evidently rejected by the first beloved. Later, in the letter of August 10, Werther gathers flowers while walking with Albert, binds them into a nosegay, and tosses them into the brook. At the most obvious level the act signifies the recognition that his love for Charlotte must pass with the flow of time. But given that water personifies the spirit of nature abandoned by Werther for Charlotte, the sacrifice of the flowers to the brook foreshadows also the necessary sacrifice of his new love to the old—as it does more openly in "Die schöne Müllerin."

Seeing the Undine paradigm in *Werther* sets Charlotte herself in a new light. If Werther abandons nature for her, she occupies the place of the faithless miller's daughter in Wilhelm Müller, or worse of the fickle beloved in "Winterreise," or of selfish Bertalda in "Undine." To be sure, this figure is occasionally positive, as in Tieck's "Runenberg," in which motherly Elisabeth owes much to the Charlotte famous for rearing her many siblings. As already seen, Charlotte interferes with Werther's ability to draw and to focus on nature; furthermore, the first result of his encounter with her is to be transported into a dream world—"I descended from the coach like a dreamer as we stopped at the pavilion, and was so lost in dreams in the hazy world arund me, that I scarcely noticed the music" (July 23–24; p. 16; ich stieg aus dem Wagen wie ein Träumender, als wir vor dem Lusthause stille hielten, und war so in Träumen rings in der dämmernden Welt verloren, daß ich auf die Musik kaum achtete; cf. his inability to distinguish night from day in the next letter, June 19). Charlotte is described virtually as a dangerous sorceress in a fairy tale about a magnetic mountain, which sucked all the metal from ships that came too close, sank them, and drowned their crews (July 26). Remove the element of magnetism and there remains Charlotte as siren, the dangerous water nixie. In this reading Charlotte is not the carrier of an ideal projected on her by Werther, but a dangerous distraction from the ideal of nature.

The mermaid image, the embodiment of nature in the reference to Melusine at the well and in the Romantic tales, is here extended to Charlotte herself, the competitor to nature. Even where the portrayal of Charlotte remains closest to the novel's roots in eighteenth-century sensibility, the siren is crucially present. In one of the most famous moments of the novel, as Werther and Charlotte stand at the window in the flush of their first evening together and watch the rain, Charlotte invokes Klopstock. Werther immediately recalls the ode she has in mind as he sinks "in the river of emotions that she poured over me with this watchword" (June 16; p. 27; in dem Strome von Empfindungen, den sie in dieser Losung über mich ausgoß). This central passage reveals the nexus: the psychological issue, *Empfindung*, is represented in the metaphor of the river in which Werther drowns. One has only to literalize the metaphor to arrive at the Romantic fairy tale, "Die schöne Müllerin," or to Eichendorff's dangerous "spring waves" (*Frühlingswellen*) in "Frühlingsfahrt"

Charlotte's association with nature is not a contradiction of the Undine paradigm, but a confirmation of it: she is the dangerous doppelgänger. Like Venus and Bianka in Eichendorff's "Das Marmorbild," it is at first hard to distinguish the moral difference—harder really in *Werther* because the moral situation is so much more complex. Thus, Charlotte is closely associated with nature, but not with the patriarchal calm of the well. In the wake of Klopstock in the scene above, or of Oliver Goldsmith in the scene beneath the walnut trees on the visit to the pastor, hers is the highly emotionalized nature of sensibility, like the moonlit garden in which Werther takes his farewell of her at the end of part 1, again replete with Klopstock allusions. In the second part of the novel her nature is dead—Werther can only write to Charlotte in the countryside in the depths of winter (January 20)—or artificial, as in her erotic parading with the tame canary that carries kisses from her lips to Werther's (September 15). The theme of kissing represents her ultimate insidious displacement of the innocent Melusine of the well. In the letter of November 24 (p. 87), Werther barely controls his desire to kiss her; she flees to the piano and Werther continues:

> Never have I seen her lips so attractive; it was as if she opened them longing to suck in the sweet tones that poured from the instrument and only the secret echo vibrated back from the sweet mouth— . . . Never will I dare to press a kiss onto you, you lips on which hover the spirits of heaven!—And yet—I want to—

> (Nie hab ich ihre Lippen so reizend gesehn; es war, als wenn sie sich lechzend öffneten, jene süßen Töne in sich zu schlürfen, die aus dem Instrument hervorquollen, und nur der heimliche Widerschall aus dem süßen Munde zurückklänge— . . . Nie will ich es wagen, einen Kuß euch einzudrücken, Lippen, auf denen die Geister des Himmels schweben.—Und doch—ich will—)

As they provide a passage for the music that flows from the piano like water, Charlotte's lips take the place of the small wall that surrounds the fountain of the letter of May 12; and like the fountain they too are guarded by hovering spirits ("wohltätige Geister schweben," 10). The language is the same but the situation is not. It now appears that kissing Malchen at the well was so appalling because it really anticipated the adulterous kisses he exchanges with Charlotte less than a month after the scene at the piano. If Ossian has displaced Homer, as Werther asserts (October 12), Charlotte has displaced the innocent spirits of nature, the child Malchen and the Melusine of the well.

At the end nature turns on Werther and takes her revenge, as in the later Romantic tales. In the letter of August 18, a final detailed loving description of the landscape is transformed into a spectacle of horror. The letter begins with the assertion that Werther's initial love for nature has been transformed into an "unbearable torturer, to a tormenting spirit that pursues me wherever I go" (51; unerträglichen Peiniger, zu einem quälenden Geist, der mich auf allen Wegen verfolgt), for all the world like Undine's angry uncle who torments Huldbrand. The same angry nature appears in the floods in which Werther madly triumphs toward the end of the novel (December 8). Nature appears also as the mourner for her lost beloved in the pathos of the Ossian translations at the end of the novel, where Ossian's figures become the voices of the desolate landscapes they haunt, mourning their lost loved ones.

But Werther dies, it may be objected, by his own hand, not overwhelmed by angry or sorrowful waters. This important difference points to the underlying significance of the connection between the Werther and the Undine paradigms. In *Werther* the vengeance and the mourning originate not with an independent external nature, but explicitly within his own psyche. In the passage cited above, it is his own love of nature that now torments him, not nature itself. And the floods at the end of the novel appeal to Werther because they seem to him to mirror his own disordered passions. Indeed, the novel depicts only a conflict in Werther's passions all along, not a conflict between some mermaid Melusine and the human Charlotte. Both the nature and the Charlotte of Werther's letters are clearly projections of his own ideals, views, and longings. This phenomenon is guaranteed by the epistolary form. That Werther does not die by water like the miller or like Huldbrand, but shoots himself instead, shows that Goethe's novel still operates in terms of the explicit rationalist psychology of the eighteenth century, which at best finds objective correlatives in nature for its passions. But the pervasive presence of the Undine paradigm reveals *Werther* teetering on the brink of a different psychology.

Allegorizing *Werther*

Romantic tales have third-person narrators, or frames to objectify the first-person narrations, instead of the radical subjectivity of Werther's epistolary mode. In the Romantic tales nature is not the objective correlative of human passion, but rather the carrier of a narrative that cannot be articulated in any other terms. The gain, of course, is access to the part of the psyche that does not operate in rational terms, what was just gaining currency as the unconscious. Where *Werther* and the eighteenth-century tradition have simile and metaphor, Romantic depth psychology is driven to what we now recognize as allegory.

But if *Werther* was teetering on the brink of a new mode of psychological representation, Goethe himself was the first to enter the new territory, in the short ballad "Der Fischer" mentioned in the previous chapter. Here a fisherman sitting calmly in his boat is accosted by a mermaid who rises from the rushing and swelling water. Siren that she is, she tempts him to his death, or at least disappearance, in the waves by offering him access to his own inner self—"doesn't your own face lure you" (l. 23; Lockt dich dein eigen Angesicht)—a self that can no longer be described in terms of passions, but only in images, in this case the reflection of the fisherman's face on the surface of the water. The ballad addresses the whole gamut of typical Romantic dichotomies—human/natural, subject/object, natural/supernatural, rational/irrational, conscious/unconscious, order/disorder, temporal/eternal—but its extraordinary perfection hides the complexity of the transition to them, which, as preceding chapters have demonstrated, Goethe explored repeatedly in the succeeding decades, in his classic plays, the *Lehrjahre*, and *Faust*.[3]

Goethe entered this territory more explicitly in 1795 in a fairy tale entitled simply "Das Märchen" at the end of a cycle of novellas dealing with the French Revolution (*Unterhaltungen deutscher Ausgewanderten* [Conversations of German Refugees, 1795]). It is generally considered the first Romantic literary fairy tale or *Kunstmärchen*, in German literature, but also usually considered so baffling that it is rarely connected to the sequence of tales discussed above. Nevertheless, it is baffling precisely because it contains the psychological elements under discussion but, as in *Werther*, not yet quite clearly articulated. Its heroine, the fair Lily, lives in a lush garden that is, however, oddly blighted. Full of greenery, it lacks flowers or fruit; in this place of stagnation and waiting the tale's hero, a prince whose realm suffers under an unexplained enchantment somehow connected to the dangerous river that divides it in two, is lured to his death. Like Charlotte, Lily is her own doppelgänger, both beloved and siren. To be sure, the dead prince is ultimately revived by the self-sacrifice of a green snake, and with his revival comes the resolution of Lily's duality into proper queen and the revival of the entire realm. The plot is set in motion by the arrival of outsiders (a pair of courtly will-o'-the-wisps) and then managed by an old man with a magic lamp. It is a straight line from him to the mysterious shape-changing Walter of Tieck's "Der blonde Eckbert." The question of failing to keep promises—betrayal—appears everywhere: the wisps don't pay their ferry fare, an old woman takes over their debt (and her hand is blackened in the river as a token) but fails to fulfill her promise, Princess Lily kills those she means to save. The mysterious prophecy of redemption familiar to all the figures does finally come to pass because the green snake agrees to sacrifice herself to prevent being sacrificed against her will. By preventing her own betrayal she saves all the others from the results of their failures to keep promises and the world can begin anew. The happy ending is tied to the ambiguous closure the tale provides for its context in the *Unterhaltungen* and to the desperation of the political circumstances it addresses. Cut off the story just before the sacrifice of the green snake, and it is *Werther* retold as a fairy tale.

Goethe's analysis of the representational issues with regard to this particular plot can be observed in his own cycle of *Müllerin* poems, first published in 1799, to which Wilhelm Müller's cycle responds. It consists of three dialogue poems arranged around a ballad, "Der Müllerin Verrat" (The Maid of the Mill's Betrayal), that Goethe had translated from a French tale called "La folle en pèlerinage," (later included in *Wilhelm Meisters Wanderjahre* as "Die pilgernde Törin" [The Deranged Pilgrim]). In that tale the ballad is sung by the mysterious young beloved of the narrator, who first met her sitting next to a well, like the mermaid Melusine. Of interest here are not the numerous verbal echoes in Wilhelm Müller's poems, but the plot of Goethe's cycle: a noble youth (*Edelknabe*) invites the pretty miller's daughter to dally with him in a bower in the fields, but she will not, because the flour dust would soil his beautiful coat and betray them. She will stick to young millers, she says. In the next poem a journeyman (*Junggesell*, the youth in disguise? the young miller referred to by the girl?) discusses his love for the miller's daughter with the sympathetic (male) brook, who also loves her. The third poem is the French ballad; it narrates how the miller's family breaks in on the young nobleman's love tryst with the girl and tries to make him marry her. He escapes with only his cloak to cover him. In the last poem the repentant girl comes to him disguised as a gypsy (painted black) to apologize for betraying him and ask for his love. Dismissed as a procuress, she reveals her identity and offers herself as his mistress; he forgives her and takes her to bed. Goethe's *Müllerin* is an ambiguous figure, both white and black, both scheming and loving (as is the pilgrim who sings the ballad in the French tale). The duality otherwise found between nature and human appears here within the girl, and it is hard for the youth to recognize (a central theme in the last two poems). With its two young lovers, the gentleman and the *Junggeselle*, the cycle stands exactly between *Werther* and Müller's "Die schöne Müllerin."

The cycle also straddles two kinds of representation. On the one hand the girl is a coquettish miller's daughter, an exaggerated version of the coquette Charlotte perhaps, a figure that Wilhelm Müller could still sanitize for the Biedermeier drawing room. On the other hand, she has also, if not yet quite a mermaid, nevertheless as gypsy, crossed the boundary from domestic reality into the realm of romance and fairy tale. Goethe originally characterized each of the poems in this group as "Old English," "Old German," "Old French," and "Old Spanish," respectively.[4] The move from north to south through the cycle corresponds to a shift from the normalcy of an eighteenth-century world in which wealthy young men seduce honest, or not so honest, working girls in bowers to the romanticism of Spanish romance. But the issue is not solely generic. In his collected poems Goethe included the group among his ballads, to which the epigraph reads: "No matter how marvelous the tale, / Poetic arts make it true" (Märchen noch so wunderbar, / Dichterkünste machens wahr). Ballads are not only associated with fairy tale, but with the realization of fairy tale, or with the revelation of their truth. Through "poetic arts" they mediate the transition from rational or "Wertherian" to the magical narrative of the Romantic tale.

If "poetic arts" sounds pretentious, it shouldn't. It should rather be taken literally—as verse. The metrical form excuses or renders acceptable the fantastic content of the fairy tale. Goethe had begun writing ballads even before he wrote *Werther*, but he returned to the ballad consciously as a form in 1797 and 1798, after two significant experiments at representing the irrational Other in prose: Mignon and the Harper in *Wilhelm Meisters Lehrjahre* and the "Märchen" just discussed above. The fairy-tale aspects of Mignon and the Harper are both mystifying and, as the narrative penetrates further into their past, shocking. Indeed, so shocking is their history compared to the rational normalcy the cured Harper had seemed to achieve, that when their past is narrated he commits suicide. The two modalities cannot exist side by side. The "Märchen" also contrasts strongly with the rational normality of its frame narrative in *Unterhaltungen*; the contrast is not shocking, as in *Wilhelm Meister*, but it is mystifying. Goethe moderates the shock into mystification by an elaborate introduction that defines the fairy tale as essentially irrational and illogical. His turn to the ballad represents, then, a formal way to isolate and thereby control the shock of the new discourse of the unconscious. When the Romantics return from the literal poetry of ballads to the prose of *Werther*, they complete the transition: without the mediation of poetic art, literally of meter, the irrational is exposed for all to see.

Ever since Freud's essay "The Uncanny" (1919), a suggestive psychoanalytic reading of E. T. A. Hoffmann's "Der Sandmann" (The Sandman), German Romantic fairy tales have been an obvious place to search for the literary predecessors of depth psychology. German literary scholarship has traditionally preferred to look away from the substantial debt the German Romantics owed to Goethe by drawing a firm distinction between the sunny clarity and humanity of German classicism (Goethe and Schiller) and the mysterious depths of dream and madness associated with Romanticism.[5] As a result, apart from the German Romantics' initially enthusiastic reception of *Wilhelm Meisters Lehrjahre* and the general acknowledgment of Goethe's "Märchen" of 1795 as the first *Kunstmärchen*, little attention has been paid, except in the most general terms, to how the single text Goethe was best known for, *Werther*, played into the development of Romantic narrative. The Werther paradigm is thus really the older, more rationalistic version of the Undine paradigm, and every once in a while it resurfaces, especially in the Biedermeier, as in "Die schöne Müllerin." From Goethe's elaborations of it in the 1790s it is but a small step to the mystified heroes of Tieck's fairy tales, whose behavior is as incomprehensible to themselves as to those around them. The Romantic tale is not a sudden irruption into or reversal of eighteenth-century psychology, but rather the logical consequence of patterns implicit in its most popular narrative.

CHAPTER 9

Goethe and the Uncanny

The trajectory from *Werther* to *Die Wahlverwandtschaften* was the starting point of this investigation because it marked so clearly the period of Goethe's struggles with Rousseau. Since *Werther* was also the starting point for the Romantics' encounter with representing depth psychology, it is only appropriate to end with *Die Wahlverwandtschaften*, where the last building block for Goethe's representations of depth psychology is set in place. This is not to say that Goethe does not advance further in his thinking; the discussions of *Faust*, part 2, in this book have already demonstrated as much. It means only that by the time of *Die Wahlverwandtschaften* Goethe himself begins to talk explicitly about the unconscious in the context of his narrative. Thus the novel provides a vantage point from which to see how, by connecting anxiety to imagination, by understanding the subconscious as a vital source of his creative power, Goethe completed his own transformation of Rousseau's interior self.

Die Wahlverwandtschaften is widely accepted today as Goethe's novel that speaks most directly to the modern or postmodern condition. It will not be news to anyone that it is fraught with anxiety and psychological complications. The novel uses the term *unbewußt* (unconscious), it knows about repression (though it does not use the term), it has become a virtual playground for Freudian readers.[1] It was Goethe's first major literary work written in a new age for Goethe—after the death of Schiller (1805) and after the collapse of the Holy Roman Empire in the wake of Napoleon's victory at Jena (1806). Central to its current popularity is its responsiveness to the categories of depth psychology and to the problems of establishing identity when religion, nation, and class seem to have lost their validity.[2] Because symbolizing and naming become so problematic in the novel, the possibility of grounding identity even in the Rousseauist interior self seems to be called into question. Preceding chapters have had occasion to discuss both the uncanny and the relation of *Werther* to Romantic fairy tale with its supernatural psychological depth. This one traces how *Die Wahlverwandtschaften* takes off from the representation of depth psychology in fairy tale and gothic narrative more generally to model what became the Freudian uncanny.[3] On that basis it becomes possible to see how it makes sense of a whole strand of writing about ghosts in Goethe's works in his classical period that has not been included in the narrative of Romantic or gothic narrative, but nevertheless illuminates clearly the early importance of repression and the uncanny in enabling Goethe to come to terms with Rousseau.

The psychic atmosphere in the novel is grim from the start. Although it begins with its hero Eduard grafting fresh shoots in early spring, the hopeful image is contradicted by a dark background. Eduard and Charlotte live isolated in a less than perfect marriage, consecrated only after each had been married for financial reasons to an older, less well-matched mate. Charlotte spends her time cleaning up the churchyard and building a moss hut, whose small size corresponds to their desire to live alone and relive Eduard's travel memories together. They have no plans for children. Outsiders, even former close friends and wards, are unwelcome to Charlotte—perhaps because she married Eduard only with hesitation after she failed to arrange a match between him and her ward Ottilie. Eduard has mysteriously changed his name; he avoids setting foot in the churchyard, as does their clumsy friend, Mittler, upon whose advice they depend for no discernible reason. Another friend, the Captain, is unable, despite his remarkable talents, to find employment or a wife. Ottilie, unsuccessful and unhappy at school, segregates herself from the world around her. The characters worry about rescuing people from drowning and protecting the village from flooding. The gentle melancholy of the opening has rapidly become angst.

The characters' anxiety arises from the fact that much in their world has been put aside, forgotten, and repressed behind symbols and symbolic objects. There has been much thoughtful discussion of the characters' tendency to misinterpret, overinterpret, or allegorize symbols in the novel, but little of their efforts to restrain and repress symbols, which seems to me equally important.[4] The concept *Wahlverwandtschaft* (elective affinity), for example, masks anxiety about divorce. When Eduard, Charlotte, and the Captain decide to invite Ottilie to the estate, the notion seems to prophesy a marriage between the Captain and Ottilie. Then, as the chemical formula is developed at length in chapter 4 (AB + CD → BC + AD = Charlotte/Eduard + Captain/

Ottilie → Eduard/Captain + Charlotte/Ottilie), the term seems to point to gender-based friendships. In both cases the real threat, an attraction between Eduard and Ottilie, remains hidden.[5] Another example of such masking is the various boxes with dangerous contents. One such is the box of fireworks set off on Ottilie's birthday; a second is the chest with Eduard's extravagant birthday gifts to Ottilie. The cornerstone of the *Lusthaus* (summer house), a third such chest, must be hastily sealed after Ottilie places in it her gold chain, the symbol of the passion neither she nor Eduard acknowledges. Graves are the extreme version of such boxes. Eduard avoids the churchyard from the very beginning. The ill-fated baby Otto, who represents the tangled relations among the four protagonists, drowns beneath the waters the others have all feared and is finally buried in the chapel on the estate, where he soon fades into the background—forgotten, repressed—by the more sensational burials of Ottilie and Eduard in the same place.[6] To be sure, Ottilie remains after her death in her glass-topped coffin in the locked chapel ornamented all over with her image, and the narrator piously hopes that she will one day awaken there. However, these details do not simply symbolize the now visible truth of the love between Eduard and Ottilie, but rather the return of the tantalizing lure of their physical union that had to be repressed. Thus Ottilie emerges as the paradigm of all these lovely and significant symbolic objects that must return in the end from the chests into which they have been repressed.[7] All anxiety in the novel, it turns out, emanates ultimately from her, and it derives from the way in which symbols around her repress as well as communicate meaning.

Die Wahlverwandtschaften as Gothic Fairy Tale

Since *Die Wahlverwandtschaften* is in so many respects a rewriting of *Werther*, and further since its melancholy and anxiety are common to the Romantic fairy tales in the tradition established by *Werther*, it needs to be read in the tradition of texts that includes Goethe's own "Märchen" of 1795, Tieck's "Der blonde Eckbert" and "Der Runenberg," and many written after *Die Wahlverwandtschaften*, such as Eichendorff's "Das Marmorbild," Fouqué's "Undine," Hoffmann's "Der goldene Topf," and even later specifically psychological fairy tales like Hugo von Hofmannsthal's "Märchen von der 672. Nacht" (Tale of the 672nd Night). In such tales protagonists typically set off in the spring on a journey away from the stagnating isolation of home into the great world, often a forest, where they are exposed to demonic forces, usually in the form of a siren or a woman in an enchanted garden space. They also encounter the lure of normal society, often represented by another woman, and ultimately must decide between the two. The decision involves somehow betraying or failing one or the other of the women, often without realizing it consciously, and then often retribution. The process of decision and retribution is generally set off by an outsider who arrives at some point. The pattern is rudimentary in *Werther*, where Lotte is the siren in the enchanted garden from which Werther fails to escape, but as suggested in the previous chapter is already present with all its elements in the "Märchen" of 1795. In the early examples, a powerful nature spirit protects the hero from the ultimate consequences of his transgression—the green snake in the "Märchen" is one such. In other tales this powerful animal spirit is murdered (the singing bird in "Der blonde Eckbert") or simply goes missing, and, like the dams in *Die Wahlverwandschaften*, the bulwarks against anxiety fall.

Although *Die Wahlverwandtschaften* appears to be a novel of manners with little action, in fact the plot engages the central motifs of Romantic fairy tale.[8] It begins in spring with the protagonists stagnating in their happy home rather like Tieck's Eckbert and Bertha: flowers appear in blossom only in the fall, when Eduard is absent and when Ottilie dies. The characters make the equivalent of Romantic journeys as they stroll around the estate, first to the moss hut, where they make the fateful decision to invite in outsiders, then, as a foursome, through the forest to an old mill, where Ottilie surrenders her father's portrait to Eduard. Ottilie quickly emerges as the demonic woman when she suggests moving the proposed *Lusthaus* out of sight of the castle into a completely other world and thereby causes Eduard to deface the Captain's carefully drawn map of the estate, the symbol of its orderliness. Like a fairy, Ottilie has such a light step that she seems weightless and she keeps the house in order as if by magic. The significance of the mill where Eduard first woos Ottilie has already been illuminated by the ballads about the *Müllerin* discussed in the previous chapter. Her fairylike qualities and the setting at the mill reveal that the seduction is not, at bottom, initiated by Eduard, as is generally assumed.[9] For most of the novel Ottilie avoids the water and shares the pervasive anxiety about drowning. And yet the plane trees planted on the day of her birth are the most important landmark on the lake and the site from which to watch the fireworks that celebrate Eduard's adulterous passion for her. Heading for these very trees she drops Eduard's son into the water. In retrospect the fear of water and drowning that Charlotte has suffered from the beginning is revealed to be her proper fear of the threat posed to her marriage by the water sprite Ottilie.

Ottilie's demonic power ensnares Charlotte as well as Eduard, so that each betrays the other. The doubling of the central betrayal of the Romantic tales may well build on the incest revealed at the end of "Der blonde Eckbert," which also deals with the crimes of both husband and wife. In accordance with this pattern, the outsiders also become insiders. The outsiders Charlotte initially fears, the Captain and Ottilie, reveal, as in Tieck, the shaky foundations on which Charlotte and Eduard's marriage was built. Unlike in Tieck, however, the two outsiders are quickly ensnared in the troubles of the marriage. As Eduard's oldest friend (to whom Eduard has ceded his birth name) and Charlotte's foster child, they are not outsiders at all, but already belong to the identities of the couple. Only because they are not acknowledged as part of their identities do they bear different names, an argument that could readily be made in Freudian readings of the Romantic tales. The illicit passions among the other four are uncovered and aggravated by dear old friends from court, the Count and the Baroness, who with their own illicit relationship also embody the return of the repressed.[10]

The tendency toward mixing and mutual betrayal becomes even more extreme with the doppelgänger. Even more than in *Tasso* all the central characters are one another's doubles, since their names all contain the same syllable. There is a certain logic in the resemblance of Eduard's and Charlotte's child to the two absent partners in their adulterous marital encounter. What could this child possibly be called other than Otto? By seeming to naturalize the doppelgänger motif, Goethe has actually made its supernaturalness stand out all the more.[11] As a result, Goethe's outsiders and his doppelgänger are the more uncanny for being familiar. The repetition of repressed childhood memories later became central to Freud's notion of the uncanny.

But another generic element requires attention first before moving closer to Freud. A major difference between German Romantic fairy tales and earlier ones in the eighteenth century is the way they incorporate elements of the newly popular gothic novel. The genre began quite suddenly in 1764 with Horace Walpole's *Castle of Otranto* and became popular in the 1790s in the wake of Ann Radcliffe's novels. Motifs such as doppelgänger, intense family problems, premonitions and omens, dream states, and of course horrifying incursions of the supernatural in these tales all derive from the popularity of the new English genre. Since Goethe first mentions Walpole in 1798, it seems at first more plausible that Tieck's "Der blonde Eckbert" picked up on the gothic than on Goethe. Nevertheless Goethe's "Märchen" of 1795 not only already shares the gothic's interest in family curses, mysterious ceremonies, and a vaguely Italian setting, but it uses two striking motifs for which the *Castle of Otranto* was particularly famous—underground vaults and dangerous giants. The *Lehrjahre*, especially the story of Mignon's ancestry in the last book, also features such gothic motifs as Italy, monks, stubborn fathers, and incest.[12] What distinguishes gothic fiction from Goethe's fairy tale—and from fairy tale in general—however, is its discursiveness. The gothic loves to describe landscapes and the feelings of its protagonists—indeed, not just their feelings but their anxieties, their anticipations, and above all their in-between dreamlike states of reverie and dread.

The same can be said of *Die Wahlverwandtschaften*. It contains obvious gothic motifs. It is preoccupied with death and places of burial; it contains elaborate ceremonies, omens, doppelgängers, a castle with secret passages, melodramatic plotting, and even dread (aroused by the face of baby Otto [HA 6:459]). It is full of the rhetoric of fate—elective affinity, higher powers, hostile demons, the "almost magical attraction" (478; fast magische Anziehungskraft) that connects Eduard and Ottilie. The substance of the novel consists not of occurrences but of description of emotions, anticipations, worries; the characters, especially Ottilie and Eduard, spend much of their time in dreamlike states of suspended or semiconsciousness. To be sure, there are no real ghosts, but Charlotte is haunted by the imaginary presence of the Captain (320), while Eduard wishes he were a ghost (473). And the novel participates fully in the gothic love of landscape.

Reading *Die Wahlverwandtschaften* as gothic brings the emotional problems of the family into perspective. The novel involves, as often in the gothic, disrupted relations between parents and children: Ottilie is motherless, and there doesn't seem to be much affection between Charlotte and her real daughter Luciane. Eduard was forced into a loveless marriage for money by his parents. At the same time Eduard can be compared to the dangerous gothic father figure who holds the pure young woman prisoner—he persuades Ottilie to set aside the guardianship of her father's portrait and in fact keeps her imprisoned on the estate by threatening to abduct her if she leaves Charlotte's care. After Eduard abandons his family, Ottilie is kept in ignorance of the true situation and becomes suspicious of Charlotte (348) as if she were being kept prisoner. Beneath the surface of this very polite novel with its exceptionally tactful narrator there lurks the den of hysterics that Ford Madox Ford was later to describe in his intense rewriting of this novel as *The Good Soldier* (1915). *Die Wahlverwandtschaften* is, in fact, a highly civilized, tamed version of a gothic novel.

The conjunction of fairy-tale and gothic elements constitutes the dark subconscious of the novel. The effect of this development comes into especially clear focus in the novella "Die wunderlichen Nachbarskinder" (The Remarkable Young Neighbors) told by visiting Englishmen to Charlotte and Ottilie in part 2. Here a marriage between neighboring families founders on the young woman's opposition; during her engagement to a second suitor of her choice, the original fiancé returns, now a blooming young hero, and the girl realizes her mistake. The hero rescues her from a suicidal plunge into the river, and they end kneeling to their assembled parents and the jilted second fiancé. The presence of fairy tale behind the narrative emerges as it moves from a bourgeois world of arranged marriages and family parties through immersion in the river into the more archaic social and emotional realm of their peasant hosts, where the protagonists recostume themselves in peasant wedding clothes and achieve the happy ending of their (presumed) engagement at the end. The tale also has more specific roots in Goethe's own "Märchen." Corresponding to the incomprehensible conflict between the two children, the "Märchen" begins with a world in unexplained conflict—the prince and his princess are separated by an enchantment, the causes of which are neither explained nor even inquired after. Both plots center on a dangerous river, and the turning point in both comes when a living being is sacrificed to the river. The heroine of the novella casts herself in, leaving only her wreath of flowers behind for the young lover; in the "Märchen" the green snake voluntarily dies to revive the prince and turns into a wreath of gems in the grass, which are then tossed into the river. The girl's sacrifice fulfills the original hopes of unifying two neighboring families, while that of the snake leads to the marriage of prince and princess, a restored society, and unification of the two sides of the river. The ends of both stories involve ceremonial changes of clothing and social roles, triple incantations of blessing, and the miraculous revelation and restoration of that which was lost. In Goethe's terms the novella is a fairy tale.

Yet the novella takes the extended interest in the emotions of its characters typical of gothic narrative. Satisfying as the redemption at the end of the "Märchen" is, its meaning remained a riddle to its listeners in the *Unterhaltungen*, as also to its contemporary readers and to most readers since. "Die wunderlichen Nachbarskinder," by contrast, evokes horror. Its English narrator sought only to make himself agreeable and is shocked by his hostess's reaction, for Charlotte immediately recognizes it as an event in the life of her beloved Captain/Major and flees from the room. Like so many unconscious motivations in the novel earlier, the novella functions here as a return of the repressed. The uncanniness is heightened by the many unclear emotions in the story. The heroine's childhood hostility toward her young neighbor is incomprehensible to her and to both families. Yet when the youth returns, the narrator's language reveals complete depth-psychological understanding of the events: "she thought she was happy and was so in a certain sense. But now, for the first time in several years, something confronted her again . . . the childish hatred, which had actually been only a dim recognition of inner value, expressed itself now in joyous amazement" (436; sie glaubte glücklich zu sein und war es auch auf gewisse Weise. Aber nun stand ihr zum erstenmal seit langer Zeit wieder etwas entgegen . . . der kindische Haß, der eigentlich nur ein dunkles Anerkennen des inneren Wertes gewesen, äußerte sich nun in frohem Erstaunen) and "She felt as if she had awakened from a dream. The feud with her young neighbor had been her first passion, and this violent struggle was really, under the form of resistance, a violent, almost innate affection. And now she could recall nothing except that she had always loved him" (437; Sie schien sich wie aus einem Traum erwacht. Der Kampf gegen ihren jungen Nachbar war die erste Leidenschaft gewesen, und dieser heftige Kampf war doch nur, unter der Form des Widerstrebens, eine heftige, gleichsam angeborne Neigung. Auch kam es ihr in der Erinnerung nicht anders vor, als daß sie ihn immer geliebt habe). The gothic focus on a bizarre emotional situation with its melodramatic happy end leads here to explicit psychological analysis of repression and the need for reversal in order to interpret it; any halfway competent depth psychologist can identify and conceptualize what appears here in narrative form.

Both genres, fairy tale and gothic novel, shape the conclusion of the novel. Echoes of the "Märchen" pervade the final catastrophe—both texts involve an accidental death caused by a devoted caretaker (of the child, of the princess's canary, and the prince), a nighttime vigil by the corpse, in each text wrapped in green, and the hope for comfort and rescue from a strong man (the Major, the old man with the lamp).[13] In the "Märchen" the old man orchestrates the sacrifice of the snake for the common good, and all then help to bring about the return of a buried temple to the world. In the novel both Eduard and the Major cannot help feeling that the baby is a necessary sacrifice to the restoration of social order, though in the absence of leadership their efforts all run astray. The substantial assemblage of parallels here may or may not mean that Goethe specifically had his "Märchen" in mind, nor does it matter. What does matter is that the mystifying plot of the "Märchen" has been fleshed out, as in the novella, with gothic narrative description of emotions and therefore now appears as a situation of which it is possible to make psychological sense. Goethe already used the blending of genres to achieve a sense of psychological depths in his classical plays (cf. above Chapter 4); the process has now reached its logical, explicit conclusion.

Ottilie: The Uncanny and Allegory Run Wild

The blend of fairy tale concreteness with gothic discursiveness is not the sole cause of uncanniness in *Die Wahlverwandtschaften*; an equally important contributor is Goethe's peculiar play with the concreteness of language. It appears most obviously in Ottilie's tendency to make the natural become supernatural at every turn and thereby generate a proliferation of symbols. Thus, for example, the Captain has to remove the floral letters that represent her initials at the celebration of the final framing of the *Lusthaus*. She and the architect paint innumerable angels on the ceiling that come ever more to resemble Ottilie, so that her image runs riot. The enthusiasm for representations then drives them to add painted wreaths to the walls the architect had originally intended to leave bare. Ottilie also has a distressing capacity to make what seemed distant or figurative become real and present. She reports to Charlotte the tragic situation of a girl who had accidently killed a sibling; after the death of baby Otto, Ottilie becomes in effect that girl, now present, not just reported. Named for a saint who cures blindness and called a "comfort for the eyes" (283; wahrer Augentrost) by the narrator, Ottilie miraculously heals her servant Nanny at the end. An earlier episode had involved *tableaux vivants*, including one of Van Dyck's blind Belisarius; by the end Ottilie herself makes the horror of that image present to the reader with her own metaphoric blindness. And after playing the Virgin Mother in the final *tableau vivant*, she appears as the literally virgin mother of Eduard's child. The confusing play between metaphoric and literal seems endless and is consistently centered on Ottilie, who embodies a dangerous force field rather like the magnetic mountain Werther used to characterize the siren Charlotte. In Ottilie's vicinity common sense and normal systems of signification acquire too much meaning, just as the box of fabric Eduard gives her cannot hold all of its contents once she has opened it, and just as she cannot return into her own "path" (*Bahn*) at the end. In her presence Mittler's thoughtless ranting becomes fatal—to the pastor at the baptism of baby Otto and at the end to Ottilie herself. Just as Goethe's first mermaid, the seductress of "Der Fischer," makes up and down, transcendence and death reverse their values, so normal logic reverses in Ottilie's presence. Nanny's fall from the upstairs window into the street brings her not death but renewed life, and yet to Eduard, who had promised himself eternal life in her arms, she brings death. The peculiar marriage in Ottilie of fairy-tale allegorical concreteness and the importance of interpreting signs that seem to emerge from the depths of gothic narrative makes her appear simultaneously full of meaning yet impenetrable—what Hillis Miller calls an empty sign, itself signified by the initial *O*, a large hole.[14]

The special uncanniness of Ottilie's destructive uncontrollable excess of meaning emerges most visibly in relation to buildings in the novel. Houses here are constantly vulnerable: the manor house is invaded almost to bursting by Luciane's swarm of guests, the Count and the Baroness, the Englishmen, the boisterous Mittler, all with their own disruptive passions. Even the deeply hidden mill and the small estate to which Eduard flees from his difficulties can be found and entered.[15] The houses in the village are subject to destruction by flooding, while the chapel and churchyard run the risk of well-intentioned restoration, for the neighboring family sees Charlotte's beautification of the churchyard as a desecration, and the architect's loving preservation of ancient artifacts depends, as Ottilie's diary attests, on desecrating tombs. It is hard to imagine that Charlotte's generous donations to the church at the end of the novel will preserve the privacy of Eduard's and Ottilie's resting place for all eternity. Worse yet, houses are subject to abandonment when family bonds fail—the English lord has left his home because his son takes no interest in it, and by the end of the novel there will be no normal family life in Eduard's own castle. In his dedication of the foundation stone for the summer house the mason makes clear that the treasures buried in it, a record of the past, can come to light only when the building, not yet even built, will be destroyed, just as the architect's treasured artifacts of the past require destruction of the tombs that preserved them for posterity. Finally, Ottilie is not safe from Eduard in the inn as she tries to return to the safety of her school—even though he does not intend to force himself upon her. Instead, their fatal confrontation follows from the malicious mischance of a door locking itself, from the instability of houses per se.

Nevertheless, the potential for destruction and death is most explicitly associated with Ottilie. Charlotte claims her moss hut can accommodate four, but the arrival of Ottilie as fourth eventually destroys the close family relations it represents; Ottilie becomes, ultimately, the ghost that destroys the home, rather as the giant ancestral ghost destroys the castle of Otranto. The summer house is consistently associated with her explosive potential—when she relocates it, at the cornerstone laying, and at the framing celebration (*Richtfest*), where her initials disrupt the preparations and where she effectively supplants Charlotte as mistress of the house. She and Charlotte between them effectively desacralize the chapel by making it an aesthetic outlet for Charlotte's landscaping and for Ottilie's painting. The chapel is ultimately not so much appropriated as a family vault, but rather forcefully transformed into a monument to adultery. It upends the notion of the church as guarantor of social order. Charlotte and Eduard intend at the beginning to establish a home (*Heim*); they spend the novel failing to create such hominess (*Heimlichkeit*) and the failure is measured by the problems of building and protecting actual homes. All they accomplish in the novel is to nearly finish the summer house. The novel turns on building a house, a home, as well as a secure marriage. In effect, the quest of the novel is to establish *Heimlichkeit*, and it fails miserably. Instead the characters build neither houses nor marriages: the world of the novel remains *unheimlich* ("not homey," but the word also means "uncanny") and the destroyer of marriage is none other than Ottilie. At the catastrophic high point, when she finally realizes the implications of her love for Eduard and refuses to agree to a divorce, she has just spent the night in a trance with her head in Charlotte's lap, a situation that reminds her of an earlier night spent the same way as she listened to Charlotte describe her situation as an orphan and prescribed rules, her orbit or *Bahn*, for herself that she now realizes she has violated. The return of the repressed comes together with the literal meaning of the imagery: Ottilie is the principle of *Unheimlichkeit*, of uncanniness, in the novel.

The novel offers a single bulwark against its swirling floods of emotion, Ottilie's firm decision to renounce her love for Eduard at the end. The term used is "renunciation" (*Entsagung*), but it only applies to feelings consciously acknowledged. It is obviously to be taken seriously and becomes a central theme in late Goethe, especially in *Wilhelm Meisters Wanderjahre*, which is subtitled "The Renunciants." Nevertheless, it is important to recognize the relation of renunciation to consciousness and also its limitations. It applies only to a self-control exerted in the face of previously unrecognized feelings that have only just been acknowledged. Thus Charlotte and the Captain, who have been aware of their attraction to one another from early on and have avoided one another, do not suffer the pain of renunciation at the end and do not, in Charlotte's eyes, deserve to marry (461). Renunciation pertains to the economy of the conscious mind, not to that of the unconscious. Furthermore, renunciation is in Goethe something very difficult, almost impossible to achieve. Ottilie can achieve it only by starving herself to death; Eduard tries to imitate her and fails. In the *Wanderjahre* renunciation is increasingly imposed by the constraints of reality. It has more to do with accepting the reality principle than with denying the id. The thrust of the argument here is not to deny the importance of renunciation, a central and properly revered concept in Goethe studies, but to demonstrate the presence of its unarticulated counterterm, repression.

Die Wahlverwandtschaften has taken events that in the 1790s Goethe and his contemporaries could still only express as sometimes bizarre fairy tales or as gothic novels and shaped them into narratives that make psychological sense. These new narratives, both the novel and its inserted novella, stage inchoate feelings that the characters do not even know they have, but that nevertheless change their lives irremediably. The characters can interpret their situation only in the antiquated language of the supernatural; they consider themselves exposed to invisible demonic forces. Only the narrator is just barely able to explain situations in psychological terms. Goethe has thus transformed the supernatural into a legible vehicle for the subconscious.

The mechanism, we now see clearly, derives from reversing the normal procedure of allegory.[16] In morality drama or in baroque and rococo art, the meaning of allegory is transparent—what you see is what it means. But in *Die Wahlverwandtschaften* seeing diverges from meaning and often opposes it. Eduard, for example, seems to take over the role of Ottilie's father when he wants to prevent an injury from the locket with her father's portrait, but really he is clearing the father out of his way. Similarly, innocent Ottilie and the mistress of love's mill appear here in the same shape. Celebrating laying the cornerstone of the *Lusthaus* and the setting of the rooftree simultaneously prepare its and the next generation's destruction. Like the word *heimlich*, which also means "unheimlich," everything in this novel means both itself and its opposite. With his maelstrom of symbols that are simultaneously literal and figurative Goethe creates a double vision of consciousness and subconsciousness that allows the reader to see both the surface and the contrary double lurking beneath, to see into the psychological depths.

From here it is a tiny step to Freud. His primary definition of the uncanny has already made its way effortlessly into the discussion—the return of the repressed. In his classic essay on the uncanny, "Das Unheimliche" (1919), Freud calls particular attention to Schelling's definition of the word: "Uncanny refers to everything that is supposed to remain a secret, in hiding, and has nevertheless emerged" (Unheimlich sei alles, was ein Geheimnis, im Verborgenen bleiben sollte und hervorgetreten ist).[17] Freud could have derived his categories for the uncanny as well from *Die Wahlverwandtschaften* as from E. T. A. Hoffmann's "Der Sandmann." His list includes fate, death, intuitions, the unclear boundary between reality and fantasy, animism and magic, the ambivalence of the doppelgänger, which is both the self and a previously overcome stage of the self (258–59). Perhaps the most important is Freud's description of the specific uncanniness of Hoffmann's gothic novel *Elixiere des Teufels* (Elixirs of the Devil, 1815): "too much of the same thing heaped up" (257; zu viel Gleichartiges gehäuft). By this he means that it contains too many repetitions of characters and names from one generation to the next. This is precisely the problem of language running riot just identified as the uncanniness of *Die Wahlverwandtschaften*.

What Freud leaves out of account explicitly, however, is the relation to fairy tale. Indeed, he denies uncanniness to the fairy tale because it makes no claims to realism (272). Evidently he did not classify the Romantic narratives so important for this argument as fairy tales. Nevertheless, the kind of representation identified here as specific to Goethe's use of fairy tale, the allegorization and concretization of not yet recognized psychological patterns, is essential to Freud's hermeneutics. He reads the mechanical doll Olimpia in "Der Sandmann," for example, as "a complex worked loose from Nathaniel that confronts him as a person" (256n; ein von Nathaniel losgelöster Komplex, die ihm als Person entgegentritt); he also recognizes the importance of children's literal understanding of idioms that adults do not take seriously (251). It is precisely the uncanniness of Ottilie to make idioms take on concrete life.

In the secularized world of the eighteenth century, the uncanny and the supernatural were acceptable only when they could be rationally explained. But to explain the supernatural is actually to explain it away, and an explanation that destroys the phenomenon it sets out to explain is absurd. The genius of Goethe's technique is to allow the reader to see the contrariness beneath the surface without describing it, without explaining it. He renders the horror of the uncanny not by describing its effect on his characters or by explaining it. Instead he frees it from the explanation that would be demanded by a rational psychology by revealing the doubleness of all language and all feeling. It is this spectacle of self-contradicting allegory upon which the Romantics built and that the nineteenth-century gradually conceptualized into the discourse of depth psychology.

Goethe's Ghosts

By revealing the doubleness of language and feeling, Goethe gives a new vitality and concreteness to the pre-Romantic discourse of the supernatural: like his use of fairy tale it transmits to the Romantics and simultaneously the moderns the language of ghosts for the subconscious. Just as Goethe is not normally considered a gothic writer (despite the reading of *Die Wahlverwandtschaften* above), he is also not considered a writer concerned with ghosts. This misconception derives in large part from the fact that improbable ghost stories model poor storytelling in *Unterhaltungen deutscher Ausgewanderten*. Nevertheless, there are significant ghosts in his work, from early to late, but especially in *Faust*, part 2.[18] The steps in his adoption of the ghost to represent internal identity serve here to recapitulate the development of his representation of the uncanny. They lead from an essentially rationalist psychology that gives way in the middle of the 1790s to metaphors for what comes from within—first memories, then increasingly what has been trying not to be remembered. At the same time they become increasingly visual and visible, and thereby reveal the essential ghostliness, the essential uncanniness of the poetic act that underlies Goethe's classicism.

The first significant ghost comes in *Triumph der Empfindsamkeit* (The Triumph of Sensibility, 1778), where the "ghost" (*Gespenst*) refers to the illusory, indeed staged, appearance of a beloved, ideal woman named Mandandane. In this satire of sentimentality the hero pining for his beloved receives the ludicrous oracle,

> When a palpable ghost dies from fair hands,
> And the linen sack hands over its innards,
> When the mended bride is wedded to her lover:
> Then shall peace and joy, o asker, enter thy house. (WA I.17:9)

> (Wenn wird ein greiflich Gespenst von schönen Händen entgeistert,
> Und der leinene Sack seine Geweide verleiht,
> Wird die geflickte Braut mit dem Verliebten vereinet:
> Dann kommt Ruhe und Glück, Fragender, über dein Haus.)

The prophecy becomes clear at the end: the "ghost" that has seemed to be a woman named Mandandane in the possession of the wrong lover is in fact a doll stuffed with sentimental novels, including *Werther*. According to the oracle, the ghost is *greiflich*, graspable with the hand. But a ghost that can be grasped is also *begreiflich*, comprehensible. The staged ghost of this early satire thus corresponds to the rationalist psychology of *Werther*. Similarly, when Jealousy is labeled a "ghost" (*Gespenst*) in the singspiel *Erwin und Elmire* (1787 version, WA 1.11:301), the metaphor documents an early explicit connection of the supernatural to the emotions. In *Wilhelm Meisters Lehrjahre* ghosts are again associated with the stage (in the *Hamlet* production, the mysterious woman [who later turns out to have been Philine] in Wilhelm's bed immediately afterward, and the Harper). They are also consistently associated with obscure, unfathomable identity, as in the earlier two texts.[19]

The development is mature in *Italienische Reise*. In Sicily, the extreme point of Goethe's penetration into the otherness of Italy, ghosts pursue him in the gardens in Palermo:

> It is truly a misfortune to be pursued and tempted by all sorts of spirits! Early this morning I went to the public garden with the firm, peaceful intention of continuing my poetic dreams, but before I realized it, I was waylaid by a different ghost that had been sneaking about after me the last few days. (HA 11:266)

> (Es ist ein wahres Unglück, wenn man von vielerlei Geistern verfolgt und versucht wird! Heute früh ging ich mit dem festen ruhigen Vorsatz, meine dichterischen Träume fortzusetzen, nach dem öffentlichen Garten, allein, eh' ich mich's versah, erhaschte mich ein anderes Gespenst, das mir schon diese Tage nachgeschlichen.)

The poetic dreams disrupted here are the plans for the drama *Nausikaa* and the ghost stalking him is none other than the *Urpflanze* (primal plant), an idea that drove his thinking about plant development for several years. *Nausikaa* was to be a classical tragedy, presumably somewhere in style between *Iphigenie* and *Die natürliche Tochter*; as the women in the two completed plays are threatened, so in this case the play itself is threatened, indeed destroyed. The ghost ironically stalking Goethe is the fate stalking *Nausikaa*. But it is also something from inside Goethe—a memory of earlier efforts, a driving interest in science that the artist blossoming in Italy was trying to put behind him as he gave rebirth to himself. It is his own repressed subself.

The ghost of Goethe's uncanny inner self leads directly to the Helena of *Faust*, part 2, an illusion that Faust makes real by embracing the paradox that illusion is the highest reality. Although she appears in act 1 (like the effigy of Mandandane) as a ghost on a stage set, he stabilizes her by repeated dreams of her conception, by fetching her shade from the underworld, and, triumphantly, by recreating her in the language of Greek tragedy, the culture that invented her. With each successive iteration she becomes both more real and more unreal, more uncanny. Although she appears as a real woman in the first scene of act 3, Mephistopheles/Phorkyas has little difficulty making her lose her sense of her own identity, and in the second scene Faust has little difficulty updating her language by a thousand years; she is a ghost at least temporarily controllable by the disciplined imagination. And her counterpart is the Sorge of act 5, who, like Helena, is "unbegreiflich." Like Goethe's *Urpflanze*, both are projections of Faust's vision onto the world around him invisible to all others, are his inner life understood as subconscious and as source of creative imagination.[20] E. T. A. Hoffmann's robot Olimpia in "Der Sandmann" returns to Goethe's earliest model of the ghost, the staged doll of *Triumph der Empfindsamkeit*, but her power is more closely related to the uncanniness and anxiety with which Goethe had invested the image in the intervening years.

The power of ghosts derives less from their uncanniness than from their visuality, since the subconscious does not operate discursively. In "Alexis und Dora," Goethe's idyllic elegy of 1796, *Sorge* makes a startlingly visual appearance just after Alexis has rushed to sea on his first independent journey moments after a routine neighborly farewell visit turned into an unexpected betrothal:

> When Care approaches, cold and horribly calm.
> Not the torch of the Furies, the baying of the dogs of hell
> Frightens the criminal so much, there in the fields of desperation,
> As the calm ghost frightens me as it shows me the fair one
> From afar: the gate of the garden is really still open!
> And another man comes! (HA 1:189, lines 138–43)

> (Wenn die Sorge sich kalt, gräßlich gelassen, mir naht.
> Nicht der Erinnyen Fackel, das Bellen der höllischen Hunde
> Schreckt den Verbrecher so, in der Verzweiflung Gefild,
> Als das gelass'ne Gespenst mich schreckt, das die Schöne von fern mir
> Zeiget: die Türe steht wirklich des Gartens noch auf!
> Und ein anderer kommt!)

The appearance of this strongly personified Sorge leads to an explosion of visual imagery—Furies, the underworld, the open garden gate, the threatening Other approaching. The images of the underworld are formally calm, *gelassen*, like the classical figures of the Orestes operas and plays, especially of Goethe's own scene of Orest's healing in his underworld of the subconscious. And the ghost creates a second dramatic scene within the first, for it shows him his beloved in an unguarded garden with another lover already approaching. Only having seen this fear as a vision from within himself can Alexis then articulate it. A letter to Charlotte von Stein from the previous decade testifies to the reality of this phenomenon as a psychological experience for Goethe; he wrote on February 18, 1782:

> And then, Lotte, I have a care in my heart a notion that torments
> me, and has worried me for a while you must allow me to tell you,
> you must reassure me. On pins and needles I await the moment
> of seeing you again. You must forgive me. It is imaginings that
> arise from my love, ghosts that terrify me, and that only you can
> disperse. (WA 4.5:262)

> (Und dann Lotte, ich habe eine Sorge auf dem Herzen eine Grille
> die mich plagt, und schon lange ängstigt du must mir erlauben daß
> ich dir sie sage, du must mich aufrichten. Mit Schmerzen erwart'
> ich die Stunde da ich dich wiedersehe. Du must mir verzeihen. Es
> sind Vorstellungen die aus meiner Liebe aufsteigen, Gespenster die
> mir furchtbaar sind, und die nur du zerstreuen kannst.)[21]

If *Sorge* is an allegory of anxiety, the ghost is an allegory of the way anxiety comes to consciousness. Goethe's great contribution was the recognition that since it was not accessible to language, it must be made visible through allegory.

Thus while older discourses readily shine through in Goethe—stoicism, melancholy, the sublime—their meaning has changed. It is no longer a matter of controlling passions or even of being transported by them. Once the subject is interiorized, the issue becomes rather simultaneously obscuring them and manifesting them, making the surface both visible and transparent. The epigraph to "Elegien II" in the collected poems—which "Alexis und Dora" immediately followed as the first text in the section—articulates the connection between the visual and passion. It reads: "Images, like passions, / Like to attach themselves to poems" (WA 1.1:263; Bilder so wie Leidenschaften / Mögen gern am Liede haften). The poem makes clear that it is actually reflecting on and redefining this apparently traditional association of imagery and passion as Alexis ruminates to himself:

> Thus the poet often places a riddle,
> Artfully twined of words, in the ear of the company.
> Everyone likes the rare combination of delicate images,
> But they still miss the word that safeguards the meaning.
> Once it is discovered, then everyone feels happy (HA 1: 185–86, lines
> 25–29)

> (So legt der Dichter ein Rätsel,
> Künstlich mit Worten verschränkt, oft der Versammlung in's Ohr.
> Jeden freuet die seltne, der zierlichen Bilder Verknüpfung,
> Aber noch fehlet das Wort, das die Bedeutung verwahrt.
> Ist es endlich entdeckt, dann heitert sich jedes Gemüth auf)

Alexis speaks of poetry as a series of visual images that suddenly fall into a pattern of meaning at a single word; he uses the simile however, to describe his just experienced recognition of his passion for Dora. Despite having known her for years, only as he departs does he realize that he has always loved her. Thus the reference of the simile is precisely the process of becoming aware of the unknown self through pictures and it confirms the relation between the imaginative and poetic processes and self-knowledge.

Correspondingly, veiling is not just hiding, but an expression of repression as positive achievement. In "Zueignung" (Dedication, 1784), the poet receives "the veil of poetry from the hand of Truth" (HA 1:152, line 96; Der Dichtung Schleier aus der Hand der Wahrheit). But Goethe was familiar with the Enlightenment usage of veiling as a negative disguise that obscures the truth. *Iphigenie* still operates largely with this version of the motif: the oracle's instructions to fetch the statue of Diana were, Orest decides, a *Schleier* (veil, blindfold) bound about their heads by the gods, and even Iphigenie's veil cannot protect Orest from the Furies. The goal of the play is to free the truth from its veils, to free Iphigenie from the repressed memories of her violent past. But such truthfulness and truth soon struck the play's readers as naive, or in Goethe's words, "verteufelt human." In this play veiling is also beneficent, particularly the repeated motif of Diana hiding Iphigenie in clouds to rescue her (as Lila in an occasional play for the court of the same name [1777] is protected from a demon by her veil). This second aspect quickly comes to the fore in Goethe's usage. Covering what is better forgotten becomes a healthy gesture, as when some well-meaning person casts an oriental tapestry over the collapsed fourth king at the end of the "Märchen." Lifting veils becomes negative, especially when the topic is science. The point is to look not under the veil, but outside of it as he asserted in the epigram "Kore," in the collection *Zahme Xenien*. Like Diana's rescuing clouds in *Iphigenie*, the veil becomes the stuff of nature, the swirling fog in *Briefe aus der Schweiz* (as also in *Hermann und Dorothea*, and again in the "Novelle" of 1827), and, finally, Helena's veil transforming itself into clouds at the beginning of act 4 of *Faust*, part 2.

Wafting veils are the stuff of later eighteenth-century classicism—in ballet, on Wedgwood vases, in the costuming of Goethe's own plays. Goethe's veiled women are not only classical, especially in the 1790s, but also often ghosts (in the singspiel *Scherz, List und Rache* [Jest, Cunning, and Revenge,1784] or Helena). Unlike Winckelmann's nude male bodies or, more importantly, Rousseau's longing for transparency, Goethe focuses on the veiled female; and unlike the Romantics, who were particularly fond of the veiled Isis, the removal of veils in Goethe rarely reveals the banality of the every day (as it does in Novalis's "Das Märchen von Hyazinth und Rosenblütchen"). The point of the veil is to hide and reveal simultaneously. The veil is not only poetry, it is also the kind of transference repression discussed in Chapter 7. As the veiling fog obscures and reveals the depths on the Furka Pass, it makes the landscape more interesting, more uncanny, more meaningful than it would seem otherwise. In effect, the veil creates the sense of interiority for the self; it makes it a place of mystery for the truth to reside in now that the heavens have been demystified. Goethe's image reveals his own sense of the necessary constructedness of our interiority. The self is not what is hidden, but what must be created by being hidden, what must be created by repression, without which there could be no Freudian processes of analysis.

It is common to associate this new serenity with Goethe's classicism, and that makes sense.[22] But the creation of the uncanny through repression is not negatively repressive: it is neither hegemonic nor escapist. By connecting the unconscious to imagination Goethe puts the finishing touch on the interior self he inherited from Rousseau. The subconscious is no longer only a dangerous source of anxiety or home of forces that must be controlled, but also the source of creative power. The self that can transform the one into the other, that can release the energy of the interior self for constructive purposes, is the fully developed, healthy self. Under these circumstances repression becomes a new kind of psychological achievement: it enables the subject to maintain its stability and even creative power in the face of elemental threats to identity and existence—a skill necessary to any thinking person in the age of the French Revolution—and after. Most important of all, this repressive style of Goethe's classicism was the first step in representing this newly complex inner self.

Classicism and Goethe's
Emotional Regime

In his autobiography Goethe revealed his works to be "fragments of a great confession"—so convincingly, that generations of readers, professional and lay alike, considered his poetry above all "poetry of experience."[1] It is known that Goethe was susceptible to powerful emotions, to great enthusiasm and to profound depression. On more than one occasion he suffered the kinds of physical and emotional collapses experienced by Werther, Tasso, Wilhelm Meister, and Faust. Even in the years of his maturity, as the privy councillor resented by the friends of his youth, he was still capable of casting himself to the floor to mourn the death of his infants,[2] or at age seventy-four of writing passionate love poetry and proposing to the nineteen-year-old Ulrike von Levetzow. He also had repeated experiences of rebirth through renunciation, of turning from passionate self-involvement to new life in the world, of accepting reality. And as his subtle analyses of anxiety and the uncanny surely demonstrate, he had considerable experience with nuances of emotion and with how to deal with them.

But the regime was not just personal. Goethe's powerful descriptions of emotional upheaval captured the attention of his age, as witnessed by his lifelong fame as the author of *Die Leiden des jungen Werther*. His importance for subsequent ages, this book has been arguing, was his depiction of repressed emotion. In his own day, only the literary avant-garde understood how his increasingly tamed, "classical" works continued the psychological labor first undertaken in *Werther*, how they replaced the cosmic referent of an older allegorical style of representation with a psychological referent. It is not that Goethe discovered or invented the interior subject; that work had been already under way for a century when he wrote *Werther*. His unique contribution to the chain was adapting the rhetoric of allegory, which made it possible to represent what was invisible or even ineffable, to what was ineffable deep within the self rather than high above it.

I have focused on Goethe's place in a narrative of the emergence of depth psychology, but he occupies an equally pivotal place in many other representative accounts of Western subjectivity, three of which I would like to describe briefly here—psychological analysis in the novel, Michel Foucault's historical analysis of subjectivity, and Norbert Elias's psychosocial analysis of the civilizing process. Thus I will conclude by pointing toward some other ways that the development demonstrated in this book made the emotional regime of the last two centuries, in part at least, Goethe's.

Most obviously, the emergence of psychological analysis in the novel of the nineteenth century—whether weighted more toward ethical and epistemological dimensions, as in George Eliot and Herman Melville, or more toward the transient nuances of thought and feeling, as in Henry James and, later, Virginia Woolf—might have already occurred to readers of my introduction. I point to it at the end, however, rather than there, because my reading of Goethe makes sense out of the strong allegorical component in much nineteenth-century fiction. The critical emphasis on realism in the period makes the allegory often harder to trace. Dickens is obviously an allegorist, but the tight connection of his allegory both to eighteenth-century satire and to gothic narrative obscure his Goethean psychological projection. Allegory emerges most clearly when it falls out of balance with explicit psychological analysis, as in late Hawthorne and Melville. While the often bizarre allegorical style of Dickens and the Americans might have been mediated in part through Thomas Carlyle's *Sartor Resartus*, these authors all knew Carlyle's translation of *Wilhelm Meister* as well.

Melville's *Pierre* (1852) offers a good example of Goethe's explicit presence behind such strange allegorizing. At the beginning of this meandering narrative the young hero is already engaged to angelic Lucy, with the approval of his beloved mother. A mysterious portrait of his recently dead father and a mysterious young woman named Isabel draw him from his initial innocent bliss; Isabel turns out to be his half sister, whose existence has been suppressed, and Pierre must choose between his passion for her and being dispossessed by his mother. He and Isabel flee to the city, where they live in poverty as Pierre tries to support her by his writing. Lucy joins them; Pierre eventually dies in prison mourned by both. Like Wilhelm Meister, Pierre seeks his identity—

not on the stage, to be sure, but in nature, in love, in philosophy, in his own writing. For any reader of Goethe, it is evident that the mysterious heroine of the novel, the musical Isabel who is both the beloved of his soul and his half sister, is modeled on the musical waif Mignon of *Wilhelm Meisters Lehrjahre*, as well as on the Beautiful Soul of the same novel and the shy Ottilie of *Die Wahlverwandtschaften* for good measure.[3] In other words, the ideal figure who embodies the inchoate goal of Pierre's quest for identity comes directly from three women in Goethe who represent the same ideal for the various men around them, who are strikingly inept at living in the world, and who are essentially inarticulate and incomprehensible figures of the self within. Only an allegorical reading of Isabel as Pierre's inchoate identity brings logic to the bizarre plot.

The book's grim position is that such a self is not to be found, and certainly not found in the depths: late in the book the narrator identifies Pierre's initial failure to realize that he is to find himself and the world not in great books, but in the "Switzerland of his soul" (331), in the "well of his childhood" (332). The passage echoes a much terser, famous line in *Werther*, "I turn back into myself and find an entire world" (HA 6:13; Ich kehre in mich selbst zurück und finde eine Welt), where Werther finds the world in himself. The narrator jeers at his hero (and presumably at the Goethe echo), "Yet now, forsooth, because Pierre began to see through the first superficiality of the world, he fondly weens he has come to the unlayered substance. But, far as any geologist has yet gone down into the world, it is found to consist of nothing but surface stratified on surface. To its axis, the world being nothing but superinduced superficies." The passage continues with the metaphor of penetrating a pyramid to find only an empty sarcophagus—"appallingly vacant as vast is the soul of a man!" (Melville 332). The skepticism about the existence of an interior self corresponds to an abrupt shift in attitude toward Goethe, who in this part of the book appears as an "inconceivable coxcomb" (352), a "gold-laced virtuoso" (353), like Plato and Spinoza, the member of a guild of "self-imposters" (245). Disparaging as the allusions are, they reveal Goethe's pervasive presence in the novel's form, goals, and ego ideal.

Goethe mattered to Melville both philosophically and stylistically. Melville not only picks up the Romantic allegorizing (above, Chapter 8), but also reflects on it and on its sources. *Pierre* travels from an almost fairy-tale pastoral world in which Pierre is the pampered son of wealth to the grim poverty of the city. In effect the novel moves from the world of German Romantic narrative to that of realistic English narrative, though the latter turns out not to be a world in which Melville is much at home. Identity is still a matter of philosophy for Melville, rather than psychology, and it remains to others like Eliot, James, and Woolf to make their less heroic, more typical characters interesting essentially for their psychology.

Goethe also has a place in Michel Foucault's grand narrative of subjectivity, the main focus of his late work. In 1981–82 Foucault delivered a series of lectures at the Collège de France published under the title *The Hermeneutics of the Subject* that placed next to "self-knowledge" (*gnothi seauton*), the traditional cornerstone of Western subjectivity, a phenomenon called "care of the self" (*epimeleia heautou*), which he considered of even greater importance. The lectures trace this tradition of care of the self from Plato to early Christianity, but the first lecture offers an overview of its longer shadow: in Plato self-knowledge appears as a subordinate concept to care of the self, which involves both soul and body; in Hellenistic and Roman Stoicism care of the self has to do with strengthening the self to encounter the vicissitudes of the world, and only in Christianity, with its recursive recuperation of Platonism, does care of the self become unambiguously self-knowledge as examination of conscience and thus more focused on ethics and epistemology than on emotional health. With what Foucault calls "the Cartesian moment," the decisive shift to a secular culture in European modernism, knowledge and spirituality part company altogether, and self-knowledge eclipses care of the self. The nineteenth century, Foucault continues, rediscovers spirituality as a form of subjectivity in Marxism and then psychoanalysis (*The Hermeneutics of the Subject*, 14–19).

In this scheme Goethe's *Faust* is a "last nostalgic expression of a knowledge of spirituality" (311)[4] descended from the tradition of care of the self. Foucault identifies the loss of spirituality registered in *Faust* as having "disappeared with the Enlightenment," so that the play is "the sad greeting of the birth of knowledge of intellectual knowledge" (311). He points to the Senecan language of the first forty-three lines of *Faust*'s opening monologue (written ca. 1772–73, thus before the sequence of texts addressed in this book). Although it does not discuss the relation to Rousseau, Foucault's narrative constitutes the perfect background for Goethe's ethical problems with Rousseau as I have outlined them. Rousseau's interior self appears as the modern turn in the development Foucault began to trace. Since, after Descartes, a self defined by knowledge but grounded in religion no longer made sense, Rousseau grounded it in psychology instead. To use Foucault's language, Goethe identified Rousseau's failure to acknowledge the ethical dimension to which the epistemological self had been subordinated by its alliance to the self to be cared for. Thus Goethe's ambivalence toward Rousseau registers that Rousseau's version of self-knowledge displaces the older, Senecan care of the self. Fortitude and moral self-culti-vation yielded to an inward retreat that required, in Goethe's view, ethical reinforcement. Foucault also does not pursue the possibility that *Faust* and Goethe's other works begin the nineteenth-century reconnection to the spiri-tuality alluded to in Marx and Freud. That would have been well beyond the scope of his book and has been, in part, the task of mine.

In any case Foucault's allusion to *Faust* not only affirms Goethe's place at the turning point to modernity invoked at the beginning of my book, but also locates his rhetoric of the unconscious in a broader historical spectrum of sub-jectivity that in turn illuminates Goethe's extension of concern for the subject to mental health. The heroine of Goethe's *Pandora*, as the fragment stands, is Epimeleia, who cares for her reflective father, Epimetheus, and galvanizes her unreflective uncle, Prometheus, into caring for others. The name "Epimeleia" does not appear among Epimetheus's daughters in Goethe's usual mythologi-cal reference source, Benjamin Hederich's *Gründliches Lexicon Mythologicum*, so that the name here shows that Goethe had the Stoic tradition described by Foucault in mind.[5] Epimeleia suffers from the unjustified jealous rage of her lover, Prometheus's own son Phileros, whose name combines two kinds of love—that which has an object (phil) and that which seeks its own satisfaction (eros). Phileros's solipsistic blindness had precipitated him into his anger at Epimeleia; his eros is corrected by a fall into the sea and subsequent rebirth.[6] Phileros is cured of Rousseau's ethical faults as Goethe understood them: he neither grounds identity exclusively in self-knowledge nor elevates jealousy of the other's hidden interior over the care of the self that leads to self-control and care for others. Inspired, finally, by Epimeleia, Prometheus unites her with her beloved. Goethe has moved *epimeleia* from Senecan ethics to psychology just when he was making selfhood psychological. As already seen, the tension between *sorgen um* (care as anxiety) and *sorgen für* (care for others) was al-ready at work in Goethe's classical plays around 1790. Heidegger also read his Goethe,[7] and the path leads further from Heidegger to Foucault.

Foucault identifies healing as a substantial part of care for the self, and healing is the crucial act of *Pandora*, as it is of most other works of what is called "Goethe's classicism" (and his later works as well). Indeed, Goethe's Pandora brings poetry and the arts into the world, not illness as in the classical myth. Goethe wasted time in his father's eyes by writing poetry in Leipzig and by studying medicine in Strasbourg when he should have been finishing his law degree. He talks repeatedly in his autobiography about the healing function of writing to master emotional devastation, and healing is a prominent theme in many of his works, especially in the works of his classical period. I have shown how Goethe's preoccupation with anxiety was associated above all with his journey to Italy, the space most identified with his classicism, which in turn is connected to control and repression, both of which turn out to be liberating, healing. That ultimately is the importance of the link demonstrated here between Goethe and Freud. Goethe acted on his nostalgia for the Stoic mode to try to heal and correct the imbalanced notion of selfhood as knowledge, as the rudderless drifting of Rousseau, rather than as process. Such healing is the essence of Goethe's classicism.

Goethe's classicism also plays a noticeable role in Norbert Elias's epic psychosocial analysis of modern Europe, *The Civilizing Process*. Using Freudian terminology, Elias argues that internal constraints to drives and affect (Freud's "superego" and what Elias also identifies as "the habit of foresight") are instilled in humans by upbringing. Socially desirable behavior becomes automatic as socially undesirable or even dangerous affects are repressed. What originally derives from fear of parents, masters, or social superiors appears to consciousness as free will (*The Civilizing Process*, 127). As social constraints are internalized, ever larger numbers of people can live together over ever larger areas with a minimum of violence and with ever increasing amounts of differentiation, or individualization. Elias identifies this "civilizing process" as characteristic of all human society but visible in its most highly developed form in the West. He locates the decisive internalization of restraint in the absolutist courts of the late seventeenth century and lays out the mechanisms by which this habitus passed from the aristocratic to the bourgeois classes.

Goethe's classicism is a prime example of the transference of court culture from aristocracy to bourgeoisie: the high bourgeois Goethe moves to court, is ennobled, produces texts that become the models of education for a century and a half in bourgeois Germany and inculcate values of civilization. So important is this example that Elias places it at the very front of his book, which otherwise ranges from the Middle Ages to the twentieth century, and discusses as the starting point of his whole endeavor the relation of the French term "civilization" to "culture" the equivalent term established in Germany by German classicism. Elias explains that emotion became more nuanced in Goethe's day as a result of increasingly complex social conditions. In this context the consummate use of repression detailed in the chapters above—not only as a tragic theme for heroes like Tasso or Faust, or as a form of education, as in

Wilhelm Meister, but above all as a technique for representing interiority, as in the chapter on anxiety—is precisely the process described by Elias.

This argument may seem inconsistent with Elias's careful avoidance of the language of interiority. The 1968 "Postscript" to *The Civilizing Process* systematically dispenses with the standard dichotomies applied to the emergent self of the eighteenth century, such as rational/irrational, individual/society, inner/outer. Indeed, it often sounds remarkably like Melville's satiric rejection of the emptiness of interiority in *Pierre*. Yet Elias grounds his resistance to such language in Goethe himself. Elias rejects the dichotomies of selfhood because, he believes, social development can be understood only in terms of process, not of alternatives, and he caps his argument with Goethe, who "once expressed the idea that nature has neither core nor shell and that in her there is neither inside nor outside. This is true of human beings as well" (480). The reference is to the following lines in Goethe's poem "Epirrhema": "Nichts ist drinnen, nichts ist draußen: / Denn was innen, das ist außen" (HA 1:358; Nothing is inside, nothing is outside: / For what is inside is also outside). For Elias, to take any of these abstract dichotomies literally is to reify a metaphor that came into being only because there did not yet exist appropriate conceptual terminology. Elias's argument about the relation of metaphor to conceptual language is the same as mine about Goethe and Freud, with the additional warning not to reify Freud's language. Conceptual language must continue to abstract and rationalize without literalizing; the conceptual language of today will appear metaphoric to a subsequent generation that lives in an even more complex, more rationalized, more civilized state of development than our own. At Elias's level of abstraction concept fades into metaphor, which is to say that science keeps getting absorbed into literature. For this strain of sociological analysis, then, Goethe becomes a figure of equal stature with Freud in the history of psychology.

The blend of abstraction and empiricism that characterizes Elias's analytical method is at bottom an outstanding example of Goethe's morphology. Elias's notion of experiment has nothing to do with hypothesis and testing; it consists rather in collecting large masses of empirical detail in order to discover the underlying pattern or law that makes sense of it—precisely the process discussed above in Chapter 5. His first specific example is an analysis of the changes in table manners in Europe over several hundred years; his arguments offer a mass of quotations, then discuss their trajectory, "the overall shape of the curve" that remains constant (90). Over and over Elias insists that periods, situations, voices, and even facts, must be understood on their own terms—as they functioned in their own time rather than in ours—and he hammers the point home by constantly shifting perspective on the same set of data from the late Middle Ages to the late eighteenth century, just as Goethe generated his experimental experiences by observing the target phenomenon from multiple viewpoints. *The Civilizing Process* is repetitive in the sense that the images in a kaleidoscope are repetitive: the small shifts and variations reveal constantly shifting symmetries and patterns whose relationship to one another are governed both by chance and also by underlying parameters that cannot be measured directly. Taken together with the frequent echoes and shadows of Goethe in *The Civilizing Process*, its subordination of humanity to the aggregates called "nature" and "society" and its resolutely secular focus on civilization as education through distancing affect control—renunciation and repression—are ultimately Goethe's values.

Healing and civilizing are the twin concerns of Goethe's classicism. Civilizing in the sense of *Kultur* and *Bildung* has always been recognized as central to it; healing has always been considered one of its important themes; and process (as in metamorphosis or the form of enhancement Goethe called "Steigerung") has always been acknowledged as its central modality. Recognizing Goethe's contribution to the thought processes of figures like Freud, Foucault, and Elias makes more evident how these three qualities go together. Civilization is a process of healing—not as Freud would have it, the discontents of civilization, but the discontents of the lack of civilization. Civilization for Goethe is learning to live in time, to live in what Hannah Arendt calls "the human condition," in which the results of action cannot be predicted. It is also the healing of anxiety, the overcoming of *Sorge* dramatized at the end of *Faust*.

To return for a moment to Goethe's most famous last word on emotion, Faust's encounter with personified anxiety ("Sorge") shortly before his death late in act 5 of part 2: Faust rejects her threat to freeze his ability to act, to deny him access to life in time.[8] By the terms of Faust's pact with Mephistopheles, "life in time" means "life in the present."[9] Anxiety distracts attention from the present to an uncertain future and is repressed, as we have seen, by focus on the eternal present of art.[10] But after Faust dismisses Sorge from his presence he does something unprecedented in *Faust*: he looks to the future. Thinking of the community that will labor to preserve its free existence on the land he has reclaimed from the sea, he pronounces the fatal satisfaction with the present moment that loses him his bet with Mephistopheles, but, however, only in anticipation, "In anticipation of such high happiness / I enjoy now the highest moment" (lines 11585–86; Im Vorgefühl von solchem hohen Glück / Genieß' ich jetzt den höchsten Augenblick). The crucial word *Vorgefühl* occurs only this once in all the twelve thousand lines of *Faust*, and indeed only seventeen times in Goethe's entire literary oeuvre. (Similarly, the word *Zukunft* [future] occurs only three times in the play and not at all in part 1). Scholarship has focused on the word *Vorgefühl* in relation to whether or not Faust loses his bet, but overlooked its crucial emotional connection to anxiety. Consistently the concept anticipates the development and exercise of one's full identity and inner powers, whether as a future member of the royal family in *Die natürliche Tochter* (HA 5: lines 473, 1089), or of one's triumph over inappropriate emotions, as in *Wilhelm Meisters Wanderjahre* (HA 8:239). Anticipation is the opposite of *Sorge*, here at the end of *Faust*, the ultimate triumph over anxiety.[11] Faust triumphs over his (and Goethe's) greatest emotional threat as the world is made a more civilized place, and both achievements result from taking charge of one's relation to time. In this much studied and much invoked moment of nineteenth-century Europe's most famous play it should now be clear how Goethe's emotional regime, German classicism, epitomizes a significant stage in the emergence of the modern subject.

NOTES

Unless otherwise noted, Goethe's works are cited to the Hamburger Ausgabe, abbreviated HA, or to the Weimarer Ausgabe, abbreviated WA. The verse dramas are cited to line number in the text of the HA. Unless otherwise noted, translations are my own.

CHAPTER 1. REPRESENTING SUBJECTIVITY

1. Arendt, *The Human Condition*, 38–39. On Goethe as the father of modernity, see, for example, Marshall Berman's *All That Is Solid Melts into Air* or the opening of Friedrich Kittler's *Aufschreibesysteme, 1800/1900*. On Rousseau as the pivotal figure, see, for example, Irving Babbitt's classic study *Rousseau and Romanticism*.

2. To be sure, Angus Nicholls argues that Goethe's centrality is a myth in "The Scientific Unconscious: Goethe's Post-Kantian Epistemology." Nevertheless, Paul Bishop makes a cogent argument in support of Goethe's importance in "The Unconscious from the Storm and Stress to Weimar Classicism," and even more importantly in his exhaustive two-volume study *Analytical Psychology and German Classical Aesthetics*.

3. Henri F. Ellenberger, *The Discovery of the Unconscious*, 571.

4. Ellenberger, *Discovery of the Unconscious*, 447, on Freud's self-identification with Goethe; cf. also the works by Paul Bishop cited above in n. 2; as well as Robert Holub, "From the Pedestal to the Couch," on how Goethe represented German identity for Freud; and, for the generally accepted view, see Henri Vermorel's piece "Goethe and Psychoanalysis."

5. On the importance of the "Nature" essay, not actually by Goethe but attributed to him in Freud's day, see, e.g., Ellenberger, *Discovery of the Unconscious*, 430. Only vols. 6 (*Hysterie und Angst*) and 9 (*Fragen der Gesellschaft, Ursprünge der Religion*) of the *Studienausgabe* seem to contain no Goethe references.

6. Theodor Reik, *Fragment of a Great Confession*, 8. The expression comes from Goethe's autobiography, *Dichtung und Wahrheit*, pt. 2, bk. 7: "Everything known about me from there [i.e. my literary works] are simply fragments of a great confession, which this little book daringly tries to make complete" (HA 9:282; Alles was daher von mir bekannt geworden, sind nur Bruchstücke einer großen Confession, welche vollständig zu machen dieses Büchlein ein gewagter Versuch ist).

7. Ellenberger, *Discovery of the Unconscious*, 727.

8. Jung, *Memories, Dreams, Reflections*, 35. See also Bishop's survey of Jung's interest in Goethe in *Analytical Psychology and German Classical Aesthetics*, 1:12–80.

9. For a history of Goethe's reputation in Germany, see Wolfgang Leppmann, *The German Image of Goethe*. David J. DeLaura has discussed his Victorian reception in "Heroic Egotism."

10. Jung and some of his followers wrote about Goethe rather more than the others. See Bishop, *Analytical Psychology and German Classical Aesthetics*.

11. Ellenberger, *Discovery of the Unconscious*, 207–8; and more recently and thoroughly, Matthew Bell, "Carl Gustav Carus and the Science of the Unconscious."

12. Carus, *Goethe: Zu dessen näherem Verständnis*, 139–40.

13. Important examples of the first category would be much of Michel Foucault's work, especially *The Hermeneutics of the Subject*, and Dror Wahrman's *The Making of the Modern Self*; major examples of the second include Charles Taylor's *Sources of the Self*; and Angus Nicholls and Martin Liebscher's collection *Thinking the Unconscious*; and of the third, work ranging from Ellenberger's *Discovery of the Unconscious* to specialized work on Moritz and late eighteenth-century psychiatry in the special section "Goethe and the Ego," edited by Fritz Breithaupt and Simon Richter in *Goethe Yearbook* 11, and Marshall Brown's *The Gothic Text*, esp. 92–111.

14. *Dichtung und Wahrheit*, part 2, book 7 (HA 9:264). This quote comes from his critique of Bodmer, published in 1811; in part 3 (1814) he refers repeatedly to psychology as the primary category of explanation and of literary attention, e.g., in book 13, 9:590 (psychology is opposed to didacticism); in book 14, 10:36 (basis for understanding others is understanding one's own "Gemüt"); in book 15, 10:72 (the tragedy in *Clavigo* is psychological rather than moral); part 4 (1833), book 17, 10:114 (interest in psychology rather than politics).

15. *Goethe's "Faust": The German Tragedy*, 145–52.

16. HA 8:486; *Wilhelm Meister's Journeyman Years*, 435.

17. Paul Bishop has blazed a trail in this direction in conceptual terms in his reading of *Faust* in relation to time and pleasure in the essay cited above, n. 2, and more fully in *Analytical Psychology*.

18. In this respect my approach differs from most of the recent work on identity, from Taylor to Wahrman, who sees it primarily as a formation of the French Revolution. I find myself closest in position to Hannah Arendt's highly nuanced description of the changes in the meaning of interiority in Western culture as developed in *The Human Condition* and especially in *The Life of the Mind*. The Goethe aphorism quoted immediately below is in fact central to Arendt's narrative.

19. Rousseau, *Discours sur l'origine et les fondements de l'inégalité, Œuvres complètes* 3:164. All subsequent references to Rousseau are to this edition, abbreviated *ŒC*; translations are my own.

20. Charles Taylor offers an effective description of how this interiority develops out of the anthropocentrism of the period, its location of being and, increasingly, causality in the self rather than in the cosmos or in a transcendent principle. It is also closely related to the development traced by Foucault in *The Order of Things*: in the course of the eighteenth century significance is increasingly located beneath surfaces rather than in the order spread out before one's eyes.

21. Indeed, do abducted women become so central in the eighteenth-century novel precisely because they offer a realistic, secular version of the necessary isolation for self-examination and the development of consciousness? This seems to me a rational alternative to gender-based explanations of the phenomenon.

22. Ernst Cassirer, *The Question of Jean-Jacques Rousseau*, 50.

23. *Reveries of the Solitary Walker*, 79.

24. As a problem of language, see, for example, Jacques Derrida, *De la grammatologie*; as psychosocial positioning, Thomas M. Kavanagh, *Writing the Truth*; as the nature of existence, Starobinski, *La transparence et l'obstacle*.

25. On Goethe's intention of *Werther* as a critique, see *Dichtung und Wahrheit*, pt. 3, bk. 13 (HA 9:578–84).

26. Only in Germany did the drama of the nineteenth century try to follow Goethe's lead in this respect, where Heinrich von Kleist, Franz Grillparzer, and Friedrich Hebbel are obvious examples; it is hard to think of dramatists of the period in English whose accomplishment compares to that of Henry James, Joseph Conrad, E. M. Forster, and Ford Maddox Ford, who brought this tradition in the novel to an end.

27. Based on my extended analysis in *The Persistence of Allegory*, chaps. 6 and 7; on opera and the emergence of Goethe's classical dramatic style, especially 201–17.

CHAPTER 2. GOETHE CONTRA ROUSSEAU ON PASSION

1. Except, of course, for Rousseau, only Chateaubriand exceeds Goethe in the number of index entries in Babbitt's classic, *Rousseau and Romanticism*.

2. See, for example, Carl Hammer, Jr., *Goethe and Rousseau*, for a general survey; the most thorough specific work on *Werther* and *Julie* is Erich Schmidt, *Richardson, Rousseau und Goethe*; and on the autobiographical works, Eugene L. Stelzig, *The Romantic Subject in Autobiography*. Gabrielle Bersier adverts frequently to *Julie* in *Goethes Rätselparodie der Romantik*, but her focus on the German Romantics makes Goethe's view of Rousseau himself less central to the study. Since the first version of this material was published, there has also appeared *Die Wahlverwandtschaften: Transformation und Kritik der Neuen Héloïse* by Anneliese Botond, which brings some new details to the discussion but rests on serious misreadings of Goethe's text. Maurice Funke's *From Saint to Psychotic* compares the texts thematically but ignores questions of influence or reaction.

3. Eric A. Blackall opened space for speculation on this topic in "Goethe's Silences." With regard specifically to the French Enlightenment, see Johann Peter Eckermann, *Gespräche mit Goethe*, 383 (January 3, 1830); Goethe commented to Eckermann: "It is unclear from my biography what an influence these men exerted on my youth and what it cost me to resist them and establish a truer relation to nature on my own" (Es geht aus meiner Biographie nicht deutlich hervor, was diese Männer für einen Einfluß auf meine Jugend gehabt und was es mich gekostet, mich gegen sie zu wehren und mich auf eigene Füße in ein wahreres Verhältnis zur Natur zu stellen). Chapter 3 below discusses how *Faust* struggles with Rousseau's definition of self in the world and in art. I have discussed how Goethe takes

issue in the *Wanderjahre* with some of Rousseau's more extreme followers of his ideas on pedagogy in *Goethe's Cyclical Narratives*, 87–97. In *The Romantic Subject in Autobiography*, Stelzig argues that Goethe's historicizing stance in *Dichtung und Wahrheit* represents a deliberate though tactfully unstated decision to avoid the excessive subjectivity of Rousseau's confessional mode (see esp. 137–48).

4. See M. Kay Flavell, "Goethe, Rousseau, and the 'Hyp.'"

5. For examples of stylization, see Hammer's somewhat random list in *Goethe and Rousseau*, 88–100; for more nuanced discussion, see Stelzig, *The Romantic Subject*.

6. The ribbon episode is the end of book 2 (*Les Confessions*, 84–86); the reference to Mme de Warens, in book 5 (195–97).

7. As the novella that grew into a novel, *Die Wahverwandtschaften* still betrays its origin in its close-knit structure; as the celebration of Goethe's victory over himself after his brief love for a woman forty years his junior, Minna Herzlieb, it is the expression of a specific stage of its author's development. For a general survey of the scholarship on the novel, see Astrida Orle Tantillo, *Goethe's "Elective Affinities" and the Critics*.

8. Eckermann, *Gespräche mit Goethe*, 545 (January 2, 1824). Nevertheless, Goethe reports having read *Werther* in a diary entry of April 30, 1780, and worked sporadically on revising it from 1782 to 1786. He refers to it more or less gratuitously in the introduction to *Briefe aus der Schweiz* (1796, publ. 1808) and reread it again in 1806 according to diary entries for September 10 and 13.

9. In *Werther* the term is *Grenzen* (HA 6:48; all further citations to both novels are to page numbers in this edition): "Human nature has its limits: it can bear joy, sorrow, pain to a certain degree and perishes as soon as it is exceeded" (Die menschliche Natur . . . hat ihre Grenzen: sie kann Freude, Leid, Schmerzen bis auf einen gewissen Grad ertragen und geht zugrunde, sobald der überstiegen ist). Compare Ottilie in *Die Wahlverwandtschaften*: "I have strayed from my path" (462; ich bin aus meiner Bahn geschritten).

10. As, for example, in the passage: "but the magistrate, *as can be easily imagined*, was not impressed by it" (96, emphasis mine; so war doch, *wie sich's leicht denken läßt*, der Amtmann dadurch nicht gerührt).

11. The most thorough discussion of this technique in *Die Wahlverwandtschaften* is to be found in H. G. Barnes, *Goethe's "Die Wahlverwandtschaften."*

12. I cite this early version of the novel from the *Neue Gesamtausgabe* 6:528.

13. Goethe connects the novel to this context in *Dichtung und Wahrheit*, pt. 3, bk. 13 (HA 9:579–85).

14. Starobinski, *La transparence et l'obstacle*, 150.

15. On the fragility of this community, see ibid., 149.

16. Hanna Fischer-Lamberg, "Charlotte von Stein, ein Bildungserlebnis Goethes."

17. I can find no explicit documentation that Goethe ever read the second half of the *Confessions*. The relationship with Mme de Warens is complete by the end of book 6. Thérèse Levasseur appears, to be sure, only beginning in book 7; however, the relationship and Rousseau's refusal to keep his children were the subject of scandal from the 1760s. Voltaire first aired the charge publicly in 1764 in the pamphlet "Le sentiment des citoyens," but it had already been circulated by Grimm, among others, in his *Correspondence lit-*

téraire, which Goethe read regularly, according to Gero von Wilpert, *Goethe-Lexikon,* 425. Rousseau treats the topic as common knowledge in the fourth promenade of the *Reveries* (*Œuvres complètes,* 1:1034), published in 1782, and Thérèse published her own defense in 1789 under the title *Plainte et défense de Thérèse Levasseur.*

18. See, e.g., Sigrid Damm, *Christiane und Goethe,* especially 132–36 on relation to court.

19. Nicholas Boyle, *Goethe: The Poet and the Age,* 2:556–67.

20. Goethe to Karl August, June 16, 1782: "In Rousseau's works there are utterly charming letters on botany in which he presents this science very clearly and elegantly to a lady" (In Rousseaus Werken finden sich ganz allerliebste Briefe über die Botanik, worin er diese Wissenschaft auf das faßlichste und zierlichste einer Dame vorträgt); cited in Hammer, *Goethe and Rousseau,* 38.

21. Sigrid Damm emphasizes how much time Goethe spent away from his family in *Christiane und Goethe.*

22. I have argued that the *Die Wahlverwandtschaften* belongs in the tradition of the English novel of manners in "*Die Wahlverwandtschaften* and the English Novel of Manners." Both Schmidt in *Richardson, Rousseau und Goethe* and Joseph Texte in *Jean-Jacques Rousseau and the Cosmopolitan Spirit in Literature* have demonstrated other relations of the novel to this tradition, which included both epistolary and third-person narratives. Cf. also Hammer, *Goethe and Rousseau,* 107–21 on the "kinship" (121) of *Die Wahlverwandtschaften* and *Julie.*

23. Starobinski, *Le transparence et l'obstacle,* 142.

24. Saint-Preux articulates as much when he says, "I constantly saw God between her and me" (*Julie,* 580; je voyais Dieu sans cesse entre elle et moi) and when he warns her against religious quietism (part 6, letter 7).

25. On the general failure of manners in the novel, see my "*Die Wahlverwandtschaften* and the English Novel of Manners."

26. Chapter 7 below will reread the water imagery in *Werther* in light of this development in *Die Wahlverwandtschaften.*

CHAPTER 3. GOETHE CONTRA ROUSSEAU ON SOCIAL RESPONSIBILITY

1. This is perhaps the only respect in which I would differ from Boyle's fine analysis of the development of Goethe's thought in the 1790s in *Goethe: The Poet and the Age,* where Rousseau plays scarcely a bit part, more in relation to Schiller than to Goethe.

2. Rousseau appears in his letters to her eight different times between 1779 and 1784; on August 4, 1780, he forwards her a copy of a letter by Rousseau, and on August 25–27, 1782, a copy of an essay about him.

3. See Boyle, *Goethe,* 1:339, on Fritz as the model for the boy in "Erlkönig."

4. Not surprisingly, Richard Friedenthal (in *Goethe, sein Leben und seine Zeit*) is the most negative, but no one seems to think Fritz led a very happy existence, not even Gero von Wilpert (*Goethe-Lexikon,* 1017). Given, however, that his own father was mostly absent

and his mother by all reports cold, it is hard to know how much to attribute to Goethe's unsystematic pedagogy and how much to other factors.

5. Boyle, *Goethe*, 2:456.

6. My description here touches only on the main aspects of the novel salient to this comparison with Rousseau. A more extensive description of the novel may be found below at the beginning of Chapter 6 as preparation for the detailed analysis that follows there.

7. See, e.g., Hammer, *Goethe and Rousseau*, 123–36, which refers almost exclusively to *Wilhelm Meisters Wanderjahre* in relation to *Emile*. Hans Robert Jauß draws a general comparison in "Rousseaus *Nouvelle Héloïse* und Goethes *Werther*," 647–52.

8. *Emile, or On Education*, trans. Allan Bloom, 201; French, *Émile, ou De l'éducation*, in *Œuvres complètes*, 4:478. Subsequent quotations will be identified by page numbers to the Bloom and *ŒC* editions in the text.

9. Cf. the attitudes of the grouchy old pedagogues Chiron, Proteus, and Nereus in act 2 of *Faust*, part 2, and also my analysis of the ironies surrounding pedagogy in the *Wanderjahre* in *Goethe's Cyclical Narratives*, 87–97.

10. Eric A. Blackall makes as good an argument as can be made that the tension between fate and chance is the central issue in *Goethe and the Novel*, 111–36.

11. HA 3:58, line 1754. Henceforth all citations to *Faust* will be by line number from this edition.

12. Rousseau, *Les rêveries du promeneur solitaire*, in *Œuvres complètes*, 1:1046; emphasis Rousseau's, translation mine.

13. Thus far I have recapitulated my own argument in *Goethe's "Faust": The German Tragedy*, 80–83.

14. Arendt's apparent preference for Goethe over Rousseau calls for analysis. I will argue below that her position follows on Goethe's struggle to achieve an ethical balance in *Faust*, and that this struggle is defined by his earlier attempts to come to terms with Rousseau's theory of socialization in *Emile*.

15. See Hannah Arendt, *On Revolution*, 38–39, which offers examples from Maximilien de Robespierre, Camille Desmoulins, Georg Forster, and Alexander Hamilton.

16. Most famous currently is the much contested case of Goethe's vote not to overturn a death sentence for infanticide in 1783, just eight years after he wrote the first version of the tragedy of the infanticide Margarete. As the facts now have been established, the issue in that case was neither the particular judgment nor approval of the death sentence in principle. At the explicit insistence of the duke Goethe was required to take a position in writing on the alternative of retaining the death sentence in such cases or lifelong imprisonment with annual public exposure of the delinquent. Documentation and analysis of the context and the history of scholarly misunderstanding are discussed extensively by Volker Wahl and René Jacques Baerlocher in *"Das Kind in meinem Leib."*

17. Argued in more detail in my *Goethe's "Faust": The German Tragedy*, 113–14, where I claim the voice is not God's but the poet's.

18. It is, of course, a play like all the actions in *Faust*, for Faust recognizes that its importance lies exclusively in its ever transient reenactment of itself in the constant effort of its inhabitants and not in a permanent stable entity.

19. For a discussion of the extreme complexity of this process, see Benjamin Bennett's *Goethe's Theory of Poetry*.

CHAPTER 4. THE THEATRICAL SELF

1. For an alternate reading of identity in *Iphigenie*, see Friedrich K. Blocher, *Identitätserfahrung*, 9–29. For a general discussion of the representation of madness in Goethe in the context of literary representation of madness in the Germany of the period, see Georg Reuchlein, *Bürgerliche Gesellschaft, Psychiatrie und Literatur*, 130–203.

2. Symptomatically, it has been figures like Ernst Cassirer (*Rousseau, Kant and Goethe*) and more recently Hans Robert Jauß ("Rousseaus *Nouvelle Héloïse* und Goethes *Werther*")—the one a philosopher, the other a specialist in Romance languages—who have placed Goethe most cogently in the context of subjectivity in the eighteenth century, while scholarship on the classic plays has more or less abandoned any claim that they have influenced important developments in European culture (with the exception of Bennett's argument on the importance of Goethe's drama in *Modern Drama and German Classicism*).

3. Goethe's work on the play is generally dated from 1775 sporadically to 1787, when he sent off the completed manuscript. Heinrich Henel ("Auf den Spuren des Uregmont") has intelligently separated different stages of the play on the basis of style, but there is practically no hard evidence for what parts of the play were written when, and no earlier versions are extant.

4. HA 4:428 (subsequent references to *Egmont* are to page numbers in this edition); HA 6:47 (letter of August 12). Parallels include motifs of drunkenness and madness, structure of repeated questions, passionate defender of the downtrodden vs. calm authoritative opponent.

5. All references to the play are to HA 5 by line number, here line 53.

6. Machiavell argues that Egmont acts openly in accordance with his conscience, while Margarete pairs Egmont with Oranien, who always acts cautiously and with secret intentions; thus she suspects in Egmont's preference for his Dutch title, Count Egmont, over his higher ranking imperial title, Prince of Gaure, a hidden intention to recover lost rights (381).

7. The same ambiguity is already raised in act 2 when the citizens praise him for being thoroughly Dutch ("Gar so nicht Spanisches," 395) but then admire the Spanish cut of his coat.

8. To Schiller, January 19, 1802, WA 4.16:11.

9. Klare's songs appear on 383 and 410 (cf. Jetter's reflection on the unconsciousness of songs, 375); on Klare's love, 385.

10. Cyrus Hamlin, "'Myth and Psychology': The Curing of Orest in Goethe's *Iphigenie auf Tauris*."

11. For more detail, see my "Orest, Orlando, Orpheus, oder Der Held von Goethes *Iphigenie*."

12. See Hellmut Ammerlahn, *Aufbau und Krise der Sinn-Gestalt*, 33–64.

13. *Dichtung und Wahrheit*, pt. 4, bk. 20 (HA 10:176–77); the remaining ten pages apply the theory to Goethe's own life. All citations will be to volume and page of this edition. On the process of revision, see Heinz Nicolai, "Goethes Schicksalsidee."

14. Cf. Bennett's argument that Egmont recovers here the heroism for which he was famous before the play began, *Modern Drama and German Classicism*, 159–60.

15. Schiller has Egmont be warned of Alba's arrival and, later, of his imminent danger from Alba, so that Egmont's refusals to flee represent deliberate political resistance rather than the refusal to act consciously.

16. In a similar vein, in Egmont's monologue in prison Goethe has him consistently address himself as "du," an objective other, while Schiller rewrites the monologue into the first person, making it conventionally subjective.

17. Carl Gustav Carus, *Psyche*, 50 and 176.

18. Cf. also Faust's double dream of the conception of Helena in act 2 and my analysis in *Goethe's "Faust": The German Tragedy*, 175–78.

19. Galatea is also anticipated in the relationship between Epimetheus and Elpore during his dream, where he cannot even see her, much less embrace her when she comes close.

20. The antecedents of *Pandora* reveal some of the tensions around using drama to represent identity. I have in mind here *Elpenor* and *Paläophron und Neoterpe*, the two other works that find their place with *Pandora* in volume 5 of the Hamburger Ausgabe among Goethe's classical dramas. Indeed, the organization of the volume reveals a certain insecurity about what constitutes classical in respect to Goethe, whether modeled on the shape of Greek drama (*Elpenor*, *Iphigenie*, *Tasso*) or whether based on classical myth (*Pandora*, otherwise shaped like a masque) or whether dealing with figures that look classical (*Paläophron und Neoterpe*). *Elpenor* is the first two acts of a Greek-style tragedy from 1781. For many years Goethe considered that he had made a major error in his choice of material, but the fact that he showed it to Schiller in 1798 suggests that he wasn't quite willing to admit it was a complete error. Although the form is that of Greek tragedy (as Goethe understood it in the early 1780s), the plot is clearly that of romance and was to involve recognition and the revelation of identities kept secret. It is based partly on Hyginus's fable supposedly based on Euripides' lost play, and partly on two Chinese texts. Since his first and successful Euripides imitation, *Iphigenie*, ended happily, there is no reason to assume that this plot too was not intended to unravel the tensions it sets up so clearly in the exposition. By shifting to a plot, however, in which the protagonist is not aware of his own identity, Goethe overlooks what was revolutionary about *Iphigenie*, the talking cure. Nevertheless, the possibilities for exploring identity in the play are intriguing. It seems evident that Elpenor has a lost first cousin who is his double, or else that Elpenor will turn out actually to be his own lost first cousin. Either way the play has set him up as a double of himself, as a self who does not know who he really is and would have found himself in an other, as do Tasso and Eugenie. What does seem evident about *Elpenor* is thus that it was grappling with problems for which Goethe could only find the solution in allegory. Accordingly, *Paläophron und Neoterpe*, a little masque written in 1800 for the birthday of the Dowager Duchess Anna Amalia, is of interest for three reasons. First, its protagonists embody opposed attitudes toward temporality and are thus a first try at the Prometheus-Epimetheus opposition in *Pandora*.

"Paläophron" means "in favor of the past"; and "Neoterpe," "taking pleasure in the future." They are uncle and niece, at loggerheads at the beginning of the play and friends by the end. They have failed to recognize their close relationship to one another because neither could bear the followers of the other. But after Paläophron sends away Griesgram and Haberecht (Grouchy and Self-Righteous), and Neoterpe likewise Gelbschnabel and Naseweis (Immature and Sassy), the two can join in their respect for Anna Amalia. In effect each figure recovers his or her true identity by sending away their personified character qualities. Even these allegorical figures have an essential identity different from their externally visible qualities. Thus the masque works allegorically, but takes account of a personality structure more complex than what could be represented by allegory.

CHAPTER 5. THE SCIENTIFIC SELF

1. On the theatricality of the love affair with Margarete, see my *Goethe's "Faust": The German Tragedy*, esp. 94–116.

2. Goethe's interest in meteorology is well documented: he wrote about it, set up a network of weather stations in the duchy of Weimar, and kept a chart of local barometric pressure pinned to the wall of his bedroom. His admiration for Howard's work is also well known; he even wrote a set of poems about it, "In Honor of Howard" (Howards Ehrengedächtnis).

3. Indeed, they remind us that the first appearance of Helena (in act 1 of part 2) as shade was even less stable.

4. "Die Einwirkung der neueren Philosophie" (The Influence of Modern Philosophy), HA 13:27. All subsequent citations to Goethe's scientific essays are to this volume. There is an extensive and distinguished scholarship on Goethe and Kant going back to Cassirer's *Rousseau, Kant and Goethe*. Starting points for the particular topic of this chapter would be Géza von Molnár's "Goethes Studium der Kritik der Urteilskraft" and the fuller book version, *Goethes Kantstudien*; Boyle's repeated discussions of their affinity in *Goethe: The Poet and the Age*, vol. 2; and Wolf von Engelhardt's penetrating analysis of Kant's impact on Goethe's scientific thinking in *Goethe im Gespräch mit der Erde*, 169–94. On the relationship of science and aesthetics in Goethe: "Der Versuch als Vermittler von Objekt und Subjekt" (The Experiment as Mediator Between Object and Subject, 1792) sees art and science as parallel in contrast (13, again 18); "Inwiefern die Idee: Schönheit sei Vollkommenheit mit Freiheit, auf organische Naturen angewendet werden könne" (To What Extent the Idea "Beauty Is Perfection with Freedom" Can Be Applied to Organic Beings), a 1794 sketch for a never published essay, attempts to capture for the natural sciences the language of aesthetics (21–23).

5. In the essay "Anschauende Urteilskraft" (Observational Judgment), which evokes the creative Earth Spirit at the loom of time (30). The ethical aspect of *Faust* also enters into these parallels, because Goethe explicitly connects the Kantian distinctions with his own principle "acting and thinking" (Tun und Denken) in "Einwirkung der neueren Philosophie" (28; Influence of Modern Philosophy).

6. See "Der Versuch als Vermittler": "I might add that knowledge, like an enclosed, spring-fed pond, gradually rises to a particular level such that the best discoveries are made not by people, but by the age" (13; Es läßt sich bemerken, daß die Kenntnisse, gleichsam wie ein eingeschlossenes aber lebendiges Wasser, sich nach und nach zu einem gewissen Niveau erheben, daß die schönsten Entdeckungen nicht sowohl durch die Menschen als durch die Zeit gemacht worden).

7. Thus Faust can also say things like "You have gained no relief unless it flows from your own soul" (568–69; Erquickung hast du nicht gewonnen, / Wenn sie dir nicht aus eigner Seele quillt), "Here I am human, here I can be so" (939; Hier bin ich Mensch, hier darf ich's sein!), "Oh, if only you could read in my inner self" (1031; O könntest du in meinem Innern lesen).

8. N.b., Faust "feels" himself to be like the Spirit, but the Spirit insists on comprehension—a different kind of self-knowledge. Faust returns to this theme in the later amplification of this passage:

I, reflection of the Godhead, who thought myself already
So near to the mirror of eternal truth,
Rejoiced in its heavenly glory and clarity,
And shook off my human body;
I, more than cherub, whose free power
To flow through the veins of nature
And, creating, in anticipation
Overstepped itself to enjoy the life of gods—how I must now atone! (614–21)

(Ich, Ebenbild der Gottheit, das sich schon
Ganz nah gedünkt dem Spiegel ew'ger Wahrheit,
Sein selbst genoß im Himmelsglanz und Klarheit,
Und abgestreift den Erdensohn;
Ich, mehr als Cherub, dessen freie Kraft
Schon durch die Adern der Natur zu fließen
Und, schaffend, Götterleben zu geneißen
Sich ahnungsvoll vermaß, wie muß ich's büßen!)

9. Wilhelm Meister takes on the role of Shakespeare's Henry V, Prince Harry, as he leads his band of actors, in outlandish costumes, into the hands of outlaws in an episode that is clearly an exercise in experimental identity (*Wilhelm Meisters Lehrjahre*, bk. 4, chap. 5).

10. In his 1999 production of both parts of *Faust* in Hannover (repeated in Berlin 2000, Vienna 2001), German theatrical director Peter Stein had the role of Mephistopheles played by two different actors with different personae, and it worked brilliantly.

11. I take this concept from the central thesis of Bennett's *Goethe's Theory of Poetry*.

12. Beginning in the fourteenth century mirrors were also used as tools by painters for developing perspective, for scaling, proportion and framing scenes to create pictures; this technical use does not, however, seem to become a metaphor for identity as other uses did.

For a survey of the history of mirrors, see Benjamin Goldberg, *The Mirror and the Man*; for an excellent history of the mirror in European culture, see Sabine Melchior-Bonnet, *The Mirror: A History*. A more specialized version may be found in Herbert Grabes, *Speculum, Mirror und Looking-Glass*. On magic mirrors, see Melchior-Bonnet, *The Mirror*, 213–15.

13. Cf. also lines 577–79:

What you call the spirit of the times,
That is at bottom the spirit of you gentlemen yourselves,
In which the times are reflected

(Was ihr den Geist der Zeiten heißt,
Das ist im Grund der Herren eigner Geist,
In dem die Zeiten sich bespiegeln)

14. Mirrors only became normally glass rather than metal or polished stone in the late sixteenth century with the spread of Venetian glass. The term consistently used in this and the seventeenth century is "crystal" (Goldberg, *The Mirror and Man*, 139; Melchoir-Bonnet, *The Mirror*, 18). The water mirror in which Narcissus is trapped is its own commonplace independent of the tradition of mirror imagery. It represents, however, not excessive subjectivity or the depths of the self, but selfishness and self-love. See Arthur Henkel and Albrecht Schöne, *Emblemata*, 1627–28.

15. Stuart P. Atkins, *Goethe's Faust*, 142.

CHAPTER 6. THE NARRATIVE SELF

1. On allegory and cosmos, see Angus Fletcher, *Allegory: The Theory of a Symbolic Mode*; on epic, Arnd Bohm, *Goethe's "Faust" and European Epic*.

2. A distinguished tradition of reading *Wilhelm Meisters Lehrjahre* as bildungsroman dates from Friedrich Schlegel's review "Über Goethes *Meister*," *Athenäum* 1.2 (1798), to, most recently, Hellmut Ammerlahn's *Imagination und Wahrheit*.

3. The name actually seems to be Goethe's cipher for his own distanced identification with his various heroes. It is well known that in *Werther* Goethe represented his own passion for Charlotte Buff Kestner, but that he also based his narrative on the diary of his friend Karl Wilhelm Jerusalem, who did actually commit suicide out of love for an engaged woman. Perhaps this is the original inspiration for Goethe's choice of the name. In his one-act play of 1776, *Die Geschwister* (Siblings), the passionate but patient hero Wilhelm eventually marries his ward Marianne, whom Wilhelm has raised as his sister and who is eventually revealed to be the daughter of a beloved Charlotte whom Wilhelm could not marry. Goethe gave the almost identical name, Mariane, to Wilhelm's first beloved in the *Lehrjahre*.

4. HA 7:9; all subsequent references are to page numbers in this edition.

5. In book 1 his elaboration of the costumes for his puppets destroys their usefulness for any coherent production (24) and his childish staging of Tasso fails, despite carefully prepared costumes and sets, because he has forgotten to tell his actors what to say. In book 3 Melina's company can take form only after Wilhelm has financed the sets and costumes.

6. I have addressed this topic in more detail in "The Theatrical Mission of the *Lehrjahre.*"

7. Peter Michelsen, "Die Problematik der Empfindungen," esp. pp. 219–20. A broader discussion of the lability of the hero of sensibility may be found in Marshall Brown, *Preromanticism*, 91–95.

8. He discovered the intermaxillary bone in the human skull in 1784 and invented the term "morphology" and identified it as a unique scientific discipline around 1795–96 (Wilpert, *Goethe-Lexikon*, 721).

9. Ammerlahn, *Imagination und Wahrheit*, 97

10. Almost any character class or motif in the novel can be arranged into a similar series, as the following table, by no means exhaustive, demonstrates:

Category	Bk. 1	Bk. 2	Bk. 3	Bk. 4	Bk. 5	Bk. 6	Bk. 7	Bk. 8
Men	Werner, Melina	Laertes, Friedrich	Harper, Jarno	uncle	Serlo	father, Narziß, Philo, uncle	Lothario	All
Natalie's family	Abbé	Friedrich, Abbé	Countess	Natalie	Abbé	Beautiful Soul	Lothario, Abbé	Natalie
Transvestite	Mariane, Chlorinde	Mignon	Baroness	Natalie	Friedrich	failed son	Therese	Mignon as angel
Theater as:	costume	costume, set	text, decor	analysis	analysis, decor	concerts	entertainment, initiation	ceremony
Prince	painting		general	Prince Hal	Hamlet			Saul

The examples reflect a shift from character to motif, from individual to social, private to public.

11. Jarno in book 3 attracts but also repels Wilhelm; in book 5 the narrator shifts perspective to reduce Serlo's stature. When Jarno reappears in book 7 he has renounced his questionable friends and company of book 3 and commands new respect as Lothario's lieutenant. Similarly, although Lothario's name clearly labels him as a rake, by the time he appears in books 7 and 8 he is ready to settle down.

12. Cf. Ammerlahn on Mignon as marionette, *Imagination und Wahrheit*, 87–88.

13. For an excellent analysis of this topic, see Jill Anne Kowalik, "Feminine Identity Formation in *Wilhelm Meisters Lehrjahre.*"

14. For extensive analysis of the importance of healing in this novel, see Robert Tobin, *Doctor's Orders.*

15. The technique was recognized and adopted immediately in the later 1790s. For examples and elaboration, see Ammerlahn, *Imagination und Wahrheit*, 263–65.

16. Cf. also the Beautiful Soul discovering her own beauty (368) and the Countess expressing her essence as a child (418, 433, 559).

17. Other examples are Mariane between her love for Wilhelm and her "duty" to Norberg, Wilhelm between his father and himself, Melina between the theater and a clerkship, Mignon between theatrical and domestic servitude.

18. Cf. Thomas P. Saine's now classic essay "Wilhelm Meister's Homecoming."

19. On the broader significance of the secret horror and its relationship to truth in this novel, see my "Im Anfang war das Bild."

20. See, for example, the model reading by Dorrit Cohn, "Wilhelm Meister's Dream."

21. I am indebted to Amy Emm for these parallels between Mignon and Philine.

22. The complex relationship of memory and forgetting in European culture has been worked out in detail by Harald Weinrich in several esays and, most comprehensively, in *Lethe: Kunst und Kritik des Vergessens.*

23. Franco Moretti overlooks the larger pattern of memory and forgetting when, commenting only on the deaths of Mignon and the Harper, he accuses Goethe of "philistinism"—"We can easily reformulate 'Remember to live!' as 'Forget the dead!' Mourning does not become Wilhelm Meister" (*The Way of the World*, 48).

24. Upon his arrival at Natalie's castle Wilhelm identifies Natalie as priestess (519). Cf. the priestess Iphigenie who remembers all through her play in order that the curse may be relegated to the past.

25. It is illuminating to locate this description of the novel in the context of broader discussions of history and memory. Thomas P. Saine has provided precise scholarly underpinnings for the *Lehrjahre*'s imprecise relation to both time and history by demonstrating that the novel does not float independent of history, but instead evokes a historical background that is mostly clearly identifiable, not just vaguely prerevolutionary (in "What Time Is It in *Wilhelm Meisters Lehrjahre?*"). In *The Way of the World* Franco Moretti offers models for how to use such knowledge, for in his view the culture of time is the essence of the "classical *Bildungsroman*," exemplified for him by *Wilhelm Meister* and Jane Austen's *Pride and Prejudice*; the bildungsroman, with its emphasis on happiness and closure, is incompatible with modernity and capitalism, the driving forces of the postrevolutionary world (24–28); by equating moral and social superiority, the classical bildungsroman disavows the French Revolution (72–73), indeed narrates, in effect, how the revolution could have been avoided (64). *Wilhelm Meister*, in this reading, does not exclude history or represent it, but participates in it. But Moretti is less convincing when he shifts from history to memory. Because the novel valorizes the existing order, the past and therefore memory take on particular significance—"*Bildung*," Moretti says, "is concluded under the sign of memory" (68). The assertion jars with his eloquent discussion of the realization of the present, where he sees in the novel's preoccupation with the everyday and the personal "a remarkable sieve against the passing of time" (54) and in its happy ending the "triumph of meaning over time" (55). Instead, I think, *Bildung* is concluded under the sign of forgetting. Natalie scarcely figures in Moretti's discussion, and, as pointed out above, Moretti resents the elimination of the passionate figures who are unable to forget from the novel. Thus his dialectic does not carry over from sociology to anthropology.

26. Harald Weinrich, "Faust's Forgetting," points to the ways in which *Faust* calls into question the morality of the shift of focus in the modern scholarly enterprise from treasuring accumulated knowledge to generating new knowledge. Weinrich's *Gibt es eine Kunst des Vergessens?* provides a larger framework for this discussion by elaborating it at both ends, but particularly to include analyses of forgetting in Nietzsche and Freud. See his *Lethe* for a longitudinal analysis of the tradition of forgetting in European culture.

27. Weinrich, *Gibt es eine Kunst des Vergessens?*, 47.

28. As I argued in *Goethe's "Faust": The German Tragedy*, esp. 251–53. On the way this ambiguity impinges on the morality of forgetting, see the analysis there of Baucis and Philemon, 233–35.

CHAPTER 7. GOETHE'S ANGST

1. In *The Anxiety of Influence*, e.g., 50–56, Harold Bloom still classed him with Shakespeare in his resistance to the otherwise all-pervasive anxiety of influence in the European tradition. For recent corrections to this account, see Meredith Lee, *Displacing Authority*, and, most closely related to what I am trying to get at here, though moving back from Freud rather than toward him, Richard Block's discussion "Fathers and Sons in Italy: The Ghosts of Goethe's Past" in *The Spell of Italy*, 49–77.

2. Damm's feminist recovery of Christiane as independent personality (*Christiane und Goethe*) draws much of its polemical energy from this traditional view of Goethe. More recently Boyle's reading of the poet in the political and social context (*Goethe: The Poet and the Age*) has offered a more vulnerable Goethe whose personal emotions extend beyond skirt chasing and irritation at personal opposition.

3. Overviews of the occurrence of *Sorge* in Goethe may be found in Wilpert's *Goethe-Lexikon*, 1002; Konrad Burdach's "Faust und die Sorge in Goethes *Faust*"; and Ellis Dye's "Sorge in Heidegger and in Goethe's *Faust*." Unlike the discussion below, all are focused on explaining the character of the same name in act 5 of *Faust*, part 2.

4. Furthermore, twenty-five occurrences of *Angst* are in translations or adaptations (*Reineke Fuchs, Benvenuto Cellini, Der Schutzgeist, Romeo und Julia*) and thus do not represent Goethe's usage. This proportion is far in excess of that of *Furcht* or *Sorge* in translations.

5. In his *Grammatisch-kritisches Wörterbuch der hochdeutschen Mundart* (*Grammatic-Critical Dictionary of the High German Dialect*, 1774–86), Johann Christoph Adelung defines *Sorge* as "actually, the discomfort associated with the *focus of the self* on the prevention of an evil or achievement of a prospective good, and the displeasure or unpleasant feeling associated with it" (Eigentlich, die mit Unruhe verbundene anhaltende *Richtung des Gemüthes* auf die Abwendung eines Übels oder Erlangung eines künftigen Gutes, und die damit verbundene Unlust oder unangenehme Empfindung), and continues: "More figuratively it is often used to refer to every serious *focus of the self* on the preservation or elimination of something" (In weiterer Bedeutung wird es oft von einer jeden ernstlichen *Richtung des Gemüthes* auf die Erhaltung oder Wegschaffung einer Sache gebraucht; emphasis mine). The repetition of "Richtung des Gemüthes" identifies the fundamentally subjective nature

of the term. Adelung also points further to the Low German usage still common in the eighteenth century of *Sorge* for "Trauer, Traurigkeit, Kummer."

6. Although Goethe uses *Angst* for a range of meanings from "Furcht, Grauen in einer gefährlichen Situation" to "Beunruhigung," "Bedenken," "Bedrückung" (today "depression"), or simply "Bedrängnis" (*Goethe-Wörterbuch*, 1:569–71), his usage tends more commonly toward the subjective end of the range. The derivative *ängstlich* leads even further in this direction from "voll Angst" to "unsicher" to "niedergedrückt, gequält" to "beschränkt" to, finally, "sorgfältig" (ibid., 573–74). The shift explains why Goethe so often supplements *Furcht* with *Schrecken*, *Angst*, or *Sorge* (dialectically opposed to *Vertrauen*, *Sehnsucht*, and *Hoffnung*) (ibid:, 3:1031). Such pairings are not repetitive but complementary: they combine the external and internal constituents of fear. Thus Goethe often uses *Furcht* together with *Angst*, but *Furcht* refers consistently to situations in which the emotion derives clearly from a cause external to the subject. The *Goethe-Wörterbuch* lists such causes as "inkalkulable Mächte, kreatürliche, archaische, abergläubische Angst vor Naturgewalten" and asserts that *Furcht* stands in a dialectical relation to *Freiheit* and *Ehrfurcht*, both words that focus on the specific absence or presence of an external power (3:1031). *Furcht* occurs in Goethe's literary works 420 times, as opposed to 450 for *Sorge*, but there is a striking absence of real fear among Goethe's literary characters. Indeed, it is difficult to think of any examples beyond Gretchen in the later parts of *Faust*, part 1. She is the one protagonist in Goethe who fears death, and her apparent embrace of it at the end of the play constitutes the anagnorisis one traditionally expects at the end of a Schiller tragedy. But this tragic Gretchen belongs to the Goethe of the 1770s. Neither Egmont nor Iphigenie knows fear, at least not of death; they rather fear any disruption that fear could cause to their inner integrity. By *Hermann und Dorothea* (1798) the paradigm is fixed; the apothecary who organizes his life around his fear of death is treated as absurd, while Hermann fears only losing the opportunity represented by Dorothea to live fully. The courage he learns is not to face death but to grasp life.

7. Heidegger devotes a chapter to "Die Sorge als Sein des Daseins," in *Sein und Zeit*, 180–230.

8. It occurs five times in *Iphigenie*, fourteen each in *Tasso* and *Die natürliche Tochter*, and twenty-two in *Die Wahlverwandtschaften*. Only the much longer *Lehrjahre* and *Wanderjahre*, with twenty-eight and twenty-three respectively, and *Faust*, part 2, with eighteen, have comparable numbers of occurrences. Although the last two works are generally associated with the last decade of Goethe's life, both were actually conceived and begun between 1800 and 1805. Similarly, most of the thirty occurrences in poems are in texts from the 1790s.

9. Wahrman explores the impact of the Revolution on the emergence of the subject in *The Making of the Modern Self*.

10. Cf. also "Süße Sorgen" of 1788, in which love replaces anxiety:

Weichet, Sorgen, von mir! — Doch ach! den sterblichen Menschen
Lässet die Sorge nicht los, eh' ihn das Leben verläßt.
Soll es einmal denn sein; so kommt ihr, Sorgen der Liebe,
Treibt die Geschwister hinaus, nehmt und behauptet mein Herz!

(WA 1.2:93; Go way from me, Cares! — But alas, Care never lets go of mortal man until Life lets him go. If it must be so, then come, Cares of Love, drive your siblings away and take over my heart!). The shift in mood seems to be motivated by the double meaning of *sorgen*: general worry (*sorgen um*) is to be replaced by the cares of love (*sorgen für*). Unfortunately the general tone of Goethe's contemporaneous love elegies, *Römische Elegien*, does not support such a reading. There the beloved is an object of which possession must be retained; she is the object of his care (*Fürsorge*) only in the form of cash gifts (Elegy 2, in HA 1:158).

11. Klingsor's fable in Novalis's *Heinrich von Ofterdingen* is an obvious example of the impact of this shift.

12. Cf. Goethe's letters, where the term occurs regularly, about twice as frequently in the meaning "sorgen um" as in that of "sorgen für."

13. The same struggle intensifies further in *Die natürliche Tochter*, where *Sorge* fluctuates irregularly between the two meanings without any resolution. The play is filled with anxiety that might better be characterized as dread; and yet the heroine, Eugenie, opts for an unwanted marriage rather than exile in order to care for the land in act 5, scene 8 ("Sorge," l.2839) and even for the king (WA 1.10:449, in a paralipomenon). At the same time she herself is helpless; for most of the last two acts she has been seeking charitable care for herself, and she enters at the end into the care of the magistrate.

14. Goethe's description of this trip in *Briefe aus der Schweiz* aroused Kleist's enthusiasm at the time he was working on his rather gothic fate tragedy *Die Familie Schroffenstein*, according to the report of Christian Gottlieb Hölder in *Meine Reise über den Gotthard im Summer 1801* (Stuttgart, 1804; cited in Helmut Sembdner, ed., *Heinrich von Kleists Lebensspuren*, 67), so that even this apparently minor text was a vehicle of transmission to the Romantic generation.

15. The first occurrence comes in part 1 and fits with the callow Wertherian language: "I climbed the Furka, the Gotthard! These sublime incomparable natural scenes will always remain present to my spirit; I read Roman history in order to experience deeply by the comparison what a wretch I am" (WA 1.19:204; Ja ich habe die Furca, den Gotthard bestiegen! Diese erhabenen unvergleichlichen Naturscenen werden immer vor meinem Geiste stehen; ja ich habe die römische Geschichte gelesen, um bei der Vergleichung recht lebhaft zu fühlen, was für ein armseliger Schlucker ich bin). The second is associated with a lower, less threatening climb and, unexpectedly, with self-control: "The passage through this defile gave me a great serene feeling. The sublime imparts to the soul a lovely serenity, it is completely filled with it, feels as great as it possibly can be. How magnificent is such a pure feeling when it reaches the extreme limit without overflowing. My eye and my soul could comprehend the objects, and since I was pure and never contradicted this feeling, they had their proper effect" (224; Mir machte der Zug durch diese Enge eine große ruhige Empfindung. Das Erhabene gibt der Seele die schöne Ruhe, sie wird ganz dadurch ausgefüllt, fühlt sich so groß als sie sein kann. Wie herrlich ist ein solches reines Gefühl, wenn es bis gegen den Rand steigt ohne überzulaufen. Mein Auge und meine Seele konnten die Gegenstände fassen, und da ich rein war, diese Empfindung nirgends falsch widerstieß, so wirkten sie was sie sollten). All subsequent references to the text are to page number in this volume.

16. In "Kennst du das Land" ("Knowest thou the land," published the same year in *Wilhelm Meisters Lehrjahre* but written 1782/83), the depths of the Swiss landscape harbor a threatening brood of dragons (*Drachenbrut*), veiled there as here by the endless gray fog.

17. See Marshall Brown, *The Gothic Text*, 156–58.

18. The linkage of the fog on the Furka to that in "Kennst du das Land" connects Mignon, singer of this poem in the *Lehrjahre*, to this anxiety. Indeed, Mignon is associated in the poem with everything that pulls Goethe toward Italy—classical art, popular theater, warmth, inarticulate naturalness. She is the very embodiment of his longing for Italy. But she stems from an ambiguous heritage that must be understood as either unnatural or supernatural; she is associated with illness and, indeed, with constant anxiety often figured as feeling cold. She thus also embodies his anxiety about Italy. The pain and freedom her death gives Wilhelm point to the significance of Italy for Goethe.

19. Hölderlin introduced the term in the preface to the publication of a fragment of his novel *Hyperion* in Schiller's journal *Thalia* in 1794.

20. Interestingly enough, the term *Bahn* was interiorized and concretized as the neurophysiological term *Bahnung* that Freud picked up from Sigmund Exner (1846–1926), where it referred to the physiological basis for memory and habitual actions. See Jochen Thermann, *Kafkas Tiere*. The multiplicity of the language here is precisely what Freud had to recreate by deconcretizing *Bahnung* back into the tortuous paths by which subconscious thoughts could be recalled to consciousness. Compare also the afterlife of the image in Paul Celan's snow poems.

21. See, for example, the elegy "Alexis und Dora," in which the hero worries about whether his newly found beloved will remain faithful to him as he sets off to sea.

22. Cf. the contrast between Iphigenie's still sanctuary of death on Tauris and the conflicts of the outside world, the sea, into which she is drawn; Tasso holds onto Antonio as the rock that destroys his ship but saves the mariner.

23. This development leads to the images of ice and skating over ice in *Die Wahlverwandtschaften* and especially in "Der Mann von funfzig Jahren" in the *Wanderjahre*. In *Die Wahlverwandtschaften* the ice melts and the violence that lurks beneath becomes visible, so that the image serves primarily as an analogy for the passions of the characters. In the *Wanderjahre* there is no distinction between the analogy and the referent; the characters are both literally and figuratively skating on thin ice.

24. In fact, *Sorge* emerges as a form of consciousness itself for Goethe as early already as 1783 in "Ilmenau," in the formulation: "I worry quietly, while you [mountain and dale] peacefully green on" (HA 1:107; Ich sorge still, indeß ihr [Berg und Tal] ruhig grünet), and again more explicitly in "Metamorphose der Tiere" (Metamorphosis of Animals, probably 1798–99): "But [Nature] experiences no worry like that of mortal women for dependable nourishment of their offspring" (HA 1:201; [Natur] aber empfindet / Keine Sorge wie sterbliche Fraun um ihrer Gebornen / Sichere Nahrung). In act 5 of *Faust*, part 2, Sorge becomes a kind of unconscious conscience—she punishes Faust's guilt but is never acknowledged as Conscience.

25. Cf. Gerhard Oberlin, who sees the discovery of the unconscious as the root of modern narcissism in his *Goethe, Schiller und das Unbewusste*.

26. See Dye's lucid discussion of the relationship of Sorge to Heidegger's *Dasein* in which he explains that both are anterior to such particular notions of existence such as "I" and "self" ("Sorge in Heidegger and in Goethe's *Faust*," 208).

27. See Schiller's objection to this scene as a *salto mortale* into opera discussed above, Chapter 4.

CHAPTER 8. "ES SINGEN WOHL DIE NIXEN"

I am indebted to my colleague Brigitte Prutti for her thoughtful critique of an early version of this material, in particular for her insistence on the miller's epistemological uncertainty and for calling my attention to the parallels between Werther's fixations on the well and on Charlotte's mouth.

1. Wilhelm Müller, *Werke* 1:42. All further references to Müller's texts are to this edition and volume by page number. The occasional minor divergences in Schubert's texts are irrelevant to this argument.

2. Eichendorff, *Werke* 1:224–25.

3. For a masterful discussion of the Romantic and depth-psychological qualities of this poem, see David Wellbery's analysis in *The Specular Moment*, 246–84. Wellbery has also demonstrated amply just how responsive *Werther* is to Freudian reading in "Morphisms of the Phantasmatic Body." His reading justifies my assertion that the beginnings of the Freudian unconscious can be documented in *Werther*. The focus on liquidity both in this essay and in *The Specular Moment* supports also the connection to the Romantic mermaids.

4. As subtitles in the original publication of 1799 in Schiller's *Musenalmanach* (except in the case of the third poem) and in a letter to Schiller included in *Reise in die Schweiz 1797* (Swiss Journey), WA 1.34.1:341.

5. The issue corresponds to a split between German scholarship, which insists on the distinction, and those who study German literature in the European context. For a recent summary of the evidence for reading Goethe as the primary German Romantic, see my "Classicism and Romanticism."

CHAPTER 9. GOETHE AND THE UNCANNY

1. Cf. already J. Harnik, "Psychoanalytisches aus und über Goethes *Wahlverwandt-schaften*." For the post-Benjamin generation it seems obvious to see the return of the repressed in the novella (as does Hillis Miller in "Interlude as Anastomosis"), and even, like Jill Anne Kowalik, to attribute to Goethe, with admiration, insights close to those of contemporary depth psychology ("Trauma and Memory in the *Wahlverwandtschaften*").

2. Insightful essays that read the novel as diagnoses of the crisis of modernity include, for example, Gabrielle Bersier, "Ottilies verlorenes Paradies," and Fritz Breithaupt, "Culture of Images."

3. The importance of considering the two genres together is illustrated by Patrick Bridgewater's recent *Kafka: Gothic and Fairytale*.

4. The most sophisticated analysis of the elusiveness of symbolic language is to be found in Claudia Brodsky's "The Coloring of Relations"; in a related vein, see Gerhard Neumann's "Wunderliche Nachbarskinder." See also, for example, Heinz Schlaffer, "Namen und Buchstaben in Goethes *Wahlverwandtschaften*"; Loisa Nygaard, "'Bild' and 'Sinnbild'"; Brigitte Peucker, "The Material Image in Goethe's *Wahlverwandtschaften*"; and Thomas Herold, "Zeichen und Zeichendeutung in Goethes *Die Wahlverwandtschaften*."

5. Brodsky points to its hidden presence under the ambiguity of Eduard's reference to Ottilie as omega in "The Coloring of Relations," 1168.

6. Cf. the fact that Rousseau's Julie finally dies by inexplicable drowning.

7. Cf. Miller on Ottilie as unknown to herself ("Interlude as Anastomosis," 116).

8. There is a line of discussion going back to Walter Benjamin's essay "Goethes Wahlverwandtschaften" about the importance of fairy tale in the novel, most recently attacked in Albert Gurganus's "Typologies of Repetition, Reflection, and Recurrence"; it focuses, however, largely on the novella "Die wunderlichen Nachbarskinder" and the question of happy ending, not on the specific phenomenology of fairy tale as it was being written in Germany in the decade and a half preceding the novel, as I do here. It is also worth noting that Jane Austen's *Mansfield Park*, a novel whose parallels to *Die Wahlverwandtschaften* I discussed at length in "*Die Wahlverwandtschaften* and the English Novel of Manners," has been analyzed in terms of its relation to "Cinderella" by Avrom Fleishman in *A Reading of "Mansfield Park,"* 57–69.

9. The same can be said of two seductresses in *Wilhelm Meisters Wanderjahre*—the "pilgernde Törin" who sings the ballad of Amor's mill, and Julia, in "Wer ist der Verräter?" (Who is the Betrayer?), who has her own miniature mill. She mercilessly takes possession of the hapless Lucidor and torments him awhile before releasing him to his beloved Lucinde.

10. The failure of the in-house adviser Mittler to comprehend or counsel effectively would seem to emphasize the importance of the outsider rather than the conscious self, the insider, for this function. He is actually less a mediator, as his name claims, than a disrupter, the embodiment of the effects of repression not mediated and carefully drawn back into consciousness. The failure of his symbolic name should be seen in the general context of misinterpretation in the novel.

11. It is the tension between natural and supernatural and its uncanniness that Schlaffer's otherwise very interesting essay overlooks in seeing the play with letters as simply the displacement of reality by mythic law ("Namen und Buchstaben," 219–22). In my view the novel moves not toward myth but toward riddle, just as the "Märchen" does. I would even argue that Goethe's move toward riddle in that tale underlies the Romantic interest in riddle that Brian Tucker argues begins the tradition of interest in obscure rhetoric that leads from Romanticism to Freud in *Reading Riddles*.

12. The giant probably derives from the statue that punishes Don Juan at the end of the various plays about him (and eventually Mozart's opera, but that is after Walpole's novel). The "Märchen" involves two likely allusions to this material. One is the erratic giant who is, in Goethe, a manifestation of the problem rather than the solution. But the fact

that the giant can act only through his shadow, not through his own might, connects him to Walpole's giant ghost that appears only in pieces. At the end he is transformed into a sundial: like the ghost in Walpole he becomes the image of order restored. Second is the fact that the underground vault in the "Märchen" contains three seated statues that eventually stand up and take power, and a fourth, originally standing, that collapses at the end into an incoherent mass. The same play of disassembly and assembly governs both texts.

13. Drowning not only is a death by water, but also resembles that of Princess Lily's canary in the "Märchen," because it is delivered inadvertently by the loving woman who cares for the tiny creature. The death of baby Otto signifies that of all the relationships among the four characters who shared his name, especially the death of Eduard for Ottilie and of the Major for Charlotte. In the "Märchen," the canary's death precedes that of the prince, who dies as the bird did by seeking refuge in Lily's death-giving arms. The two are placed in a magic basket surrounded by the snake and watched through the night by the anxious Lily and her followers. Charlotte watches similarly beside her dead infant in a basket covered with a green blanket (green because the canary in the "Märchen" is wrapped in leaves [226]). Lily is rescued by an old man with a magic lamp, who directs all the action in the "Märchen." Charlotte receives a comforting visit from the Major, though he is unable to provide equivalent leadership and solve all the problems. Charlotte, strikingly, agrees to all his suggestions so long as she does not have to act on her own.

14. "Interlude as Anastomosis," 118. In "The Coloring of Relations" Brodsky offers a more accurate description of the ambiguous "emptiness" of the sign.

15. Compare Claudia Brodsky's profound meditation on the process of building in the novel and its relation both to memory and to signification, *In the Place of Language*, a discussion I find very sympathetic. For a thoughtful, but more predictably deconstructionist, analysis of architecture and meaning in the novel, see Susan Bernstein's *Housing Problems*, 73–88.

16. Again, I work here with a historical definition of allegory as it operated in drama from the late Middle Ages through the nineteenth century, not with the currently more popular Benjaminian concept that really is a theory of the ghostly afterlife of allegory in the wake of the secularized modernity whose advent is best marked by the French Revolution. It does not automatically imbricate the kind of political ideology so thoughtfully teased out by, for example, Bersier ("Ottilies verlorenes Paradies") under the rubric of allegory.

17. I cite to "Das Unheimliche," in *Studienausgabe* 4:240–74, here 248–49. Translation mine. All further references to this essay are to this text.

18. Cf. Marshall Brown and Jane K. Brown on the gothic in *Faust* in Marshall Brown, *The Gothic Text*, 209–22.

19. In *Die natürliche Tochter* frequent references to "Gespenst" render the political circumstances uncanny (HA 5, lines 657, 1127, 1674, 2837).

20. As invisible projection, cf. "Are they dreams? Are they memories?" (*Faust*, part 2, line 7275; Sind's Träume? Sind's Erinnerungen?"); as subconscious, cf. Jane K. Brown on descent into the self in acts 1 and 2 in *Goethe's "Faust": The German Tragedy*. A link from the Helena of act 3 to Sorge appears in the cloud monologue at the beginning of act 4, where both Helena and Gretchen are evoked in clouds; Goethe's poem about clouds, "Howards

Ehrengedächtnis" (1820) uses the phrase, "a ghost forming ghosts" (HA 1:350, line 26; ein Gespenst Gespenster bildend).

21. *Sorge* is consistently used in this sense in the letters to Charlotte von Stein, 1782–84.

22. Cf. Wilpert, *Goethe-Lexikon*, 139–40.

CONCLUSION

1. On "Fragments," see Introduction, note 6; poetry of experience as *Erlebnisdichtung* is a generally accepted shorthand for the reading of Goethe's poetry propounded by Wilhelm Dilthey in *Das Erlebnis und die Dichtung*.

2. Boyle, *Goethe: The Poet and the Age*, 2:199.

3. In Melville, *Pierre*, 24; Mignon allusions, 150, 177, 421; beautiful soul, 167; Ottilie, 180. Furthermore, Aunt Dorothea, from whom Pierre first learns the history of his father's portrait in the context of a tale about refugees from the French Revolution, has the same name as the heroine of Goethe's *Hermann und Dorothea*, whose heroine is herself a beautiful refugee of the Revolution (Melville 92). All further citations are to this edition.

4. Cf. Harald Weinrich, "Faust's Forgetting," where intellectual knowledge is what must be processed by the devil. Carus is still so caught up in Goethe's imagery that he uses the cosmic, mystical language of *Naturphilosophie*.

5. Hederich calls them Prophasin and Metameleam, and dismisses both as obvious fictions (Hederich, *Gründliches mythologisches Lexikon*, 826).

6. He is identified as an "Anadyomen" (epithet for Aphrodite) at line 1027, and the correction of his vision is announced by none other than Eos, the dawn and bringer of light. It is tempting to see the dropped *r* as a literal correction of "eros."

7. Heidegger virtually says as much in his note on Konrad Burdach's essay on Sorge in chapter 7 in *Sein und Zeit*, 197n. Cf. also Dye's "Sorge in Heidegger and in Goethe's *Faust*."

8. Cf. above, Chapter 7; Burdach, "Faust und die Sorge in Goethes *Faust*"; and Dye, "Sorge in Heidegger and in Goethe's *Faust*."

9. See, for example, Deirdre Vincent, *The Eternity of Being*, 164. For an extensive overview of the issue and thorough bibliography of this much discussed topic, see Andreas Anglet, *Der "ewige" Augenblick*.

10. Cf. my reading of art and the eternal present at the end of *Faust* in *Goethe's "Faust": The German Tragedy*, 241.

11. In this respect my reading diverges from readings of Sorge as some aspect of Faust's conscience (a tradition already established by Burdach's time) and/or fear of death, most recently represented by Matthew Bell, "Sorge, Epicurean Psychology and the Classical Faust."

Adelung, Johann Christoph. *Grammatisch-kritisches Wörterbuch der hochdeutschen Mundart mit beständiger Vergleichung der übrigen Mundarten, besonders aber der oberdeutschen.* Ausgabe letzter Hand. Leipzig, 1793–1801. Elektronische Volltext- und Faksimile-Edition. Digitale Bibliothek. Bd. 40. Berlin: DirectMedia, 2001.

Akademie der Wissenschaften der DDR, Akademie der Wissenschaften in Göttingen, Heidelberger Akademie der Wissenschaften, Berlin-Brandenburgische Akademie der Wissenschaften. *Goethe-Wörterbuch.* Stuttgart: Kohlhammer, 1978.

Ammerlahn, Hellmut. *Aufbau und Krise der Sinn-Gestalt: Tasso und die Prinzessin im Kontext der Goetheschen Werke.* New York: Peter Lang, 1990.

———. *Imagination und Wahrheit: Goethes Künstler-Bildungsroman "Wilhelm Meisters Lehrjahre"; Struktur, Symbolik, Poetologie.* Würzburg: Königshausen & Neumann, 2003.

Anglet, Andreas. *Der "ewige" Augenblick: Studien zur Struktur und Funktion eines Denkbildes bei Goethe.* Cologne: Böhlau, 1991.

Arendt, Hannah. *The Human Condition.* Chicago: University of Chicago Press, 1958.

———. *The Life of the Mind.* New York: Harcourt Brace Jovanovich, 1978.

———. *On Revolution.* New York: Penguin, 2006.

Atkins, Stuart P. *Goethe's Faust: A Literary Analysis.* Cambridge, Mass.: Harvard University Press, 1964.

Babbitt, Irving. *Rousseau and Romanticism.* Boston: Houghton Mifflin, 1919.

Barnes, H. G. *Goethe's "Die Wahlverwandtschaften": A Literary Interpretation.* Oxford: Clarendon Press, 1967.

Bell, Matthew. "Carl Gustav Carus and the Science of the Unconscious." In *Thinking the Unconscious: Nineteenth-Century German Thought,* ed. Angus Nicholls and Martin Liebscher. New York: Cambridge University Press, 2010. 156–72.

———. "Sorge, Epicurean Psychology and the Classical Faust." *Oxford German Studies* 28 (1999): 82–130.

Benjamin, Walter. "Goethes Wahlverwandtschaften." In *Gesammelte Schriften,* vol. 1.1, ed. Rolf Tiedemann and Hermann Schweppenhäuser. Frankfurt am Main: Suhrkamp, 1991. 123–202.

Bennett, Benjamin. *Goethe's Theory of Poetry: Faust and the Regeneration of Language.* Ithaca, N.Y.: Cornell University Press, 1986.

———. *Modern Drama and German Classicism*. Ithaca, N.Y.: Cornell University Press, 1979.

Berman, Marshall. *All That Is Solid Melts into Air: The Experience of Modernity*. New York: Simon and Schuster, 1982.

Bernstein, Susan. *Housing Problems: Writing and Architecture in Goethe, Walpole, Freud, and Heidegger*. Stanford, Calif.: Stanford University Press, 2008.

Bersier, Gabrielle. *Goethes Rätselparodie der Romantik: Eine neue Lesart der "Wahlverwandtschaften."* Tübingen: Niemeyer, 1997.

———. "Ottilies verlorenes Paradies: Zur Funktion der Allegorie in den *Wahlverwandtschaften*; Wieland-Brentano-Goethe." *Goethe Yearbook* 4 (1988): 137–60.

Bishop, Paul. *Analytical Psychology and German Classical Aesthetics: Goethe, Schiller, and Jung*. 2 vols. London: Routledge, 2008–9.

———. "The Unconscious from the Storm and Stress to Weimar Classicism: The Dialectic of Time and Pleasure." In *Thinking the Unconscious: Nineteenth-Century German Thought*, ed. Angus Nicholls and Martin Liebscher. New York: Cambridge University Press, 2010. 26–56.

Blackall, Eric A. *Goethe and the Novel*. Ithaca, N.Y.: Cornell University Press, 1976.

———. "Goethe's Silences." In *Geist und Zeichen: Festschrift für Arthur Henkel*, ed. Herbert Anton, Bernhard Gajek, and Peter Pfaff. Heidelberg: Carl Winter Universitätsverlag, 1977. 39–51.

Blocher, Friedrich K. *Identitätserfahrung: Literarische Beiträge von Goethe bis zu Walser*. Cologne: Pahl-Rugenstein, 1984.

Block, Richard. *The Spell of Italy: Vacation, Magic, and the Attraction of Goethe*. Detroit: Wayne State University Press, 2006.

Bloom, Harold. *The Anxiety of Influence: A Theory of Poetry*. New York: Oxford, 1997.

Bohm, Arnd. *Goethe's "Faust" and European Epic: Forgetting the Future*. Rochester, N.Y.: Camden House, 2007.

Botond, Anneliese. *Die Wahlverwandtschaften: Transformation und Kritik der Neuen Héloïse*. Würzburg: Königshausen & Neumann, 2006.

Boyle, Nicholas. *Goethe: The Poet and the Age*. 2 vols. Oxford: Clarendon Press, 1991, 2000.

Breithaupt, Fritz. "Culture of Images: Limitation in Goethe's *Wahlverwandtschaften*." *Monatshefte* 92 (2000): 302–20.

Breithaupt, Fritz, and Simon Richter, eds. "Goethe and the Ego." Special section in *Goethe Yearbook* 11 (2002): 77–278.

Bridgewater, Patrick. *Kafka: Gothic and Fairytale*. Amsterdam: Rodopi, 2003.

Brodsky, Claudia. "The Coloring of Relations: *Die Wahlverwandtschaften* as *Farbenlehre*." *MLN* 97.5 (December 1982): 1147–79.

———. *In the Place of Language: Literature and the Architecture of the Referent*. Princeton, N.J.: Princeton University Press, 2009.

Brown, Jane K. "Classicism and Romanticism." In *Cambridge Companion to German Romanticism*, ed. N. D. B. Saul. Cambridge: Cambridge University Press, 2009. 119–31.

———. "*Die Wahlverwandtschaften* and the English Novel of Manners." *Comparative Literature* 28 (1976): 97–108.

————. *Goethe's Cyclical Narratives: "Die Unterhaltungen deutscher Ausgewanderten" and "Wilhelm Meisters Wanderjahre."* University of North Carolina Studies in the Germanic Languages and Literatures 82. Chapel Hill: University of North Carolina Press, 1975.

————. *Goethe's "Faust": The German Tragedy.* Ithaca, N.Y.: Cornell University Press, 1986.

————. "Im Anfang war das Bild: Wilhelm Meister und die Bibel." In *Goethe und die Bibel*, ed. Johannes Anderegg and Edith Anna Kunz. Stuttgart: Deutsche Bibelgesellschaft, 2005. 241–59.

————. "Orest, Orlando, Orpheus, oder Der Held von Goethes *Iphigenie*." In *Getauft auf Musik: Festschrift für Dieter Borchmeyer*, ed. Udo Bermbach and Hans Rudolf Vaget. Würzburg: Königshausen & Neumann, 2006. 55–65.

————. *The Persistence of Allegory: Drama and Neoclassicism from Shakespeare to Wagner.* Philadelphia: University of Pennsylvania Press, 2007.

————. "The Theatrical Mission of the *Lehrjahre*." In *Goethe's Narrative Fiction: The Irvine Goethe Symposium*. Berlin: De Gruyter, 1983. 66–84.

Brown, Marshall. *The Gothic Text.* Stanford, Calif.: Stanford University Press, 2005.

————. *Preromanticism.* Stanford, Calif.: Stanford University Press, 1991.

Burdach, Konrad. "Faust und die Sorge in Goethes *Faust*." *Deutsche Vierteljahrsschrift für Literaturwissenschaft und Geistesgeschichte* 1 (1923): 1–60.

Carus, Carl Gustav. *Goethe: Zu dessen näherem Verständnis.* Ed. Hans Friedrich Wöhrmann. Herford: Die Arche, 1948.

————. *Psyche: Zur Entwicklungsgeschichte der Seele.* Darmstadt: Wissenschaftliche Buchgesellschaft, 1964.

Cassirer, Ernst. *The Question of Jean-Jacques Rousseau.* Trans. Peter Gay. Bloomington: Indiana University Press, 1967.

————. *Rousseau, Kant and Goethe.* Trans. James Gutmann, Paul Oskar Kristeller, and John Herman Randall, Jr. New York: Harper Torchbooks, 1963.

Cohn, Dorrit. "Wilhelm Meister's Dream: Reading Goethe with Freud." *German Quarterly* 62.4 (1989): 459–72.

Damm, Sigrid. *Christiane und Goethe: Eine Recherche.* Frankfurt am Main: Insel, 1998.

DeLaura, David J. "Heroic Egotism: Goethe and the Fortunes of *Bildung* in Victorian England." In *Johann Wolfgang von Goethe: One Hundred and Fifty Years of Continuing Vitality*, ed. Ulrich Goebel and Wolodymyr T. Zyla. Lubbock: Texas Tech Press, 1984. 41–60.

Derrida, Jacques. *De la grammatologie.* Paris: Minuit, 1967.

Dilthey, Wilhelm. *Das Erlebnis und die Dichtung: Lessing, Goethe, Novalis, Hölderlin; Vier Aufsätze.* Leipzig: B. G. Teubner, 1906.

Dye, Ellis. "Sorge in Heidegger and in Goethe's *Faust*." *Goethe Yearbook* 16 (2009): 207–18.

Eckermann, Johann Peter. *Gespräche mit Goethe in den letzten Jahren seines Lebens.* Zurich: Artemis, 1948.

Eichendorff, Joseph von. *Werke.* Vol. 1. Ed. Hartwig Schultz. Frankfurt am Main: Deutsche Klassiker, 1987

Elias, Norbert. *The Civilizing Process: Sociogenetic and Psychogenetic Investigations.* Oxford: Blackwell, 2000.

————. *Über die Zeit*. Trans. Holger Fliessbach and Michael Schröter. Frankfurt am Main: Suhrkamp, 1988.

Ellenberger, Henri F. *The Discovery of the Unconscious: The History and Evolution of Dynamic Psychiatry*. New York: Basic Books, 1970.

Engelhardt, Wolf von. *Goethe im Gespräch mit der Erde: Landschaft, Gesteine, Mineralien und Erdgeschichte in seinem Leben und Werk*. Weimar: Hermann Böhlaus Nachfolger, 2003.

Fischer-Lamberg, Hanna. "Charlotte von Stein, ein Bildungserlebnis Goethes." *Deutsche Vierteljahrsschrift für Literaturwissenschaft und Geistesgeschichte* 15 (1937): 385–402.

Flavell, M. Kay. "Goethe, Rousseau, and the 'Hyp.'" *Oxford German Studies* 7 (1972–73): 5–23.

Fleishman, Avrom. *A Reading of "Mansfield Park": An Essay in Critical Synthesis*. Baltimore: Johns Hopkins University Press, 1970.

Fletcher, Angus. *Allegory: The Theory of a Symbolic Mode*. Ithaca, N.Y.: Cornell University Press, 1964.

Foucault, Michel. *The Hermeneutics of the Subject*. Trans. Graham Burchell. New York: Picador, 2005.

————. *The Order of Things*. New York: Vintage, 1973.

Freud, Sigmund. *Studienausgabe*. 11 vols. Ed. Alexander Mitscherlich, Angela Richards, and James Strachey. Frankfurt am Main: Fischer, 2000.

Friedenthal, Richard. *Goethe, sein Leben und seine Zeit*. Munich: Piper, 1963.

Funke, Maurice. *From Saint to Psychotic: The Crisis of Human Identity in the Late 18th Century; A Comparative Study of Clarissa, La Nouvelle Héloïse, Die Leiden des Jungen Werthers*. New York: P. Lang, 1983.

Goethe, Johann Wolfgang. *Goethes Werke*, Hamburger Ausgabe. 14 vols. Ed. Erich Trunz. Munich: C. H. Beck, 1982–2008.

————. *Neue Gesamtausgabe der Werke und Schriften*. 22 vols. Stuttgart: Cotta, 1950–68.

————. *Werke*. Hrsg. im Auftrage der Grossherzogin Sophie von Sachsen (Weimarer Ausgabe). 144 vols. Weimar: H. Böhlau, 1887–1919.

————. *Wilhelm Meister's Journeyman Years, or The Renunciants*. Trans. Krishna Winston. New York: Suhrkamp, 1989.

Goldberg, Benjamin. *The Mirror and the Man*. Charlottesville: University Press of Virginia, 1985.

Grabes, Herbert. *Speculum, Mirror und Looking-Glass: Kontinuität und Originalität der Spiegelmetapher in den Buchtiteln des Mittelalters und der englischen Literatur des 13. bis 17. Jahrhunderts*. Tübingen: Niemeyer, 1973.

Gurganus, Albert. "Typologies of Repetition, Reflection, and Recurrence: Interpreting the Novella in Goethe's *Wahlverwandtschaften*." *Goethe Yearbook* 15 (2008): 99–114.

Hamlin, Cyrus. "'Myth and Psychology': The Curing of Orest in Goethe's *Iphigenie auf Tauris*." *Goethe Yearbook* 12 (2004): 59–80.

Hammer, Carl, Jr. *Goethe and Rousseau: Resonances of the Mind*. Lexington: University Press of Kentucky, 1973.

Harnik, J. "Psychoanalytisches aus und über Goethes *Wahlverwandtschaften*." *Imago* 1 (1912): 507–18.

Hederich, Benjamin. *Gründliches mythologisches Lexikon*. Leipzig: Gleditsch, 1770. Facsimile edition, Darmstadt: Wissenschaftliche Buchgesellschaft, 1967.

Heidegger, Martin. *Sein und Zeit.* Tübingen: Niemeyer, 1967.

Henel, Heinrich. "Auf den Spuren des Uregmont." In *Goethezeit: Ausgewählte Aufsätze von Heinrich Henel.* Frankfurt am Main: Insel, 1980. 102–29.

Henkel, Arthur, and Albrecht Schöne. *Emblemata: Handbuch zur Sinnbildkunst d. XVI. u. XVII. Jahrhunderts.* Stuttgart: Metzler, 1976.

Herold, Thomas. "Zeichen und Zeichendeutung in Goethes *Die Wahlverwandtschaften.*" *Seminar* 45.1 (February 2009): 1–15.

Holub, Robert. "From the Pedestal to the Couch: Goethe, Freud and Jewish Assimilation." Accessed July 15, 2010. http://www.vanderbilt.edu/AnS/Germanic-Slavic/german/germandept2/Goethe-Freud.htm.

Jauß, Hans Robert. "Rousseaus *Nouvelle Héloïse* und Goethes *Werther* im Horizontwandel zwischen französischer Aufklärung und deutschem Idealismus." In his *Ästhetische Erfahrung und literarische Hermeneutik.* Frankfurt am Main: Suhrkamp, 1982. 589–653.

Jung, C. G. *Memories, Dreams, Reflections.* Recorded and ed. Aniela Jaffé, trans. Richard and Clara Winston. New York: Vintage, 1965.

Kavanagh, Thomas M. *Writing the Truth: Authority and Desire in the Works of Rousseau.* Berkeley: University of California Press, 1987.

Kittler, Friedrich. *Aufschreibesysteme, 1800/1900.* Munich: Fink, 1985.

Kleist, Heinrich von. *Sämtliche Werke und Briefe.* 2 vols. Ed Helmut Sembdner. Munich: 1964.

Kowalik, Jill Anne. "Feminine Identity Formation in *Wilhelm Meisters Lehrjahre.*" *Modern Language Quarterly* 53.2 (1992): 149–72.

———. "Trauma and Memory in the *Wahlverwandtschaften.*" *Goethe Yearbook* 12 (2004): 129–40.

Lee, Meredith. *Displacing Authority: Goethe's Poetic Reception of Klopstock.* Heidelberg: C. Winter, 1999.

Leppmann, Wolfgang. *The German Image of Goethe.* Oxford: Clarendon Press, 1961.

Melchior-Bonnet, Sabine. *The Mirror: A History.* Trans. Katharine H. Jewett. New York: Routledge, 2001.

Melville, Herman. *Pierre, Israel Potter, The Piazza Tales, The Confidence-Man, Uncollected Prose, Billy Budd, Sailor.* Library of America 24. New York: Library of America, 1984.

Michelsen, Peter. "Die Problematik der Empfindungen: Zu Lessings 'Miß Sara Sampson.'" In his *Der unruhige Bürger: Studien zu Lessing und zur Literatur des achtzehnten Jahrhunderts.* Würzburg: Königshausen & Neumann, 1990. 163–220.

Miller, J. Hillis. "Interlude as Anastomosis in *Die Wahlverwandtschaften.*" *Goethe Yearbook* 6 (1992): 115–22.

Molnár, Géza von. *Goethes Kantstudien: Eine Zusammenstellung nach Eintragungen in seinen Handexemplaren der "Kritik der reinen Vernunft" und der "Kritik der Urteilskraft."* Weimar: Hermann Böhlaus Nachfolger, 1994.

———. "Goethes Studium der Kritik der Urteilskraft: Eine Zusammenstellung nach den Eintragungen in seinem Handexemplar." *Goethe Yearbook* 2 (1984): 137–222.

Moretti, Franco. *The Way of the World: The Bildungsroman in European Culture.* London: Verso, 1987.

Müller, Wilhelm. *Werke. Tagebücher. Briefe.* 6 vols. Ed. Maria-Verena Leistner. Berlin: Mathias Gatza, 1994.

Neumann, Gerhard. "Wunderliche Nachbarskinder: Zur Instanzierung von Wissen und Erzählen in Goethes *Wahlverwandtschaften*." In *Erzählen und Wissen: Paradigmen und Aporien ihrer Inszenierung in Goethes "Wahlverwandtschaften,"* ed. Gabriele Brandstetter. Freiburg: Rombach, 2003. 15–40.

Nicholls, Angus. "The Scientific Unconscious: Goethe's Post-Kantian Epistemology." In *Thinking the Unconscious: Nineteenth-Century German Thought*, ed. Angus Nicholls and Martin Liebscher. New York: Cambridge University Press, 2010. 87–120.

Nicholls, Angus, and Martin Liebscher, eds. *Thinking the Unconscious: Nineteenth-Century German Thought*. New York: Cambridge University Press, 2010.

Nicolai, Heinz. "Goethes Schicksalsidee." *Goethe* 26 (1964): 77–91.

Novalis. *Schriften.* Vol. 3. Ed. Richard Samuel, Hans-Joachim Mähl, and Gerhard Schulz. Darmstadt: Wissenschaftliche Buchgesellschaft, 1968.

Nygaard, Loisa. "'Bild' and 'Sinnbild': The Problem of the Symbol in Goethe's *Wahlverwandtschaften*." *Germanic Review* 63.2 (Spring 1988): 58–76.

Oberlin, Gerhard. *Goethe, Schiller und das Unbewusste.* Giessen: Psychosozial Verlag, 2007.

Peucker, Brigitte. "The Material Image in Goethe's *Wahlverwandtschaften*." *Germanic Review* 74.3 (Summer 1999): 195–213.

Reik, Theodor. *Fragment of a Great Confession: A Psychoanalytic Autobiography.* New York: Farrar Straus, 1949.

Reuchlein, Georg. *Bürgerliche Gesellschaft, Psychiatrie und Literatur: Zur Entwicklung der Wahnsinnsthematik.* Munich: W. Fink, 1986.

Rousseau, Jean-Jacques. *Les Confessions.* In *Œuvres complètes*, vol. 1., ed. Bernard Gagnebin, Robert Osmont, and Marcel Raymond. Paris: Gallimard, 1959.

———. *Discours sur l'origine et les fondements de l'inégalité.* In *Œuvres complètes*, vol 3. Ed. Bernard Gagnebin and Marcel Raymond. Paris: Gallimard, 1964.

———. *Emile, ou De l'éducation.* In *Œuvres complètes*, vol. 4. Ed. Bernard Gagnebin, Robert Osmont, and Marcel Raymond. Paris: Gallimard, 1969. English citations from *Emile, or On Education*, trans. Allan Bloom (New York: Basic Books, 1979).

———. *Julie, ou La nouvelle Héloïse.* In *Œuvres complètes*, vol. 2. Ed. Bernard Gagnebin, Robert Osmont, and Marcel Raymond. Paris: Gallimard, 1961.

———. *Les rêveries du promeneur solitaire.* In *Œuvres complètes*, vol. 1. Ed. Bernard Gagnebin, Robert Osmont, and Marcel Raymond. Paris: Gallimard, 1959. English citations from *Reveries of the Solitary Walker*, trans. Peter France (Harmondsworth: Penguin, 1981).

———. *Œuvres complètes.* 4 vols. Ed. Bernard Gagnebin, Robert Osmont, and Marcel Raymond. Paris: Gallimard, 1959–69. Abbreviated *ŒC.*

Saine, Thomas P. "What Time Is It in *Wilhelm Meisters Lehrjahre?*" In *Horizonte: Festschrift für Herbert Lehnert zum 65. Geburtstag*, ed. Hannelore Mundt, Egon Schwarz, and William J. Lillyman. Tübingen: Niemeyer, 1990. 52–69.

———. "Wilhelm Meister's Homecoming." *Journal of English and Germanic Philology* 69 (1970): 450–69.

Schiller, Friedrich. *Schillers Sämtliche Werke*. Vol. 5. Ed. Gerhard Fricke and Herbert G. Göpfert. Munich: Hanser, 1960.

Schlaffer, Heinz. "Namen und Buchstaben in Goethes *Wahlverwandtschaften*." In Norbert W. Bolz, *Goethes Wahlverwandtschaften: Kritische Modelle und Diskursanalysen zum Mythos Literatur*. Hildesheim: Gerstenberg, 1981. 211–29.

Schmidt, Erich. *Richardson, Rousseau und Goethe: Ein Beitrag zur Geschichte des Romans im 18. Jahrhundert*. Jena: E. Frommann, 1924.

Sembdner, Helmut, ed. *Heinrich von Kleists Lebensspuren*. Munich: Hanser, 1996.

Starobinski, Jean. *Jean-Jacques Rousseau: La transparence et l'obstacle; Suivi de sept essais sur Rousseau*. Paris: Gallimard, 1971.

Stelzig, Eugene L. *The Romantic Subject in Autobiography: Rousseau and Goethe*. Charlottesville: University Press of Virginia, 2000.

Tantillo, Astrida Orle. *Goethe's "Elective Affinities" and the Critics*. Rochester, N.Y.: Camden House, 2001.

Taylor, Charles. *Sources of the Self: The Making of the Modern Identity*. Cambridge, Mass.: Harvard University Press, 1989.

Texte, Joseph. *Jean-Jacques Rousseau and the Cosmopolitan Spirit in Literature*. New York: B. Franklin, 1963.

Thermann, Jochen. *Kafkas Tiere: Fährten, Bahnen und Wege der Sprache*. Marburg: Tectum-Verlag, 2010.

Tobin, Robert. *Doctor's Orders: Goethe and Enlightenment Thought*. Lewisburg, Pa.: Bucknell University Press, 2001.

Tucker, Brian. *Reading Riddles: Rhetorics of Obscurity from Romanticism to Freud*. Lewisburg, Pa.: Bucknell University Press, 2011.

Vermorel, Henri. "Goethe and Psychoanalysis." Accessed July 15, 2010. http://www.answers.com/topic/goethe-and-psychoanalysis.

Vincent, Deirdre. *The Eternity of Being: On the Experience of Time in Goethe's "Faust."* Bonn: Bouvier, 1987.

Wahl, Volker, and René Jacques Baerlocher. *"Das Kind in meinem Leib": Sittlichkeitsdelikte und Kindsmord in Sachsen-Weimar-Eisenach unter Carl August; Eine Quellenedition, 1777–1786*. Weimar: Hermann Böhlaus Nachfolger, 2004.

Wahrman, Dror. *The Making of the Modern Self: Identity and Culture in Eighteenth-Century England*. New Haven, Conn.: Yale University Press, 2004.

Weinrich, Harald. "Faust's Forgetting." *Modern Language Quarterly* 55.3 (1994): 281–95.

———. *Gibt es eine Kunst des Vergessens?* Jacob Burckhardt-Gespräche auf Castelen 1. Basel: Schwabe, 1996.

———. *Lethe: Kunst und Kritik des Vergessens*. Munich: C. H. Beck, 1997.

Wellbery, David. "Morphisms of the Phantasmatic Body: Goethe's *The Sorrows of Young Werther*." In *Body and Text in the Eighteenth Century*, ed. Veronica Kelly and Dorothea von Mücke. Stanford, Calif.: Stanford University Press, 1994. 181–208.

———. *The Specular Moment: Goethe's Early Lyric and the Beginnings of Romanticism*. Stanford, Calif.: Stanford University Press, 1996.

Wilpert, Gero von. *Goethe-Lexikon*. Stuttgart: Alfred Kröner Verlag, 1998.

ACKNOWLEDGMENTS

The earliest section of this book was first drafted in 1976, so a list of the colleagues, friends, and students who offered suggestions and support would overwhelm the book itself, even if I could reconstruct it. Instead I can point only to a few especially bright beacons and devoted encouragers along the way of its specific development—my supportive editor Jerry Singerman; the graduate students at the University of Washington and Rutgers who responded with special enthusiasm to my seminars on *Wilhelm Meister*; my colleagues Hellmut Ammerlahn and Brigitte Prutti, who offered incisive criticisms and suggestions at different times; Dorrit Cohn, who read an early version of the initial material; lifelong friends Meredith Lee, Clark Muenzer, Simon Richter, and Tom Saine, all of whom created many opportunities to work out and present various pieces of this manuscript and always helped to profile what it had to offer; and Cyrus Hamlin, without whose lifelong faith in my work none of it would have been written. I owe a special debt of gratitude to Jürgen Schröder for his support and interest that led to the Humboldt Preis that supported the writing of several chapters and the final assembly of the work. Above all, my children Dorrit and Benedict have generously shared their mother's devotion with Goethe for literally their entire lifetimes, and my husband Marshall, as colleague, critic, chef, companion, and everything else, has actively shared in the creation of this manuscript at every stage. Among the three of them they have contributed more than a century of love and support.

Chapters 2, 5, and 8 have previously appeared in print as "Goethe, Rousseau, the Novel, and the Origins of Psychoanalysis," in *Goethe Yearbook* 12 (2004): 111–228; "Theatricality and Experiment: Identity in *Faust*," in *Goethe's Faust: Theatre of Modernity*, ed. Hans Schulte, John Noyes, and Pia Kleber (Cambridge: Cambridge University Press, 2011), 235–52; "Es singen wohl die Nixen: *Werther* and the Romantic Tale," in *Rereading Romanticism*, ed.

Martha Helfer (Amsterdam: Rodopi, 2000), 11–25. Chapters 3 and 4 contain small amounts of material from essays previously published in German in *Goethe Jahrbuch* (2009) and in my own collection *Ironie und Objektivität* (Königshausen & Neumann, 1999). I am grateful to all of these publishers for permission to publish the material here.